MW01380086

Emily

Work Hard, Be Kind

A Memoir
by
Jerome R. Cox, Jr.
2022

Work Hard, Be Kind

Publisher: Pesca Publishing and Productions, LLC

ISBN 979-8-9865287-0-0

About the Cover
The cover art is taken from a painting of me by a talented artist, Theresa Cox-Kendig. Theresa was married to my half-brother, Ferris Randall (Randy) Cox who died in 2012 after a fall on the stairs in their home. Theresa has remarried and now lives near Erie, Pennsylvania. She created the painting recently from a photograph taken in the 1980s and I always liked the result. So it pleases me very much to use it for my book's cover.

To my wonderful family

CONTENTS

Foreword ii

Preface iv

Chapter 1: The Early Years | 1925–1939 1

Chapter 2: High School | 1939–1943 14

Chapter 3: The Army | 1943–1944 25

Chapter 4: MIT | 1944–1947 34

Chapter 5: Bobby | 1947–1952 51

Chapter 6: Doctoral Dissertation | 1952–1954 64

Chapter 7: Central Institute for the Deaf | 1954–1961 75

Chapter 8: Going Digital | 1961–1964 87

Chapter 9: Biomedical Computer Laboratory | 1964–1969 102

Chapter 10: Positron Emission Tomography | 1969–1975 120

Chapter 11: An Adventure in Moscow | 1972 136

Chapter 12: Computers in Cardiology | 1974– 144

Chapter 13: Computer Science | 1975–1991 153

Chapter 14: Two Thrilling Trips | 1973 and 1979 168

Chapter 15: Electronic Radiology and Project Zeus | 1977–1997 180

Chapter 16: Committee Work | 1982–1997 190

Chapter 17: Growth Networks | 1997–2000 199

Chapter 18: Bobby's Last Days | 2000–2006 210

Chapter 19: Blendics | 2004– 216

Chapter 20: Q-Net Security | 2015– 227

Chapter 21: Music, the Auditory System, and My Belief | 2021– 234

Chapter 22: My Family | 1951– 240

Chapter 23: Epilogue | 2022 245

Acknowledgments 247

QR Codes 248

Index 250

Tributes 261

FOREWORD

We have known and worked with Jerry Cox as a friend and colleague for some 50 years, and we are delighted that he has authored this well-researched memoir. It provides engaging stories of his life, his family, and what he calls his "adventures." Chronological accounts of his professional endeavors are interleaved with stories of his past and present family, who, along with influential friends, he introduces fondly as real, multi-dimensional people.

As a preamble to his student years at MIT, Jerry's childhood stories report an early curiosity about how things work (such as trains and radios). In graduate school, he studied and made contributions to the field of acoustics. From there, he branched out to do seminal work in digital computing, medical imaging, advanced digital networking, and most recently in network security. We are thankful that he joined Washington University in St. Louis (WU), where he is among the most respected faculty members and recently an award-winning entrepreneur.

A turning point was his research at the Central Institute for the Deaf (a WU affiliate) in which Jerry created "HAVOC" (one of his whimsical acronyms). It was a special-purpose digital computer for testing infants' hearing. That led him to a group at MIT, who were the designers of a ground-breaking laboratory computer called the "LINC." He amuses us with "The Prime Number Drop" that he fell for on an MIT visit.

While still a junior member of the WU faculty, he conceived of a new, independent laboratory to explore medical computer applications more broadly. In record time, he gained permission from the medical-school dean, secured substantial funding from the NIH, and lured the LINC group from MIT to WU. Thus, in 1964, the Biomedical Computer Laboratory (BCL) and the Computer Systems Laboratory (CSL) were born. A related story tells of a silent, mysterious stranger lurking in a corner during his pitch to the dean.

Once BCL and CSL were established, collaborations blossomed. A few of their research areas in the early years were radiation treatment planning, electrocardiography, neurosurgery, and nuclear medicine imaging. It was a time when computer applications in the field of medicine were uncommon. So, before long, BCL was widely known as the most advanced center for medical computer applications nationally, a stunning success for a young faculty member.

Many important complex needs were addressed by the BCL. In the early 1970s, the first cross-sectional imaging devices were introduced, and WU was heavily involved. Jerry, with others, developed and patented methods to reconstruct images for the earliest CT scanners. Although WU was not properly recognized, the methods were used by some of the largest scanner manufacturers. The same methods were also useful in WU's building of the first PET scanners.

Jerry envisioned more clearly than the rest of us how trends in technology would unfold, and he drew on his prescience to develop over-the-horizon solutions. He recognized, for example, that simple terminals linked to a central computer would soon be obsolete, and instead he installed networked computer workstations in the Computer Science Department. Also, he anticipated that early computer networks would be too slow for medical image distribution, so he led pioneering work to establish WU as a national leader in high-speed networking.

Key to Jerry's success is his leadership style. He is skillful in bringing people together to solve problems or to take on emerging opportunities. He has been a collaborator, a facilitator, a team builder. He leads but is quick to share credit for success with others. Everyone enjoys working with him.

When Jerry retired in his mid-sixties, his productivity did not wane. He has since taken on three different complex technical problems, and for each, he created a company to solve them. The intellectual properties of two have been acquired by a larger entity. The third, Q-Net Security, continues, and its novel system is under serious consideration by a foreign country and by several major companies.

Jerry is highly admired and liked by all whose lives he touches. His quiet, easy-going style, his thoughtfulness, his enthusiasm, and his creativity all make him a delight to know. Those qualities, and his proven ability to solve difficult problems, make him a sought-after consultant. He has been a valuable leader on countless committees nationally and internationally.

WU and the wider world are better off because Jerry Cox has graced them with his well-lived life. There's much to savor here.

Enjoy!

R. Gilbert Jost, M.D.[1]
Donald L. Snyder, Ph.D.[2]
Lewis J. Thomas, Jr., M.D.[3]

PREFACE

My license plates read *WHBK* and stand for the phrase, "Work Hard, Be Kind." I realized late in life that this phrase encapsulates the approach to living that had come into focus for me in recent years. Yes, work hard, but do it because you have found something you love to do. Then, working hard is a joy and not a burden. It also helps if your work has an unselfish motive. Whatever you do, don't turn down an invitation for an adventure. They do not all work out as you wish, but each adventure has its own savory story and will live in your memory.

The words, "Be Kind," have surprisingly powerful implications that go well beyond being nice to family, friends, and neighbors. Each member of the human race wants to be somebody and will take offense if his or her path is repeatedly blocked by others. Barriers to opportunity, whether virtual or physical, will occasionally lead to devious or violent attempts to break through by those on the wrong side of the barrier, and that is particularly true if that barrier seems unfair. So, when you don't know exactly what is fair, be kind and compassionate. For those whose culture is based on honor, family pride, or narrow religious belief, that advice may seem like mental mush because it does not always even the score. But who is counting? It should be both parties or no one.

I have been blessed in many ways, but my greatest good fortune was to encounter so many wonderful people along the way. This book tells stories about many of them, but four stand out and are the major motivation for putting my fingers to this keyboard: my beloved wife, Hallowell Davis, Wesley Clark, and William Danforth.

My late wife Bobby, formally Barbara Jane Lueders Cox, helped me in too many ways to document here. It was love at first talk, and that love never slackened from our first date in 1948 until her death in 2006. Hallowell Davis was my mentor in my early professional life, showing me how to seize adventure without compromising my principles. Wesley A. Clark—a remarkable innovator, wonderful friend, and underappreciated computer pioneer—affected my career in more ways than I can count. In fact, if my effort to tell stories about Wes brightens his memory for others, that will have made this book worthwhile. William Danforth saw Washington University through the transformative journey of becoming a nationally ranked research university.

The following chapters are composed of many stories from my past, but as you read them be aware of my favorite line about memory that was told to me by the great memory researcher and professor, Henry "Roddy" Roediger: "Oh memory—you sly deceiver." At least, that is how I remember what Roddy told me. My stories are written as best I can remember. However, since I have told them many times, it's hard to decide whether I'm remembering the event itself or its most recent retelling. Where possible, I have consulted paper or digital records—but alas, that is not always possible. So, savor the stories. In my mind they are all true.

In these stories, there are a remarkable number of coincidences. You can take the view of the famous physicist, Richard Feynman, that there is always a physical explanation. It is just that our minds automatically seek explanation and resort to mysticism or religion if the physical explanation is not readily apparent. This later explanation is neatly encapsulated in a friend's statement, "Coincidence is God's way of remaining anonymous." I am less ready to accept that reasoning, but my goodness, I have seen a lot of such odd coincidences, more than can be attributed to random processes and hidden physical events, it would seem. You may wonder whether religion has played a part in my life. I will try to answer that question in Chapter 21.

The book's chapter titles are chronologically ordered—well, actually, they are only partially ordered, which allows me to tell stories that happened concurrently but fit best when told in different chapters. I will identify these temporal jumps wherever they occur. The book is largely composed of stories with only enough historical narrative to serve as the connective tissue between the stories. This is not a "tell all" book. There are no family secrets revealed—just stories that I have told and, in some cases retold, many times.

There will be 23 chapters. Why 23? Because 23 is my favorite number:

- I was 23 years old when I first met my wife, Bobby.

- The number 23 is the ninth prime.

- The number 23 is composed of two consecutive primes, 2 and 3.

- My office was on the 23rd floor of the University Tower when Wes Clark and I conceived of a way to build "unhackable" computer systems.

- There are 23 human chromosome pairs.
- The number 23 played an important role in the "prime number drop" mentioned in Chapter 9.
- I like my martinis "shaken and not stirred" and prefer them shaken just 23 times.
- My youngest son's birthday is 23 October 1965.

It is now time for me to move out of lecture mode and into story-telling mode.

Chapter 1
The Early Years | 1925-1939

I have said that I value work and kindness as deeply important values and ones that have informed my entire life. As I look back, I think I learned their importance in my early childhood, which contained a good deal of both. On the whole, it was a very happy childhood; I was surrounded by a loving family, a doting nanny, and a group of wonderful friends who stood in as the siblings I didn't have. My family was prosperous and remained relatively unscathed by the miseries of the Great Depression. In addition to our home in South Bend, Indiana, we had a cottage on the shore of Lake Michigan, where I spent magical days playing in the water, in the dunes, and in the nearby woods. The major and abiding sorrow of my early days came in 1936. When I was 11, I suffered the death of my beloved mother, which changed everything.

But let me start with my paternal grandparents, though I know little about them. My paternal grandfather, Jerome A. Cox, was a grocer who owned the general store in Preston, a small town on the Eastern Shore of Maryland. His wife and my grandmother was Lillian Cox, whose maiden name was Rockhold, the source of my middle name. They both passed away before I could have had any memory of them, in 1921 and 1926.

I know a great deal more about my maternal grandparents, the Rev. Seth A. Mills and his wife, Mary Dunscombe Mills. Mary Dunscombe, who was born in 1852 in County Cork, Ireland, had moved to Canada at age 30. Rev. Mills was born in Quebec, Canada, in 1864, ordained as an Episcopal priest in 1889, and married to Mary Dunscombe in 1890; they moved to Troy, New

York in 1905 to take over a church there. They had three children: Ada Mills who died at a young age; my mother, Jane Mills; and my uncle, Harold Mills, who were all born in Canada in 1891, 1893, and 1895, respectively. Tragically, Uncle Harold was killed in the Battle of Belleau Wood, the bloodiest and most ferocious battle that U.S. forces fought during World War I. He was a 2nd Lieutenant in the 1st Battalion, 6th Marines, which relieved the 3rd Battalion on 7-8 June 1918. The Germans were attacked in the woods six times by the Marines before they were expelled on 26 June, but sadly Uncle Harold died on 17 June and was buried in France. I know him only through my grandmother. His death was a heavy burden for her, one that I was aware of, even as a child. More about her later.

My mother, Helena Jane Mills, was known to me as "Mom," of course, but her friends and my father always called her "Jane," and I did not know about the name Helena until recently. From her diary, I learned that she wanted to be a nurse, but she came back early from an initial year in nursing school in New York City, disappointed that it had not worked out. Her diary was not clear as to why. Instead, she went to the New York State Normal College in Albany where she majored in Household Economics, graduating in June 1913. She took a secretarial job when the family of three moved from Troy to a new church in Hyattsville, Maryland, in 1921. I believe her job was at the State Department near the White House. She joined a hiking club based in Washington, DC, where she met my father.

Because of my mother's untimely death, I have more stories from my father about these early years. He was sent to Western Maryland University at age 15 because, as he told me, his high school teachers felt they had nothing more to teach him. He did well there and returned to Preston to teach English at the high school. That would have been in 1914 when he was barely older than his students. About that experience, he said simply that it "just did not work out," but in a few years along came World War I, and in 1917 he enlisted in the Army Air Corps. He was trained to be an observer in a two-seat biplane, with the pilot in the front seat and the observer, both of them officers, in the rear. The pilot, of course, flew the plane, and the observer took notes on ground movements and conditions. In 1918, my father was commissioned a 2nd Lieutenant in Arkansas, where he had flight training. He told me that veteran pilots would take advantage of the newcomers by practicing a bit of hazing. The pilot would do a slow roll and, if the observer was unprepared, he would fall out of the plane to the end of his seatbelt, his clipboard trailing to the end of its cord, and the pencil used to record observations yet further down. It was a primitive arrangement that today's air travelers would find hard to comprehend.

My father was not posted overseas, and he returned to civilian life in early 1919, determined to find a different career. He entered George Washington University Law School and specialized in patent law, perhaps because it was technical and allowed him to apply the law to a new and exciting field that he had tasted in the Army Air Corps. During those law school years, he joined a hiking organization, Red Triangle Outing Club, where he met my mother. Their romance blossomed, and they met for lunch frequently at the All States Cafeteria, a mutually convenient spot near the White House. She was working at the State Department, and in 1922, after graduating with his LLB, he interned at the Patent Office, then located in the nearby Department of Commerce building. In 1923 they married, and I was born in a hospital in the District of Columbia on 24 May 1925. Their budget was tight, so my parents lived with my grandparents in Hyattsville, a near suburb of Washington, DC.

My first personal recollection occurred when I was just 3 years old, but that memory was certainly enhanced by my parents reminding me of the event when I was older. I was curious about the commuter trains that stopped at the downtown Hyattsville station, and I took an unaccompanied walk to watch the action. I clearly remember the joy in my parents' faces once I was collected and brought back onto my grand-

My mother and me at the house in Hyattsville

3

My tricycle and me behind our house in Hempstead

parents' grand front porch. That porch was only a couple blocks from the station and had one of the then-popular wide porch swings. I do not remember being chastised—only happiness.

Soon my father left the patent office for a job with Pratt & Whitney, a manufacturer of aircraft engines in Hartford, Connecticut, but that job was short-lived. Within a year, we moved to Long Island so that he could work for Curtiss-Wright, another rapidly growing company in the aircraft business. We lived in an apartment just off Queens Blvd., then in Garden City, and finally in Hempstead, each step bringing increasingly large quarters.

Two adventures there remain in my memory. In the first, my curiosity again led to family distress. I poked a stick into a hornet's nest on the back of our house in Hempstead. I sustained a number of bites but was immediately comforted by my mother. It was painful—but only briefly. The second adventure was not of my making. My father took me on an airplane ride out of nearby Floyd Bennett Field. It was in a two-seater plane with me in my father's lap. I am guessing the year was 1929, when I was only four years old. It was exciting for me, but I have no report of my mother's reaction to this flight, though I can guess.

At some point during these early years my mother suffered a strep throat infection, which led to rheumatic fever and heart-valve damage. I was completely unaware of this illness and of the fact that, if it was not treated with antibiotics, the effect can lurk in the heart for years. In the 1920s and early 1930s, antibiotics were unknown. My mother's lingering but dormant illness may have been the reason that I was an only child.

In 1930, my father's work as a patent attorney led him to move the family in order to take a new job with Bendix Aircraft in South

Bend, Indiana. We never talked about why he changed jobs, but I expect it was a step up, because we rented a bigger house at 103 N. Sunnyside Avenue about 10 blocks east of downtown. The house is still there, as can be seen courtesy of Google Maps, though it certainly has been remodeled at least once since then. It was and remains a lovely single-story bungalow. South Bend was a manufacturing city of about 100,000 people. Then, in addition to Bendix Aviation, it had Studebaker automobiles, South Bend Lathes, and many other smaller companies. South Bend is also the home of Notre Dame University and its nationally famous football team.

While in Hempstead, I had started kindergarten in the spring of 1930, and I continued in the fall when we reached South Bend, which had a one-room portable school building that contained grades K through 5. I walked by myself or with schoolmates the six blocks east from our house to school. The schoolroom was small: about 25 feet on a side with a single teacher attending to the total of 20 or so students in all the grades. She would give assignments to the three or four in each grade and come back to see how we were doing after visiting the students at other levels. My memories of that time are pleasant. I was eager to move on to the next grade as soon as possible but got in step with schoolmates by spending a year and a half in kindergarten. In later years, I would jokingly tell friends that I had been held back upon moving to South Bend and had to repeat kindergarten. A distinct recollection from that time is the partial eclipse of the sun in August 1932. The family stood in the

I started kindergarten in Hempstead and continued in South Bend.

front yard and observed the event with dark glasses. My father explained what was happening, but I cannot say it was a turning point toward science for me. After all, I was only seven.

During the previous year, Rev. Mills had passed away in Maryland, and it was not long before my grandmother moved near us in South Bend. There was not enough room in the house on Sunnyside, so later that year we moved just north of downtown to a larger house at 803 Forest Avenue. My grandmother joined us there, and I got to know her.

My grandmother and me shortly after she moved in with us on Forest Avenue

At her knee, I heard stories of her family's grand home in County Cork, the winning of prizes for her watercolors, and the ownership of the Blarney Castle by her uncles. When I was older, it occurred to me that the latter story might be a bit of blarney itself, but more of that later. I did not hear about her move from County Cork to Canada in 1884, her meeting with my grandfather, their marriage in 1890, or the death of Ada, their oldest child, but I discovered all that through records on the Ancestry site. Also, she did not discuss how her birth year happened to move forward a year or two upon each census. However, she never criticized me but was always warm and cheerful, except when she talked about the loss of my Uncle Harold in World War I.

My parents were duplicate bridge zealots, and they had several tables of bridge players at the house monthly, each table with its green-felt card holders set up on bridge night. I was supposed to be in bed but would creep to the top of the stairs and peek through the balustrade to see the action. It was through these monthly occasions and through St. James Episcopal Church that I met the Skillern family. Dr. Penn Skillern was a local surgeon whose wife Lisa had a charming Danish accent. Dr. Skillern had been a naval surgeon during the war and had plucked Lisa from a chance encounter in Copenhagen, bringing her back to the States to marry her. However, I was most interested in the three Skillern children: young Penn and young Lisa were older than I, but Scott was just about my age. The Skillerns became fast friends of my parents, a friendship that has endured among the surviving Skillern family members over many years.

The move to Forest Avenue meant a new school for me: James Madison Grade School, with classes that ran from kindergarten through 9th grade. I had a short walk through an alley, down a hill, and through a playground—just a few blocks. Several memories stand out from those days. I was in 3rd grade when there was an epidemic of chickenpox. My teacher seized the opportunity for the class to learn about poetry, and I received many variations on:

Jerry Cox
Is a sly fox
He has the
Chicken pox

I had a dog, Zipper, a dwarf collie and my constant companion when I was at home. Of course, it was a dreadful loss when Zipper passed away, but the move to 827 Forest Avenue was a fortunate distraction. It was a bigger house, with eight rooms and a bath and a half. My father owned this house after renting the previous two in South Bend. But

Zipper and me outside 803 Forest Avenue

the biggest attraction was the Myers family who lived next door. There were six Myers children: Larry, Phil, Elizabeth, Ralph, Paul, and Mary. Mrs. Myers was a widow, whose late husband had been a professor of English at Notre Dame. She supported this large family on her late husband's pension and her salary as a high school English teacher.

Amusements for an only child with such neighbor kids were many: a tin-can telephone between the two houses; a miniature theatre with puppets in my playroom; memorized fragments of children's poetry from A.A. Milne, Lewis Carroll, Ogden Nash, and Leigh Hunt; a large sandbox in the yard that separated the two houses; and rubber-gun battles in our four-car garage. Helicopter parenting was unknown, particularly for a working widow, so we would build our own rubber guns from short pieces of 1" x 4" wood, slices of inner tubes for bullets, and a wooden clothes-pin trigger to fire the "bullets" at the enemy. Amazingly, without parental oversight, we would climb into the rafters of the garage, shooting the inner-tube bullets down at the invaders. Of course, if you were hit by an inner-tube bullet, you were out of action, even though they hardly stung the victim. What fun it was, and I do not remember serious injury or parental complaint. Did it build an appetite for literature and adventure? Maybe so.

In the winter, my mother and I would go to the Colfax Movie Theater in downtown South Bend on Saturday nights to see the first-run movies there. After the show, we would visit a nearby soda fountain and splurge on a sundae, just the two of us. I don't remember for sure but expect my father was working. Sometimes we would get a hamburger at the White Castle franchise across the street from the Colfax Theater before the show.

In the summer, without air conditioning, my mother and I would retreat to a rented cottage on Eagle Lake, a small lake in Michigan just northeast of South Bend. My father would join us on weekends and on some Wednesday nights, returning to South Bend on Thursday mornings. Subsequently, I came down with painful headaches, and Dr. Skillern suggested that it might be an allergy to something in the lake water. My parents were eager to find a cure, because I would frequently wake them in the night, moaning, and nothing could relieve my pain. My father found a cottage on Lake Michigan, just 35 miles northwest of South Bend at Rosemary

Running with a football at Rosemary Beach

Beach. It was a new beach with only a few cottages, and the one we rented in 1935 we named the "Jays' Nest": Jerome, Jane, and Jerry. It had an outhouse, a one-cylinder engine to operate the pump on a well, no running water, no electricity, and just three rooms.

It was wonderful for me. The headaches were gone, and playing and swimming in Lake Michigan was exciting with its occasional huge waves. Even more exciting was exploring by myself new trails through the woods, which grew out of the sandy dunes that ran for about a mile eastward from the

This is the gang at the "Jay's Nest." From the right are my mother and father, the Skillerns, and me between two neighbors.

lakefront. I could blaze new trails that seemed to be through completely uncharted hills and valleys. We all liked it so much that my father decided to build a lakefront cottage in a new section that Mr. Reiner, the owner of Rosemary Beach, had recently opened for development. That cottage was to be constructed in the summer of 1936, while my mother and I drove to Canada by way of Detroit, Windsor, Ontario, and the Bruce Peninsula to Manitoulin Island, where her uncle was the road commissioner. It was just the two of us in her Model A Ford, a great trip.

It was a memorable adventure. I was the navigator and was able to deal with the AAA TripTik Maps that laid out each turn and point of interest along our route. Finally, we reached the ferry at the tip of the Bruce Peninsula that brought us to the island. A car ferry was a new experience for me. Being the navigator was a task that gave me a sense of accomplishment as the miles rolled by. But most of all, talking and being alone with my mother was extremely fulfilling. She was always warm and serene. I do not remember her ever criticizing me or being upset. That was in contrast to my Aunt Katherine, my father's sister. Whenever she visited South Bend, my table manners and grammar were always on trial.

❧

Once on Manitoulin Island, we fished and saw the sights under the guidance of my great-uncle, returning to South Bend before school started. I was 11 and entering the 6th grade. Then everything changed. Just after school began, my mother became ill and was confined to bed in the front room downstairs at 827 Forest Avenue. I was not told the nature of her illness but visited her frequently at her bedside. She died on 15 November 1936. My grandmother died two days later, her death clearly caused by a broken heart. Her

My arms are akimbo as I stand next to my mother, great-uncle, and aunt.

three children and her husband were now all gone. At the time, I did not appreciate the depth of that tragedy.

Many questions remain, ones that an 11-year-old did not have the sense to ask. What exactly precipitated my mother's untimely death? Because her heart was damaged, did she know it was coming, and had she scheduled the trip to Manitoulin Island in order to have some final time with me? Did my father and grandmother know she might die? I wish I knew, but these are the kinds of questions that linger in a family for decades without answers.

After her death, my father asked me to be brave, and I attempted to do that by going to school the next day. However, when my teacher tried to comfort me, I burst into tears and went home to

Bessie and me sitting on a bench at the head of the stairs at Rosemary Beach

Bessie, our new housekeeper. Bessie Plummer, hired by my father to help take care of me and my mother, was a godsend at this moment in my life. She was short, round, about 30 years old, and a good cook. She cared for me as if I were her own, and her love for me saw me through the difficult years from ages 11 to 15.

During 5th grade, I discovered the school library and the magical book, *The Wonderful Wizard of Oz*. Frank Baum's delightful novel captivated me and opened my eyes to the joys of reading. I read every Oz book the library had and several other books I found there, including *WE* by Charles Lindbergh. The great pleasure of reading continued from the 5th grade throughout my life, but today my choices are almost exclusively non-fiction works.

By the next summer, the new lakefront cottage was complete, with electric power, indoor plumbing, running water, and enough room to sleep eight or ten in a pinch. The Myers kids were there, the Skillern kids were there, and even Dr. and Mrs. Skillern. Another

From left to right are Lisa Skillern, me, and Larry Myers, with Dr. Skillern peeking through the screen door.

My smile reflects my love for Rosemary Beach.

frequent visitor was George Yak, my best friend from grade school. Summers were wonderful with no shortage of things to do. For example, at the age of 13 I asked my father if I could add more electrical outlets to the kitchen, which only had one. I ordered all the parts myself, and my arms were small enough to reach into the concrete blocks in the basement kitchen wall to install several new outlets. I believe they would have passed code, had there been inspectors to inspect them. The Sears, Roebuck and Co. catalog of the day gave me enough of a description of the electrical product options that when I coupled that knowledge with what I had learned from books, I felt confident my wiring installation was going to be first class.

Let me jump ahead to 1980. My family and I—including my wife; my younger son, Randall (Randy); my daughter Nancy, her husband, and my one-month-old grand-daughter, Kim—were enjoying a two-week vaca-tion at the cottage. It was then owned by the Skillerns, who had purchased it from my father when he moved away from South Bend. Because of the rich history between the families, the Skillerns would not take any rent from me. In search of some way to compensate the Skillerns, we decided that there were still insufficient outlets in the downstairs kitchen. I commissioned Randy, then 14, to install a few more. His arm fit inside the cement blocks just as mine had done 42 years before. Working under my supervision, he wrapped up the job quickly and soundly. I could not possibly have gotten my adult arms into those concrete blocks.

Jumping back to 1938, the beach was wide that summer. Its width varied year by year depending on the annual precipitation and the runoff allowed through the Chicago River. Between swims, it was pleasant to lie on the beach observing the waves and the seagulls. One day, a young woman from a nearby beachfront home joined me and introduced herself as Elrose Randall. After several minutes of conversation, she asked whether I had ever played the game Hangman, which involved trying to guess a word given a set of blanks and gallows marked in the sand. It was fun, and it increased my vocabulary. For example, Elrose choose the word "syzygy." A usual tactic was to guess the five vowels first and I did so without scoring a single letter. Now I had 19 consonants to choose from and quickly lost the game because I did not know the obscure word, "syzygy"; however, I soon learned that it pertains to alignment of the planets. I added it to my vocabulary to cut my future losses. Elrose and I had many vocabulary-enhancing rounds of Hangman on successive days, and during one of them my father joined us. I introduced him to Elrose, never dreaming of the consequences that would arise within a year.

Chapter 2
High School | 1939-1943

By 1939, my father was courting three women as widely diverse in background, age, and temperament as one could imagine. I do not remember the names of two of them, perhaps because I did not like them. The first was a widow from a farm near Goshen, just southeast of South Bend. She was plain and sturdy. While her interactions with me were gentle and pleasant, they were uninteresting. The second was a high-society widow living in Washington, DC. My father took me on a driving trip to Washington to meet her. I could tell she was very interested in my father but clearly had no interest whatsoever in me. Then, there was Elrose.

Elrose was born in 1913 and my father in 1896, a 17-year difference, but in early 1939, I was 13 and she was 25, only a 12-year difference. Naturally, among the three, I was drawn to her. So, when

Elrose standing in front of 827 Forest Avenue in South Bend

my father took me aside and asked which of the three women I preferred, I unhesitatingly said, "Elrose!" Within a month or two my father left on a trip, not an unusual occurrence. Within a few days, Bessie received a telegram from him announcing that he had married Elrose in Florida on Valentine's Day. She read the telegram to me, and it was a shock. I burst into tears—and I do not exactly know why. Perhaps I expected to be part of the ceremony, but I certainly did not regret his choice. Elrose and my father returned to South Bend. I fretted that I had been responsible for an important decision in his life, but I tried to convince myself that he had made up his own mind and just wanted to be sure I agreed.

Elrose and my father made plans for their honeymoon in Mexico as soon as spring break had begun. Surprisingly, I was invited along for the first part of the drive, travelling with them all the way to Monterey, Mexico. I then returned to South Bend, shepherded back by Tom LaPlante, a junior colleague of my father at Bendix. I cannot remember the logistics, except that gas for LaPlante's car was only 15 cents a gallon. Upon the return of Elrose and my father from Mexico, Bessie left our household for her long-deferred wedding. I was extremely sorry to see her leave but understood that she felt her job was over and could now pursue her own life. In my later years, I often think of her and feel grateful for the important role she played at such a vulnerable time for me.

As always, summer 1939 at Lake Michigan was a joy. Some weeks, George Yak and I were at the cottage by ourselves. Elrose and my father would come on Wednesday nights but return to South Bend on Thursday mornings. She was pregnant, but I did not realize it at the time. George and I ran a pretend radio station complete with commercials and comedy shows in the big front room at the cottage. We also listened faithfully to the Gary Moore radio show on Chicago's WLS; it was an amazing tour de force in which he and his sidekick Durward Kirby provided a couple hours of humor each weekday. We swam, explored, cooked Kraft's macaroni and cheese, and talked about our futures. George wanted to be a radio announcer. I was vacillating between becoming a cartoonist, a playwright, a humorist, and an engineer. I am convinced that those summer days gave me an important sense of independence and a thirst for adventure.

When fall 1939 came, I started 9th grade at James Madison with some classes at Central High School. Latin, English, and Introductory Algebra were at Madison and Electrical Circuits and Machine Shop at Central. I continued my interest in radio shows, sometimes listening with George at his home but more often at night in my home. Programs that I enjoyed most came on at 9:00 p.m. Central Time, but I was to be in bed by then. I had been given a small plastic Crosley radio that I smuggled under the covers to listen to Fred Allen, Jack Benny, and the Lux Radio Theatre. However, my father could see the pilot light glowing through the covers and demanded that I turn it off. So, one weekend morning, I took the radio apart seeking the pilot light. To my delight, it was easy to unscrew the bulb, but my disassembly revealed something even more exciting: a set of amazing parts that included vacuum tubes, resistors, a transformer, and a large variable capacitor. I sat on the stairs, showing the disassembled radio to Elrose, exclaiming about the magic I had found. Soon I tracked down the local radio store and bought the American Radio Relay League (ARRL) Handbook, which told me in terms I could understand what those parts did. I was hooked. Not only could I listen to my radio secretly at night, but I also knew that I wanted to be an electrical engineer.

This decision was confirmed when my father took me on a trip to a testing agency in Chicago. We later received the report that I had good structural visualization and good math skills, so I would do well as an engineer. On that same trip, my father and I visited the Museum of Science and Industry, and the exhibits there—the coal mine, the German submarine, and the displays of electrical phenomena—only reinforced my conviction that engineering was what I wanted to do.

In December 1939, Elrose presented my father with a baby boy, Ferris Randall Rockhold Cox. I had occasional baby-sitting duties, and I must confess that my parents' trust in me was misplaced. I viewed Ferris as amusement for me rather than an amazing but fragile demonstration of life's continuity. Fortunately, he grew up to be my friend and chose, understandably, to forsake "Ferris," a first name from Elrose's family. Instead, he used her last name, Randall, and became Randy to friends and family.

I felt no jealousy of Randy, perhaps because the age difference was so great. I did miss Bessie but quickly adapted to confiding in Elrose. For example, Elrose helped me construct my "swindle sheet," an expense report that explained how I had spent my weekly allowance. My father insisted I produce this report before he doled out the next week's allowance installment. I missed my mother, but the acute period for that longing had been bridged by Bessie's presence from 1936-38. As far as a 14-year-old boy could tell, my father and Elrose got along well. She was also accepted by Mrs. Skillern, though Dr. Skillern, as was his custom, remained aloof.

The summer of 1940, like those before, flew by at Lake Michigan. George Yak and I had our pretend radio station. At times, the older Myers kids and the Skillern family, including Dr. and Mrs. Skillern, were there. I was noticing girls but did not know what to do about it. I particularly noticed young Lisa Skillern who was then 17, while I was only 15. She was gorgeous, and it was hard for me to keep my eyes off her in the short shorts she wore around the cottage. Young Penn, who was a year older than Lisa, was dating another Rosemary Beach beauty, Margot Meckel. To keep that romance under control, Mrs. Skillern posted me in the back seat of Dr. Skillern's big Buick while Penn and Margot enjoyed hugs and kisses in the front seat. The car was parked in the road at Margot's parents' cottage, and the radio played the song "Where or When" by Hal Kemp. I felt no awkwardness and perhaps even felt a bit elated by the responsibility placed on me. Penn and Margot? Not so much, I'm sure.

That summer, my father sat me down for "the talk." I believe he felt even more awkward than I did. He used proper anatomical names for the relevant body parts, and a few of those names were new to me. I mostly listened, and he seemed relieved when he had finished. In some ways, I was not ready for "the talk," so I never got answers to the questions that came to me later; in other ways, it was "old news" because of things I had inferred from conversation with friends. I think the method the next generation had for the transmission of this information was much better. *Everything You Always Wanted to Know about Sex* (*But Were Afraid to Ask)*, the book by Dr. David Reuben, was published in 1969, and a teenager could absorb the information at his or her own pace and be more fully informed than by a brief talk.

In the fall, I was expecting to be a full-time sophomore at Central High School, but my father had a surprise in store: He had arranged for me to attend James Whitcomb Riley High School on the south side of South Bend. Since we lived far north of the Riley district, I

Before World War II, my father—Jerome Cox., Sr.—was a patent attorney working for Bendix Aircraft in South Bend, Indiana.

have no idea how he made my registration at Riley happen, but Mrs. Myers, who taught English at Riley, must have been involved. My father may have been motivated by the racial composition of the two schools. Although Central had a large percentage of African Americans, Riley was entirely white. Also, the Skillern children had all attended or were attending Riley, since they lived on the south side of town.

It was an important decision for me. It broke me free of my humble social ranking at James Madison. At that point, I was not good at anything that mattered socially—marbles, sports, playground stunts, talking to girls. As a result, I had a liability among my Madison classmates that I would have carried with me to Central High. Those classes at Central High that I had already taken did not involve the Madison social upper crust, just techies like me. The Madison neighborhood was stable and in fact quite well off. Looking back, I see that the switch to Riley made possible a social "do over" for me.

In the morning I rode to Riley with Mrs. Myers, while in the afternoon I took the bus, waited for Mrs. Myers, or walked the three miles home. Somehow, I was invited to join a boy's social club, the Hermits. Embroidered on the back of our jackets was Al Capp's hermit character, Earthquake McGoon, from his daily cartoon strip, *Li'l Abner*. About a dozen of us were in the Hermits, and it was an anti-jock club, since none of us were athletic. Most of us did well academically. I was in the top 10% of students, but not straight A. I graduated on the honor roll as did half the Hermits. We kept our distance from the popular football players. Fellow member Allen Dewart and I decided, mostly as a joke, to run for vice president and president of the Student Council with the slogan, "Go on the rocks with Dewart and Cox." To our surprise we won, demonstrating to me the power of a catchy trademark. To my great surprise, I was popular and so were my fellow Hermits. I think our club, along with our female confederates, the SubDebs, included a critical mass of students interested in student government, drama, the student newspaper, band, and glee club—all extra-curricular activities not readily available at Madison.

In my junior year, I took geometry from Mary Alice Kitson. It was possibly the most important event in my entire high school career. I loved every minute of it, and Miss Kitson saw that I did. That year, there was a statewide math contest for juniors at the University of Indiana in Bloomington, and Miss Kitson entered three of us: Arlen Brown, Dick White, and me. It was a great adventure. Geometry opened a vista on mathematics that algebra had not done. Now, I could see its beauty and truth. Arlen scored 1st in the state, Dick 12th, and I came in 13th.

Later, Arlen became a well-known professor of mathematics at Indiana University and is now emeritus; some years ago, he reported to me that he could look down from his office window to the room

Dick White and I are pictured as we test an airplane wing in aeronautics class at Riley High School during our junior year. Dick, a lifelong friend, is pictured on the right.

where we had taken that test in 1941. Dick was a member of our high school Hermits and a lifelong friend until his death in July 2007. More about his life later. Miss Kitson, I have learned recently, enlisted in the Marines in August 1943, shortly after I graduated from high school, and served until January 1945. She married in 1958 when she was 51 and died in January 2000. I remember her fondly for her pivotal impact on my life.

I became active in the Riley Drama Club and had bit parts in *Mrs. Miniver, Green Chartreuse, Stage Door*, and some crazy skits that George Yak and I wrote. George was enrolled at Central High, but we saw each other frequently since he lived only a 10-minute walk from my house. One of those skits was a parody of Shakespeare's *As You Like It*. I remember only a fragment:

All the world's a beachball,
And all the men and women are merely picnickers.
They have their fires and fumes
And one man in his time burns many marshmallows....
Sands in teeth, sands in eyes, sands in taste, sands in everything.

I was vice president of the Drama Club at Riley, and that may have had an improper influence on what we produced. In any case, my participation foreshadowed my love for live theater that survives to this day.

In December 1941, the mood of the country changed dramatically. FDR came on the radio in our living room to announce that Sunday, December 7, was "a date which will live in infamy." My father was greatly worried and understood the implications much better than I did. Life did not change for me, so I did not see what was ahead. George and I wrote skits promoting the war effort: One suggested that saving gasoline aided our troops and another that Halloween pranks aided the enemy. Neither of us realized how our lives were going to be disrupted.

The Notre Dame campus was a two-mile walk from our house, and during my high school years, I had many occasions to make that walk. Most frequently, I headed to the football stadium on Saturday afternoons to strap on a heavy, ice-cooled box so that I could sell ice cream in the stands. Goodness, that box was heavy, particularly for a skinny kid trudging up and down the stairs in the packed stadium! But it was fun to see my favorite football team play, even if it was from the end zone steps. I did not make much selling ice cream or from any of the other part-time jobs I had in high school, but they did give me spending money beyond my allowance.

During the war, I made another trip to Notre Dame to see a physics professor recommended by Mrs. Myers. My reading about radio waves had suggested to me that they could be used to detect enemy planes in the sky. I explained my idea to the professor, and he reassured me that it was being taken care of. He did not mention the word "radar" or indicate anything about how such a detection system might work, but about a year later, in the summer of 1943, I saw a strange white dome on the top of Building 8 at MIT. Only much later did I learn it was a radome, and then I realized that the Brits and MIT were playing central roles in the development of radar.

Despite the war effort, summers for me were spent at Rosemary Beach. During most weeks, George Yak and I were again there without a car. Each day, we would walk the 3/4 mile to the milk box where the milk man would deliver milk bottles encased in ice to a lined hole in the ground; then, the Rosemary Beach residents collected them. Everything was on the honor system, and it worked without a hitch. Once or twice a month, we walked 2.5 miles to the Jerico, Michigan, general store for supplies, mostly macaroni and cheese. My father, Elrose, Randy, and their new red-headed baby girl, Candy (Elrose Katharine) came on most weekends, as did the Skillerns. Gas was limited, so we had to minimize travel. But there

Dr. and Mrs. Skillern along with Elrose and her two toddlers, Randy and Candy

was plenty of room for everyone: two bedrooms with double beds, a sleeping loft with double bed, and a back porch with two double beds—altogether, room for ten, not counting the cots that could be set up in the big living room overlooking the lake.

Sunsets were often dramatic, with the sun sinking slowly into the lake, but thunderstorms were frightening as the wind off the lake blew the rain through the cracks between the cabin's log siding. After a storm, the waves could be as high as those in the ocean, and that was enticing to George and me. We dove into them head over heels, with our tumbling accelerated by the crashing waves. We hiked often in the woods, and we could usually discover a hill with a new wild blueberry patch a half mile or so from the lakefront. Our make-believe radio station continued. The independence, opportunity, and adventure of Rosemary Beach were formative, I believe, for me and for George.

George went on to become a radio station announcer, spinning records in Central City, Pennsylvania, a small town I visited years later. The station, WCCL, was much the same as we had imagined during our summers at Rosemary Beach. Regrettably, I lost track of George after that.

Coincidentally, I discovered much later that three colleagues I met through Central Institute for the Deaf (CID) had also purchased cottages at Rosemary Beach and loved it. Ward Halstead had a big house overlooking the lake several lots north of ours; Dewey Neff had purchased Mr. Reiner's place; and Don Eldredge had a cottage just east of ours. Digging deeper, I found that Neff was Halstead's colleague on the faculty of the University of Chicago, and only later did Dewey move to a professorship at Indiana University. Don grew up in South Bend, becoming a physician interested in auditory physiology and eventually landing at CID. These links make the coincidence less amazing, but still, how did Rosemary Beach become a hotbed of auditory-neurophysiological research?

Back at Riley for my senior year in 1942-43, my interest in girls grew. I dated Nancy Feldman, Carol Knepp, and Mary Ellen Keyes. Nancy was the first girl I kissed, while Mary Ellen and I were dating at the time of my graduation in 1943. For a date with Mary Ellen in October 1942, my father had lent me his prize possession, a Packard sedan. Somehow the hour had grown later than I realized as I drove into the designated slot in the garage behind our house. I was trying to be quiet, but my foot slipped off the brake, and I bumped the garage wall with a thump. I waited, but since the house remained dark, I thought it safe to enter. To be extra careful, I took off my shoes and carried them in my hands. As I reached the stairs, the living room light flashed on. There was my father sitting in a chair with a remarkably stern expression. As he wrote in his diary for that day, "I got very angry and did not get to sleep until 4."

Unsurprisingly, I was grounded with extra chores. He, of course, thought I must have been up to dangerous behaviors, and nothing I could say would ease his mind. Fortunately, the extra work—tending to the coal furnace, cleaning the basement, and losing some of my allowance—were all I had to endure. There was no damage to the Packard, and the garage wall was something I could repair. My father was always the stern disciplinarian. My mother, Bessie, and Elrose could be counted on to take my side. Later, after I left home, my father softened, and his love for me became clear.

By spring 1943, the tide had turned in the Pacific at the battle of Midway, and the Axis had surrendered in North Africa. The war effort at home was in full swing. Many factories in South Bend had converted to producing wartime products. Draft boards were calling up young men, but my friends were not yet 18, and only a few sought their parent's permission to sign up at 17. Gasoline was scarce, of course, as were tires. Other than these and a few other shortages, life went on for us in Riley's senior class with little privation.

That spring, my plan was to enlist in the Navy V12 program and attend engineering classes at Purdue University, only 100 miles southwest of South Bend. Purdue was, and is, an excellent engineering school, and several of my Hermit friends were planning to do the same. The V12 program was an officer-training program and would have kept me out of combat until I graduated. I wanted to be in the service but having a bed to sleep in seemed like a good idea. The Navy needed technically trained officers for the many shipboard tasks in the new, electronically oriented military, and that seemed better than the infantry.

The Navy accepted me into the program, but my plans soon took a surprising turn. To increase my fitness, I was exercising on the monkey bars behind Riley when I fell and straight-armed the ground. A broken wrist was the only damage, but the Navy declared I was not physically fit, and the V12 program was no longer available to me. With my father's help, I reviewed my alternatives. I had also been considering MIT, an engineering school in Cambridge, Massachusetts, that was unfamiliar to me but seemed well-known to some of my father's friends. It was not nearly so highly rated nationally as it is now, but I followed my father's advice, applied, and was accepted. My high school record was good (honor roll) but not outstanding. Dick White was valedictorian of our class and Wilbur Campbell was salutatorian—both Hermits and good friends.

Tuition at MIT was cheap, only $600 a semester, so in late May 1943—shortly after graduation and my 18th birthday—my father and I boarded a train for Boston. All academic schedules were accelerated during the war with three semesters a year and classes on Saturday and many holidays. When my father and I arrived at Boston's Back Bay station, we crossed the Charles River and were housed at the MIT Grad House. I was awakened early the next morning by Brent Kuhnle and John Fisher, members of the Lambda Chi Alpha fraternity. I was rushed and joined as a pledge. My father returned to South Bend, and I have trouble imagining what must have been in his mind at that time. Was he worried about how I would manage at the fraternity? Was he feeling sorrow at his partially empty nest? Did he fear what was in store for me regarding military service?

I found MIT a challenge but one that I enjoyed. Classes were dominated by students in the MIT version of the V12 program. The fraternity provided social support, and hazing was not a problem. While I suffered some from homesickness, there was little time to think about that. We had the mandatory lecture from Professor "Perfect Circle" Sears in MIT's big lecture hall, 10-250. He announced, "Look at the man on your left and the man on your right. Next semester one of the three of you will not be here." He had the nickname "Perfect Circle" because he could draw a perfect circle with a flick of his wrist; he was also the author of the freshman physics text and an exemplary lecturer.

In the late summer of 1943, my life at MIT was rudely interrupted by a draft notice. To my father's distress, I withdrew from MIT, packed up my belongings, and boarded a train for South Bend. My father felt I should have sought a change of address with the draft board, thereby delaying my induction. But I wanted to eliminate the uncertainty and get on with whatever came next in my life.

Chapter 3
The Army | 1943-1944

After returning to South Bend in August 1943, I spent only a few weeks at home seeing friends and dating before boarding a bus to Fort Benjamin Harrison, just southeast of Indianapolis. The enlistment officer had my test results and my history, including my short tenure at MIT. He chose to focus on the fact that I had studied cornet in grade school and ignored my time at MIT. So, I was sent by train to Camp Blanding, Florida, for basic training in a company of recruits intended to become infantry buglers.

Camp Blanding is midway between Jacksonville and Gainesville, Florida, and the terrain is mostly sand. Buglers were to be assigned to infantry regimental headquarters companies; traditionally, they relayed orders to the troops from the regimental commanders by bugle call. By WWII, their role had evolved beyond playing "Reveille," "Mess Call," and "Taps" to also transmitting orders to the company commanders in other non-musical ways. However, it was still necessary to learn to play the bugle. It was considered a good assignment in the infantry.

My first morning, I was awakened by "Reveille," followed quickly by "First Call." I had barely enough time to dress and put on my puttees, a cloth legging that is bound tightly around the lower leg by a hook-and-lace scheme. We had been given our new army fatigues the night before, including shirts, boots, GI

Here I am dressed in my newly issued army uniform.

underwear, and a cap. I had no time to think about my new uniform but managed to get it on and race for the barracks door. Just as I stepped outside, my legs locked together, and I plunged headfirst into the company street. My sergeant took his whistle out of his mouth and yelled, "There's always one in every new batch." Only then did I realize that the hooks go on the outside of the calf, not on the inside facing the contralateral calf. The two rows of hooks had locked together on my legs provoking laughter throughout the company as they struggled to come to attention in the company street. Not an auspicious beginning as we fell into formation for the first time. The episode also gave a new meaning to the traditional Army command, "Fall out!"

The training for the enlistees in my company of buglers was the same as other infantry basic training, except that we were issued bugles and practiced the various bugle calls for an hour every day. We had hikes, calisthenics, KP, short-arm inspection, and rifle practice. The first time I had to fire my M-1 rifle at a target with the outline of a man on it, I had a meltdown. Until then, I had never fired anything more lethal than a BB gun. Tears ran down my face, and my sergeant was very kind to me. Instead of shouting, he talked to me in a comforting way, and soon I was at least pulling the trigger, if not hitting the target. He must have seen that reaction before in sheltered 18-year-old recruits.

Shortly after our arrival at Camp Blanding, an announcement was made to the recruits in each recently composed company that we could apply to join the Army Specialized Training Program (ASTP), the Army's equivalent of the Navy V-12. I applied, was one of the few accepted, and immediately was transferred to a regular infantry basic training company. The ASTP program would have sent me back to college, where I would emerge as an officer in a few years—clearly a better deal than being an infantry private. The explanation I received for the transfer to a regular infantry company was that they did not want to waste the bugler training on someone who, as an officer, was not going to blow a bugle. The training was the same in my new company except for the absence of bugling, and they took away our horns. Even though I would be one of the few destined for officer training, I had to undergo basic training with the rest of the recruits. The training was intense and left little time to worry about more than the next exercise.

I learned after the war that the ASTP program had been bitterly fought over in the U.S. Congress. Universities and some generals argued that it was important to train men to become officers, particularly in an increasingly technical conflict. Other generals argued that the infantry needed replacements at the rank of private—and needed them soon for anticipated action in Europe. They further argued that it was more important to have replacements for casualties now than to have officers in three or four years when the war might be over. That argument carried the day, and ASTP for all fresh recruits was cancelled just a month before I finished basic training.

In a few weeks, basic training was over, and I, along with the other members of my new basic training company, were given orders to report to Newport News, Virginia, with a five-day delay en route. I travelled by rail from Camp Blanding to South Bend and then, after the delay, to Newport News. The trip was over the holidays, so I was able to spend the five days with my family. After about a month and a half in Newport News waiting for transport, we shipped out on a large troop carrier. It was fast enough that it sailed without an escort of any kind because, as we were told, the German U-boats could not catch us.

The first day at sea I stood on deck and lit up a cigarette. I had never smoked because my father was exceedingly strong in his opposition to smoking. I don't know where his conviction came from, because almost everyone smoked in those days, and packs were free in all the services. The medical evidence against smoking had not yet appeared. Where my father had grown up on the eastern shore of Maryland, tobacco farming has been a staple crop for more than 300 years. However, he considered smoking a "dirty habit," and I knew that a tobacco taint on my breath would lead to the most serious of punishments. But here I was, "standing between my father and the perilous foe." If I was old enough to do that, then I was old enough to choose to smoke. I lit up and almost immediately got sick. Was it the tobacco, the ship motion, or the combination of the two? I don't know, but I am so grateful for that moment. I have never tried to smoke since and admire my father's prescience for saving me from the dirty habit.

It is almost 3,000 miles from Newport News to Casablanca, Morocco. However, because of the zig-zag route we followed to minimize the danger of a U-boat attack, the trip took us about two weeks. We did not see Rick's Café, Humphrey Bogart, or any part of downtown Casablanca, but we were immediately delivered to an army encampment on the outskirts of town. In contrast to the 1942 movie, the squalor across the road from us was startling. Hundreds of families were living in one-room hovels crowded along narrow walking streets. Their walls were made of flattened tin cans and other discarded items—just a single room, with kids playing in the streets. It was a dramatic sight for a young soldier from South Bend. Some of my comrades sought out the nearby house of ill repute, but I did not even venture across the street. In a week or two, we were herded onto a train with no announcement of our destination. We travelled in boxcars with "40 Men and 8 Horses" plainly displayed on the side of each one. It was possible to sit but not to move around. The train would stop from time to time, allowing us to leave our boxcar to stretch, get some exercise, and deal with bodily functions. We carried K-rations but were very relieved to arrive in Oran, Algeria, after an almost two-day, 500-mile trip.

Oran is an Algerian port on the Mediterranean near the border with Morocco. We had no idea where or what our final destination would be, and the commanders of our unit wanted it that way to avoid providing the Germans with any useful information. We camped overnight at the edge of Oran, had a decent meal, and embarked on a British troopship the next morning. Instead of bunks three high, as we had on the Atlantic crossing, we now had bunks five high. It was necessary to climb the ladder, swing your feet in, and make yourself horizontal to squeeze in between the man below and the man above. After a couple of days at sea, we arrived at Naples on Easter Sunday, 1944. We then travelled by truck to Caserta, Italy, not far from Monte Cassino.

At Caserta, the army had established a replacement depot or "repo depot" in the jargon of the time. Thousands of fresh troops arriving from the U.S. were staged at Caserta and then dispatched to active divisions to replace the wounded and the dead. We drilled and hiked at Caserta, knowing that we would be called into front-line infantry service, but not knowing where or when. Fortunately, we were with buddies from basic training who helped the grave time pass.

Not far from us was the Monte Cassino abbey, which dates from

Courtesy of the Imperial War Museum

Monte Cassino Abbey overlooking the Rapido River, where the German Forces held off the Allies until May 1944

529 AD and overlooks the Rapido River. It was a pivotal element in the German defense known as the Gustav Line. The Allies had attacked these defenses four times during the first four months of 1944. Finally, the abbey was bombed by the Allies, and the German defenders were driven from their position, retreating northward to Rome. I did not know this history, of course, in 1944. In mid-May, I was assigned to a company in the 88th Infantry Division, and we crossed the Rapido and started chasing the Germans north along Route 6.

At first it was easy going. We marched along the highway, and my only problem was the Browning Automatic Rifle (BAR) I was assigned to carry. I suppose the BAR was given to me, an infantry private, since the man I replaced, who was also a private, had carried it.

US Marine Corps Photograph

The BAR (Browning Automatic Rifle) was a relic from World War I but an effective weapon.

The rifle had two front legs about 10 inches long that were raised for transport and secured with thumbscrews. When firing the weapon, the soldier lay on the ground, extended the legs perpendicular to the barrel, and adjusted the length of the legs so that they supported the weapon's barrel at the right height to reach the target.

I was not able to get those thumbscrews tight enough, because after a few miles the legs would swing loose and bang me in the ear as I walked. Practice allowed me to walk farther between stops to tighten the thumbscrews, but these stops did not sit well with my sergeant. Eventually, we left the paved road and proceeded on a narrow trail into the mountains. We came under enemy fire from German 88 mm guns mounted on their retreating tanks. The muzzle velocity was about 2.5 times that of sound, so the shells arrived before the sound of their firing. Thus, if you heard it, you were safe. The Germans were primarily firing the 88 at Allied tanks deployed along Route 6 and not on the mountain trails. Thankfully, we heard the shells.

We slept on the trail, but I was feeling increasingly lightheaded. The combat medic assigned to our company took my temperature, declared I was sick, and said I should return to the rear where I could get medical attention. I traded in my BAR for a lighter M1 rifle. My orders were to return along the winding path we had followed into the mountains and report to the unit stationed where we left the highway. On the way, I slept in an Italian farmer's barn and then managed to make it to the highway the next day without incident. Italy had surrendered the previous year, provoking a German invasion of the peninsula and the welcoming of Allied troops by Italian peasants. As a result, I had no fear of being attacked by the Italian farmer whose barn I had briefly appropriated.

When I reached the military unit at the intersection of the trail and the highway, a medic again took my temperature, and I was driven to a mobile hospital where my diagnosis was declared to be malaria. After a few doses of a malaria drug and 10 days in the hospital, I was discharged and returned to my unit then stationed at Civitavecchia, the port of Rome. The malaria diagnosis was probably a mistake because my symptoms have never returned. In my absence, the Allies—including my company—had taken Rome on 4 June 1944. The 88th was having some relief from the war, regrouping from losses sustained in the advance north along the mountain path parallel to Route 6. The taking of Rome was eclipsed in the headlines around the world by the landing at Normandy two days later. Fortunately, none of my friends in the squad had been killed or wounded, but that cannot be said for the 88th in general.

A large bundle of mail caught up with me at Civitavecchia. My father had written me faithfully every day since I was inducted, so there were many letters from him stretching back to early May when I was at the repo depot in Caserta. These letters clearly expressed his love and were in contrast to the stern disciplinarian I had experienced in high school days. There were also letters from Elizabeth Myers, my neighbor, and from Mary Ellen Keyes, my high school crush. I had time to write letters to each of these correspondents and to

Mary Ellen Keyes sent me pictures of herself while I was in Italy.

relax with my company mates. Our duties were light.

Before long, my left foot began to swell, becoming exceedingly painful. Examination by a medic resulted in my transfer to an army hospital that had been set up in an abandoned Italian hospital in Rome, not far from the Vatican. I was diagnosed with osteomyelitis, an infection in the footbone, and put on crutches. Antibacterial drugs were yet to be widely available, so treatment was conservative: Use crutches and stay off the foot. I learned how to play ping pong on crutches, wrote letters, read, and visited the Vatican with a group of other GIs. The Pope appeared and gave us all a blessing.

By August 1944, I was told I no longer needed the crutches; I should report to the re-assignment officer, a young MD, who would determine my next posting. I entered his office and saluted. After a bit, he looked up from the papers he was reading and returned my salute asking, "Soldier, if you were discharged, what would you do?" I replied without hesitation, "I would go back to MIT, sir." He replied, "That's all, soldier." The interview was over, and I left his office having no idea where my next assignment would be.

To my great astonishment, I soon received orders to return to the U.S. to be discharged, "at the convenience of the government." I shall never know if the reassignment officer thought I could better serve the country at MIT, was a useless soldier, had an incapacitating injury, or some combination of those reasons. It was one of those life-altering moments, over in a flash, but setting a completely different trajectory for my life. I never learned his name and did not understand until years later the difference those few moments meant to me. Then I read about the heavy losses the 88th division had sustained in combat in northern Italy—fighting that raged from mid-September until November 1944. By then, the 88th had lost 6,000 of its 14,000 men. My chances of surviving that fall campaign unharmed were poor, and instead I was on my way home, thanks to the quick decision of that reassignment officer.

The next stop was the "racetrack" just east of Naples. It had been taken over by the Allies as a staging area for troops and supplies. I was stationed there for about a month, on KP 12 hours a day, serving coffee from a large 32-gallon can like those used today for trash. A cloth sack filled with coffee beans was draped over the side and a 6-inch-high heater placed underneath. A large ladle was in my hand to deliver the brew to the line of soldiers that never seemed to end. Somehow that experience has given me a lifetime aversion to coffee that is more physiological than gustatory.

A month after beginning my coffee service, I boarded a troopship for the U.S., where our group of early-returning GIs was delivered to southern Florida and housed at a luxurious Miami Beach hotel. It was an early version of a combat readjustment facility in which our only duty was to lie on the beach and check the bulletin board once a day. I was 19, enjoyed the girls our age who flocked to the beach, learned to consume alcoholic beverages, and took advantage of our undemanding assignment. I longed to see Mary Ellen, who had been a faithful correspondent while I was overseas.

The day arrived when the bulletin board advised that I should declare the post at which I would prefer to be discharged. I chose Fort Sheridan just outside Chicago. This was a great disappointment to my father but enthusiastically received by Mary Ellen. My father, Elrose, and the two children were living in Bethesda, Maryland, where my father commuted to a job with a downtown patent law firm. In retrospect, I had made an insensitive mistake, but one that turned out best for me.

After my discharge at Fort Sheridan, Mary Ellen and I arranged by phone for a night out on the town. I wore my new civilian clothes, and she was greatly disappointed, having expected to be able to show off her returning war hero in his uniform. I knew I was no hero and did not want to pretend to be one. We fought, I saw her home, and I left immediately by train for Bethesda. I suppose it ended well for me. Mary Ellen was definitely out of my system, and I could turn my attention to MIT. By great good fortune, a semester was just beginning that November. The wartime accelerated schedule had upended the traditional college semester dates, and I was quickly accepted into the freshman class. I spent a few weeks with my family and then took the train from Washington,

DC, to Boston, Massachusetts, only to find that the fraternity house was closed. I had spent only 13 months in the Army and was looking forward to the next chapter in my life. But with the fraternity closed, what to do next?

Chapter 4
MIT | 1944–1947

Unsure where to find housing, I walked across the Harvard Bridge, which spans the Charles River and links Cambridge and Boston. I was on Massachusetts Avenue, known fondly as "Mass Ave," a busy thoroughfare that runs through Back Bay Boston, across the Harvard Bridge, past MIT in Cambridge, and then about 1.6 miles to Harvard and Harvard Square. Curiously, the bridge is named for the Reverend John Harvard and has nothing to do with its proximity, or lack thereof, to Harvard College. On the east side of Mass Ave at the Cambridge end of the bridge stands the familiar and massive MIT buildings. The less-familiar MIT Grad House (now Fariberz Maseeth Hall) is an old brick building just opposite on the west side of Mass Ave. I thought there might be housing at the Grad House, where I had stayed with my father on our arrival at MIT in early summer 1943. However, when I inquired, I was informed that all housing on the MIT campus in the late fall of 1944 was occupied by a large influx of Navy V-12 students. I was on my own. So, with my small suitcase in hand, I headed back across the bridge to Boston.

At the MIT Grad House, a staff member had suggested that a room might be available in the Delta Upsilon (DU) fraternity house, 526 Beacon Street. The now-closed Lambda Chi Alpha (LXA) fraternity house that I had pledged in 1943 had been at 441 Beacon Street, and the two fraternity houses were roughly equidistant from Mass Ave, though on opposite sides of that street. I met with the DU house manager, Irv Dearnley, and discovered, to my relief, that they had space in a double room. Then he introduced me

to John Adams, my new roommate, in the second-floor front.
John was a Navy ensign attending
Radar School, one of many non-
DUs filling the DU house during
wartime. Irv and another resident,
Dick Best, worked at the MIT
Radiation Laboratory, known as
the "Rad Lab." Irv had previously
been initiated as a DU at the University of Rochester.

So, I had dealt with the housing problem, but I still had to
figure out how to come up with
tuition and my house bill. From a
visit to the MIT bursar's office, I
learned that Congress had recently
enacted Public Law 16 to benefit

John Adams, my new roommate, and me
at the beach

returning disabled veterans. Although I had not received a medical
discharge, I had received a 10% veteran's disability because of my
injured foot. Since the GI bill was not yet functioning, the existence
of PL 16 was great good fortune. To augment the PL 16 tuition
benefit, I took a job serving food to the V-12 students at the Grad
House. Now my three immediate problems were solved.

Right away, I liked my new roommate John Adams, a good-
humored young man who was 6'3", thin, and wiry, with a legendary
appetite. He had a fondness for adventure, even mischief. Once
he had carried out a "midnight requisition" of a welding machine
from MIT, welded the gates to Harvard yard shut, and, as a final
flourish, hung his MIT tie over the gates. John returned the welding
machine to MIT and, as far as I know, got away with this caper,
one of many in a long-running series carried out by students from
both schools and tolerated, if not occasionally smiled upon, by the
administration.

Soon he involved me in our own adventure: the purchase of a
1928 straight-eight Studebaker, an automobile that did not run. We
did not really need a car, but we both thought it would be fun. So
why buy a non-running automobile, you ask? It was spring 1945,
the war was still on, and inexpensive used cars with good tires were

My grandson-in-law Troy recently restored this 1928 Studebaker in his automotive shop, and we celebrated the reincarnation of the adventures John Adams and I had with our 1928 Studie. (Pictured: My son Randy and daughter Nancy, with me behind the wheel)

non-existent. An engine that did not run could be fixed, but there was no way to fix bad tires—the rubber was just not available. Together, we toured several used car lots, found the Studebaker, and had it towed to a spot behind the DU house. We then set to work replacing the engine's bearings. Neither of us had the necessary experience, but we plunged ahead anyway, working after our classes. Soon we were finished, and we eagerly attempted to turn the crank to start the car, which had been made before electric starters were commonplace. What a disappointment! The crank was impossible to turn, even with both of us leaning on it. Reluctantly, we disassembled the engine again and shimmed all the bearings, making them looser. This time, the car started right up, and we proudly drove it down Beacon Street.

It ran so well that we planned a weekend trip to New London, Connecticut, where John's parents were living. On the road, we nursed the car along at no more than 40 miles per hour, enjoying the smooth ride. But near Willimantic, Connecticut, we suddenly had trouble. I gave the old Studie the gas—and instead of accelerating, it whimpered to a stop. Around us, we saw mostly fields, but in the distance, there was an airport with a single Lockheed Super Constellation on the runway. I stayed with the car while John wandered over there. When he came back, he had learned that the Super Constellation had had an engine fire and made a successful emergency landing at the small Windham Airport. A half dozen mechanics were working to repair the engine. John had talked one of them into lending us his toolbox. Just imagine that happening today!

When we took the engine apart, we discovered a stripped fiber-timing gear, so John hitchhiked into Willimantic, found the part in a junkyard, and returned with it about 45 minutes later. We installed the replacement timing gear, started the Studie back up— and in a moment, it was purring as before. After we returned the toolbox to the mechanic, we were off to New London. What still amazes me today is the number of lucky coincidences that had to fall into place for our car trouble to be a brief interruption in our trip rather than a major fiasco! However, that was the way it was with John. He just expected everything to work out—and it usually did.

Another story that became a favorite around the DU house that spring is worth repeating because of an incredible coincidence that occurred a few years later. On the first floor in the rear of the DU house was a two-person study and bedroom, but in order to get to that room, you had to pass through the adjoining bathroom first. George Procyk, a DU brother who always wore a derby hat to hide his receding hairline, lived in that room, and his roommate was a newly arrived freshman. One day, the eager freshman decided to show off his room to his young date—and there was George on the commode, with his trousers around his ankles and his derby in place. The freshman, uncertain how to proceed, introduced George, who tipped his hat and, without missing a beat, quipped: "You'll pardon me if I don't get up." Of course, that story flew around the house. However, the small-world twist is that the Katharine Gibbs School graduate who was to become my wife repeated the story to me shortly after we met. One of her Katy Gibbs friends was the date who got that unusual introduction!

All of us at the DU house worked hard during the week and on Saturday mornings. A few were civilian students, such as Arthur Armstrong, George Procyk, and me; or staff members on campus like Irv and Dick Best. Many, including John Adams and Marty

Amsler, were in the Navy going to radar school. After the Germans lost the Battle of the Bulge in January, we thought that Hitler would give up at any moment, but he held on. So, it was somewhat anticlimactic when the war in Europe finally ended in early May 1945. That summer, the action shifted to the Pacific with a very uncertain future.

On Sundays during that summer, a group of us would sometimes ride by train to the beach at Lynn, Massachusetts. That was better than driving because there was no place to park nearby, and the train station was within walking distance. Those in radar school were college graduates and officers, while Arthur, George, and I were undergrads. However, we were all good friends, and there was no class distinction or discrimination among us that I was aware of. We wore our bathing suits under our street clothes on the train and then took off our outer clothing, swam, and played in the sand. We

Foolishness on the beach at Lynn, Massachusetts

could look across the bay to Nahant, a small town connected to the mainland north of Lynn by a long, thin peninsula. The whole adventure was great fun. When we were dry and ready to return, we rode by train back to North Station and then by MTA to "Mass Station," just a few blocks from Beacon Street.

It was a very eclectic crowd at the DU house. There was no common thread except that many felt the need to relieve the wartime stress with nonsense of one kind or another. Arthur Armstrong, for example, was a civilian student from the Midwest, who had a curious hobby. Whenever he visited a new city or town, he would consult the phone book (remember those?). If he found an Arthur A. Armstrong there, he would call the number, and the dialogue would go something like this:

Our Arthur: This is Arthur A. Armstrong
Responding Party: Yes.
Our Arthur: No, *this* is Arthur A. Armstrong

The conversation would generally become a hilarious exchange that frequently led to a date for lunch and an effort to uncover any common ancestors.

In August 1945, the war ended, and the DU house would soon be filled by returning brothers. This was a big transition, since radar school, V-12, and Rad Lab were all coming to an end, and most of the occupants of the DU house would be scattering. The uncertainties of the war were replaced by much less disturbing post-war uncertainties, such as what to do with the Studebaker; John was going home, and I wasn't sure where I would be living, since I was not a DU. So, we sold the Studebaker, and Art Galusha, a Lambda Chi brother, showed up and solved my housing problem. He managed to get me sworn in as a full-fledged Lambda Chi through the Brown University chapter in Providence, which had not closed during the war. I was able to skip any serious hazing and moved in at Lambda Chi, just a block east of the DU house, on the other side of Mass Ave. In the transition, most of the wartime occupants of the DU house moved away, and I lost track of the friends I had made in my first year back at MIT. Quickly, I was able to replace them with Lambda Chi brothers like Galusha, Brent Kuhnle, and John Fisher, whom I had met in the summer of 1943 before receiving my draft notice.

My status as the first combat veteran to return to MIT was quickly overshadowed by returning veterans of all grade levels and military experience, and as a result the LXA house filled rapidly. The school was still operating on the wartime accelerated schedule of three semesters a year to help the returnees catch up. I was in my sophomore year and had started taking some electrical engineering courses, enjoying them enough to earn all Hs that semester. In those years, grades at MIT were uniquely labeled: H, C, P, L, and F, standing for Honors, Credit, Pass, Low, and Fail. There was also a double F grade or FF that stood for a failure of both the course work and the final exam. This unusual system of grading at MIT has now yielded to the more familiar A, B, C, D, and F.

One of the new Lambda Chi pledges, Sherwood Johnson, had more money than was good for him, since his father and mother had done well in the sugar market years before. Not only did he drive a Jaguar XK120, but he also had a Chris-Craft that he once bought to impress a date and then docked it, unattended, on the Charles River near the fraternity house. In his freshman year, he managed to get all FF grades except for an F in physical education, a course that had no final exam. Needless to say, he was not back for his sophomore year. Instead, he switched to auto racing in his Jaguar and did very well, winning the National Sports Car Championship in 1952 and 1955 and finishing in the money at three Grand Prix events worldwide between 1953 and 1955.

One returning combat veteran was Harry Lighthall, who had lost an arm in France. Harry had outfitted his car with a knob on the steering wheel so that he could drive with one hand to turn and one knee to steady the wheel. He managed very well. All the brothers loved Harry. One of his dates mistakenly introduced him to her friends as Harry Lightbulb, and ever after he was known as "Bulb" to all in the house.

A great story about Harry involved a Lambda Chi house party. When he complained that he did not have a date, two brothers who were bringing Wellesley girls said they would fix him up. That Saturday night, as they were all coming back to the house from Wellesley, his date was in the rear seat with one couple while Harry sat in the front seat with the driver and the driver's date. When he got to the fraternity house and took a good look at his extremely unattractive date, he went straight to the bar where there was a large bowl of deadly, sloe-gin punch. He did not realize his "date" was actually his roommate, George Shultz, made up and dressed as a girl. As the evening wore on and Harry continued to drown his sorrow in the punch, George could not stand it any longer and said in his normal voice, "Bulb, it's me!" Harry could only say, "Oh, my" and slump into a chair. We all had a good laugh, including Harry.

A less-lighthearted story also involves drinking. Harry and two other fraternity brothers who had imbibed too much on a visit to a friend living in Athol, Massachusetts, were involved in an auto accident in Leominster, a small town on the route back to Boston. The driver, not Harry, failed to turn when he reached the town square and hit a granite watering trough head on. The EMTs arrived to find a bloody scene. One of them reported later that he had spent considerable time looking for Harry's missing arm, not realizing that he would have to go to France to find it. Fortunately, all three brothers recovered within a few weeks in the Leominster hospital. Harry went on to graduate, enroll in graduate school at Brown, finish a doctoral degree in mathematics, and become a professor of mathematics at the University of Vermont. He and his wife had a lovely home facing Lake Champlain, only a short drive from Burlington, Vermont.

Still another drinking story involved Bill Shuman, who was seeing a woman several blocks east of the fraternity. One Saturday night, he returned to the fraternity and climbed into his usual bunk above me in our dormitory. Shortly thereafter, I realized that he had climbed out of his bunk, and I turned to see him crawl out of the open dorm window. I ran over and saw him lying on the ground three stories below. I yelled, "Shuman just went out the window." Normally, you could blow a bugle in the dorm, and everyone would grumble and turn over. However, there must have been something in my voice that caused all 20 or so of the sleepers to jump up. We called the EMTs who came promptly and took Bill to the hospital. Luckily, the diagnosis was only a dislocated cervical vertebra in his neck, and Bill recovered completely in a few weeks.

When he returned to the house, we asked Bill whether he remembered why he had jumped out of the window. To our astonishment, he explained that he had had too much to drink at his lady friend's first-floor apartment, but he managed to make it home and fall asleep. In his dream, he was still at her apartment when they heard someone at the door. So, he jumped up and went to the window, which he believed to be on the first floor, and jumped. Thus, his state of inebriation probably got him out of his bunk in the first place, but it also may have minimized his injuries.

Drinking was an integral part of fraternity life in those postwar days. Although most of us were a year or two older than ordinary college students, our judgment with respect to alcohol was dreadful. Fortunately, these three stories ended without loss of life, but that was not the case for Jim Graziadei, a fraternity brother who died in an alcohol-related auto accident while at home in New York City for Christmas break in 1950. Today's heavy-handed monitoring of fraternities by universities pushes the open use of alcohol out of fraternities, but it continues to be a problem—just one that is not as easily linked to the university. Both the DU and LXA houses are currently banned from MIT for recent alcohol-related problems, and it is not clear that they will ever be able to return. Still, I felt that fraternity life was an essential part of my maturation while at MIT.

Another good Lambda Chi story requires a jump in time to more than a decade later. In 1958, one of the brothers was looking for a novel and harmless pledge-hazing idea, and he settled on measuring the span of the Harvard Bridge in units that represented the length of a pledge-class member's body. His choice was obvious: Oliver Smoot, the shortest member of the pledge class at 5' 7." So, Oliver lay down on the bridge sidewalk at its Boston beginning, and his pledge-mates painted a mark on the sidewalk at his feet and at the top of his head. Then Oliver would get up and put his feet on

Photo courtesy of John Ohlson and Oliver Smoot

Oliver Smoot with his feet at a recently painted "Smoot Mark" and about to have the next mark laid down at his head

the previous head mark, and his colleagues painted a new "Smoot Mark" above his head. They repeated this process 364 times before reaching the Cambridge side of the bridge. Surprisingly, these Smoot marks and their numbers became so popular that they have been repainted annually by Lambda Chi pledges and alums, and they rate a Wikipedia page of their own.[1] Even the city of Boston has found them useful, since the police can, for example, radio to

1   https://en.wikipedia.org/wiki/Smoot

police cars: "There has been an accident at Smoot 289." When the city resurfaced the bridge and sidewalks, they repainted the Smoot marks without assistance from Lambda Chi. Oliver Smoot himself graduated in 1962, became a lawyer, served as chairman of the American National Standards Institute (ANSI), and later was president of the International Organization for Standardization (ISO). Today, MIT's student-run radio station broadcasts at the wavelength of two Smoots,

Courtesy John D. C. Little

This is the cover of a memorial edition of *Voo Doo*, created by John D. C. Little.

and the Smoot is a recognized standard unit of length used by Google. The word "Smoot" now appears in the American Heritage Dictionary.

In my junior year, I started working for *Voo Doo*, "MIT's only intentionally humorous campus publication," which had a friendly

Among these members of the board of *Voo Doo*, I am third from the right, pretending to smoke a cigar.

rivalry with *The Tech*, a weekly MIT student newspaper. As a staff associate, my job was to collect jokes to print in the magazine. My colleagues and I reviewed the dozens of college humor magazines that arrived monthly from other schools and selected jokes that we would like to see in *Voo Doo*. Sometimes we inserted our own original jokes, which were then likely to circulate around the nation's colleges. It was a humorous ecosystem that had no formal rules or concerns for intellectual property. Here are a couple of examples:

Use Lumpo Soap. Doesn't lather.
Doesn't bubble. Doesn't clean.
Just good company in the tub.

"Do you smoke?"
"No, I don't smoke."
"Do you drink?"
"No, I don't."
"Do you neck?"
"No, I don't."
"Well, what do you do?"
"Tell lies."

In addition to jokes, *Voo Doo* also had humorous stories, cartoons, and a few ads. But the most fun of being associated with *Voo Doo* were the capers, which we would now call hacks.

Here is one example. In the postwar period, buildings were going up across the MIT campus. Every parking lot was in danger of being commandeered. One day, we got advance warning that Dr. Karl T. Compton, the MIT president, was to conduct a ground-breaking ceremony at one of the endangered parking lots. So, the night before, several of the *Voo Doo* staff members dug a large hole in a likely spot on that lot and erected a sign that said, in large letters, "Dig Here, Karl." Benign, but slightly uncomfortable for the official party that arrived the next morning. Compton could no longer turn over the first spade-ful of dirt at the site, but he gallantly carried on.

A more ambitious caper was the witch-burning that we staged in Salem, Massachusetts, to celebrate the 255th anniversary of that infamous event. One *Voo Doo* staff member asked a lovely student from a Boston modeling school to participate; *Life* magazine was also invited. That evening, the *Voo Doo* staff, the "witch," the *Life* photographer, and various students marched up the hill where these legendary events had taken place. We had arranged with the city to have a bonfire, and a large pile of flammable boxes was waiting for us, with a rickety gallows structure at the top. After a mock trial, the "witch" was hoisted a short way up the pyre. Then, while the crowd's attention was diverted by the fire, the live model was released and a dummy substituted. When the dummy reached the top and the flames consumed the gallows and the dummy, everyone cheered except the *Life* photographer. He wanted us all to go back down the hill and come up again, since he had missed a shot he felt was needed. We declined, and the story never ran in the magazine.

In those days, John DC Little was the general manager of *Voo Doo*, and he went on to a still more illustrious career. He created "Little's Law," a 1960 proof that applies to many queuing-theory problems, such as how long you should expect to wait in a grocery store line based both on the number of customers in line and the customer arrival rate. *Voo Doo* is still published at MIT, though I don't know whether its office is still in 303 Walker Memorial Hall. Back in 1947, I took my turn selling the monthly magazine in that Great Hall just outside Room 10-250, where I had my first physics class, taught by Professor "Perfect Circle" Sears. *Voo Doo* is still sold monthly in the Great Hall.

In my senior year, I was elected president of the MIT chapter of Lambda Chi. As president, my major accomplishment was constructing, from a kit, the fraternity's first television set, which had a screen that only measured ten inches diagonally. It was 1947, and television sets were expensive and rare. But I could buy a kit for $195.50 that, when assembled, gave us a complete RCA 630TS television. We crowded into the second-floor front library, adjacent to my room, to watch the

An RCA 630TS television assembled from an inexpensive kit and enjoyed by all the brothers in 1947

infant industry begin with Ed Sullivan and Milton Berle. Later, we all gladly took a break from our studies on weeknights to watch, listen, and laugh at the beginnings of late-night television with Morey Amsterdam and Jerry Lester.

I enjoyed almost all my courses, from freshman physics to a senior electronics course. In my junior year, I took a statistical mechanics course from Professor Bernard Feld, who delivered his lectures in a large, sloping lecture hall to some 50 students. MIT then had a system of bells that rang five minutes before the hour and again five minutes after. This allowed students to make their way from one classroom to another in the 10-minute interval. Feld was notorious for continuing his lecture well past the first bell, so that it was difficult to get to the next class on time. One day, after the first bell, Feld said, "I'll just put up this triple summation," a particularly dense mathematical form. A student in the very back row stood up, pulled out a gun, put it to his head, and cried out loudly, "Oh no!" Then he pulled the trigger and slumped into his chair. The report startled everybody, including Feld. When we all realized it was joke, the entire class broke into sustained laughter. Feld had to give up on the triple summation—and thereafter he was more cautious about the timing of his lectures.

Over Christmas break of my senior year, I hitchhiked to Columbus, Ohio, where my father and family had moved at the end of the war. The patent practice in Washington, DC, had let him go as their partners had returned from the service. An attorney in Columbus was looking for a partner to help with his growing practice, and my father accepted the opportunity.

The Studie was not available to me since John Adams and I had sold it. The "thumb" was a much more common way to find transport then, since we had all fought a war together, and most drivers were happy to be helpful. Just west of Harrisburg, Pennsylvania, another hitchhiker and I joined forces at the ramp to the Pennsylvania Turnpike. A driver stopped and we both jumped in, with me in the front seat and my new friend in the back. We quickly learned that the driver was drunk because he would speed up to 70 mph, put the car in neutral, coast to 30 mph, and then repeat the process. I asked what he was doing, and his brief answer was, "Saving gas." My friend in the back and I managed to talk him out of driving. Blessedly, he agreed and lay down in the backseat. My hitchhiking friend moved to the front, and we took turns driving west on the Turnpike.

When we reached the end of turnpike, the gas gauge was close to empty, so we pulled into a service station. The car owner in the back seat was sound asleep and could not be awakened. My hitch-hiking partner and I split the cost of the tank of gas, and then we got back into the front seat and drove off. As we crossed into Ohio, we wanted to know his destination and tried again to wake him but only got a grunt. I was going to Bexley, Ohio, the Columbus suburb where my parents lived, and my friend was going to Chicago, Illinois. We proceeded west on route U. S. 40 making good time except for stops to try to wake the owner in the back. I bid the two of them goodbye as we entered Bexley. I have no idea when our sleeping owner woke up or where he was going but hope we were heading toward his destination. After a wonderful holiday visit, my thumb also provided an uneventful return to MIT and the last semester of my senior year.

The only course I really did not like at MIT was AC machinery, which I took in that last semester. There was too much for me to memorize and not many fundamental formulae I could use to guide me. I got my only P in my undergraduate career in that course; all the rest were H and C grades (equivalent to As and Bs). The senior-year course I enjoyed the most, one on advanced electronic circuits, was taught by Professor Harold Edgerton, known by one and all as "Doc" Edgerton. He was a delightful lecturer with stories about flash photography and underwater exploration. Doc had made major contributions to each of those fields, including the invention of the photographic flash tube so widely used today.

During my last undergraduate semester in spring 1947, it seemed prudent to take a few days off to explore

AP Photo/Bill Chaplis

"Doc" Edgerton is holding an early version of his invention, the flash tube, which is now seen on all cameras and on the wingtips of all planes.

employment opportunities. Unfortunately, the only openings available to me then were in the defense industry, but I dutifully followed up on several opportunities in New York and Boston that the MIT placement office suggested. Soon I concluded that, after my days in the infantry, I did not want to take a job with any company making things that went BOOM. So, when Doc pulled me aside after class one day and asked, "Have you ever considered going to graduate school?" I was all ears. I had not seriously considered graduate school until that moment.

Doc explained that there were openings at the MIT Acoustics Lab, and they included a graduate stipend. I found that PL 16 would pay my tuition, so I was all set to continue my engineering education when the fall semester began. In May 1947, my father, Elrose, and Candy came to see me march in my cap and gown to get my diploma. Afterwards, we drove together through the White Mountains of New Hampshire and back to Columbus, Ohio.

It was great to relax in Columbus, but before too long I became restless and announced I was going to visit South Bend to see old friends. Again, I hitchhiked, and I set off by way of Toledo, Ohio. One ride I picked up just south of Toledo seemed fine at first, but soon my driver drifted into the left lane of the two-lane highway. As we approached an oncoming car in that lane, I decided it was time for action: I grabbed the wheel, steering us back to the right lane. My driver woke up suddenly and said he was grateful, explaining that he had been driving for about 30 hours straight to Florida and back. So, before we got to Toledo, I decided to tell the driver, "Well, here is my stop," and I got out, thankful to have my feet on the ground. The rest of the trip was uneventful, with only a couple more rides required to reach South Bend.

Upon reaching South Bend that evening, I needed a place to sleep so I checked in at the YMCA, but I awakened early with a fever and swollen glands in my neck. On the drive home from MIT, I had caught the mumps from my half-sister Candy. Not knowing what else to do, I called Dr. Skillern, who promptly came to get me, putting me up in his daughter Lisa's bed at 1014 East Fox Street. Since young Lisa was off at college, the room was available. After the most dangerous phase of the disease had passed, my father drove to South Bend to retrieve me, and I completed my convalescence in Columbus. This was the first of many encounters with the generous

Skillerns that took place after our days at the cottage.

In fall 1947, I returned to MIT to take up my assistantship in the Acoustics Lab. It was located at the east end of Building 20, the celebrated two-story, wooden structure that had housed the Rad Lab, where much of the U.S. development of radar had taken place between 1940 and 1946. In fact, the Rad Lab had installed the early experimental radome I had seen on the roof of Building 8 in 1943, during my first enrollment at MIT. In fall 1947, the Rad Lab building housed the Research Lab of Electronics (RLE), a mixture of mostly independent research laboratories.

At the Acoustics Lab, Professor Leo Beranek became my advisor. He had been recruited from Harvard after the war to join physics professor Richard Bolt in the lab's establishment, which was primarily made possible by funding from several large Navy contracts related to underwater sound and sonar. It was already well populated with both staff and graduate students. I was assigned a desk in a multi-student office, where I was asked to work out the acoustic equivalent circuit of a particular sound source.

Soon Professor Beranek also asked me to help out with some consulting work he was doing for the National Advisory Committee on Aeronautics (NACA), the predecessor of NASA, at their facility

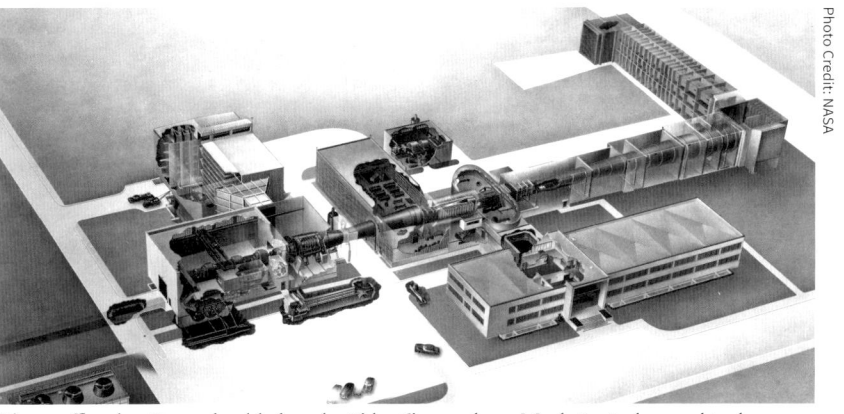

Photo Credit: NASA

The muffler that Beranek added to the 8' by 6' open loop Mach 2 wind tunnel is shown jutting upward at right angles to the main wind tunnel expansion section. Without the muffler, the expansion section pointed directly at downtown Cleveland.

in Cleveland, Ohio. The problem was that NACA had just built a large wind tunnel at the Cleveland airport, but the tunnel was immediately shut down because of noise complaints from the city. The wind tunnel had an 8'-high-by 6'-wide cross section, and it was unique in that it could test aircraft engines at supersonic speeds up to Mach 2. Testing engines required that the wind tunnel be "open loop," that is, the exhaust-laden air must not be recycled. For this reason, the 8'x6' test section was followed by a horn-shaped expansion section to slow down the air from speeds greater than that of sound—roughly 1,000 feet per second to a mere whoosh at about 15 feet per second—before it was exhausted into the surrounding neighborhood. Unfortunately, this huge exponential horn resembled, "an 87,000-horsepower bugle aimed at the heart of Cleveland." The only time when sufficient electric power was available to operate the huge wind tunnel blowers for their first trial was after midnight on Saturday night. Almost all of Cleveland was awakened to the sound of that initial trial, and legal injunctions were hurled at NACA by the city. Professor Beranek was hired with the simple mandate: "Fix it."

He had done that by adding to the horn a large U-turn muffler section, pointed away from Cleveland, which was acoustically treated. Several other graduate students and I were asked to make noise measurements both inside and outside the 8'x6' wind tunnel when performance tests at supersonic speeds were run on a huge experimental jet engine. The project was exciting. Again, the tests took place on a Saturday night, and the city had granted special dispensation for NACA to prove they had fixed the problem. Happily, Beranek's solution worked, and our noise measurements were testimony to that accomplishment. This was my introduction to life at the MIT Acoustics Lab and the many challenging projects that Beranek laid out over the years for me and my fellow graduate students.

Chapter 5
Bobby | 1947–1952

In the early fall of 1947, in parallel with my work at the Acoustics Lab, I began graduate course work in electrical engineering (EE). Since the Lambda Chi house was not fully occupied, I could stay in my room on the second floor behind the library. From our window, my roommate, Zenas (Zee) Crocker, and I had a view of an apartment building that fronted on Hereford Street, which runs perpendicular to Beacon Street. Hereford is the last of the alphabetically named streets that begin with Arlington at the Boston Public Garden and run parallel to each other through the alphabet, A through H, spanning almost all of Back Bay in Boston.

In that apartment building lived a young lady who chose to lie in her bed minimally clothed during the hot, late summer evenings. Her window was almost directly opposite ours, and had the fraternity house not been solidly built, it surely would have tipped in that direction, since all the brothers gathered at our window to inspect her and her boudoir. Did she know what interest she aroused next door? I suspect she did.

I discovered that one of my instructors, Sam Mason, and his wife Jeannie, lived in that same apartment building, but several floors above the second floor—and with more discreet window treatment. Sam was an electrical engineering doctoral student who was just about to finish his dissertation. It was not unusual, then as now, for doctoral students to be assigned teaching duties, and I very much enjoyed the course that Sam taught. He had a flair that few MIT instructors had. One day, he brought to class what appeared to be several sticks of colored chalk and laid them in the tray at the bottom of the chalkboard. Picking one up as he talked, he would almost start writing on the board but then would turn to the class to lecture a bit more. After repeating this routine several times, he amazed the class by lighting up the "chalk" he held in his hand—which was actually a colored cigarette. The fact that Sam smoked was not unusual; it was an accepted habit in 1947. He used the occasion to emphasize to the class how important it was to check your implicit assumptions.

Occasionally, Sam and I walked across the Harvard Bridge together back to our residences. I discovered that he liked to play ping pong, and we had a table in our fraternity's basement. I thought I was pretty good at it, but to my dismay Sam trounced me and everyone in the fraternity who dared to challenge him. He later confessed that he had won some kind of ping pong championship in New Jersey. In 1942, Sam had graduated from Rutgers in engineering and then come to MIT to work at the Rad Lab; after the war, he chose to pursue a doctorate in EE. Sam integrated well into the fraternity, not only with ping pong but also with help sessions and advice for younger fraternity members. In fact, the relationship worked so well that the fraternity made Sam an honorary member of the MIT chapter of Lambda Chi.

We all enjoyed the vibrant music scene in Boston during the late 1940s. The Savoy Café on Mass Ave just south of Symphony Hall, as well as the Ken Club downtown on Warrenton Street, were featuring many of the big names in traditional jazz at the time. Big Band music was available at a few hotels, but the music at the RKO Boston, a first-run movie theater, was particularly exciting. After the movie, the screen would go up, and there would be Tommy Dorsey and his band rising up out of the orchestra pit on an elevator stage and belting out "Well, Git It." It was dramatic and memorable, an experience that thrilled me then; even now, the memory still pleases me. It wasn't only Dorsey either, but a new Big Band would be booked every week or so.

For a while I dated a girl, Jay Sperlinga, who sang with a Big Band in the ballroom of the Bradford Hotel on Tremont Street in the Boston theater district. She was backed up by identical-twin female singers, and it was great fun for me to sit in the back and watch the trio perform; afterwards, I would go out to a late dinner with Jay. The Bradford is now gone, and our relationship did not work out. One reason was that my father met her on a trip to Boston and delicately disapproved. Zee Crocker was going out with a nurse in training and suggested that I date her roommate, Corky LaQuess, another nurse in training.

Corky was voluptuous and very attractive but not much of a conversationalist. After she graduated from nursing school, she was in search of a Boston apartment. I asked around among young ladies I had met on the staff at MIT and was referred to a group of three girls with a four-person studio apartment at 27 Saint Botolph Street, just off Copley Square, who were looking for a fourth. Corky and I visited, and I was tactfully informed later that Corky had not made the cut.

A few days later, on a Sunday afternoon, Bill Shuman, my fraternity brother who had long since recovered from his climb out the dorm window of our fraternity, and I were standing and chatting on the steps to MIT at 77 Mass Ave. As we chatted, one of those three girls, Bobby Lueders, walked out of the building, crossed the street, and turned to wait for the Mass Ave bus. She was in jeans, having come in on a Sunday to do some cleaning of file cabinets in her office. From across the street, I could see that she was petite. As I discovered later, she was never more than 110 pounds, wore a size 4 or 6, had brown hair with blonde streaks and lovely hazel eyes. She had graduated from Katharine Gibbs, the prominent finishing and secretarial school with a location in Back Bay Boston. That Sunday, from my viewpoint across Mass Ave, I was only reminded of her attractive face, smile, and figure as seen during the apartment visit just days before—but something clicked in my head. All thoughts of Corky disappeared.

The next day, I found her in her office, where she was secretary to EE Professor Richard Taylor, and boldly asked whether she liked jazz. To my great elation, she said "yes," and we made a date for the next Friday night to visit the Ken Club, where Max Kaminsky was playing. After an enjoyable Friday evening together, we went back to her apartment, sat at the dining room table, and talked until the early hours of the morning. I learned a number of things: that talking to a girl did not have to be difficult; that Bobby had never listened to jazz before; that she felt Corky LaQuess should have her name in lights at a burlesque theater; that she had just broken an engagement with another MIT EE graduate student, Keith

Hunton; and that her name was Bobby, not Bobbie, since that was one letter cheaper on the charm bracelet she had purchased in grade school. The other two girls in the apartment were Ann Page and Dottie Chadwick, and they were still searching for a fourth. I can't remember what else we discussed, but it had all been so completely natural and easy that the hours had flown by.

I was so thrilled about our date that the next morning I announced to Zee that I was going to marry Bobby, if she would have me. He nodded his head lazily, doubting my seriousness. But Bobby and I dated regularly: a hiking trip to Walden Pond, the movies, dinner at Howard Johnson's, and sometimes just quiet times at the apartment. It had a huge living room with a high ceiling and great light from four tall narrow windows that fronted on St. Botolph. It probably had been an artist's studio at some time in the past. Two small bedrooms were at the rear of the living room, and all the other rooms—kitchen, laundry, dining room, and bathroom—were downstairs below the level of the street, the front entrance, and the living room.

Frequently, fraternity friends and their dates, including Sam and his wife, Jeannie, would show up on Sunday afternoons to build human pyramids, practice singing, and play charades in the studio/living room. Ann and Dottie had steady boyfriends and would only occasionally participate; however, the girl who had by then filled the fourth spot, Joy Reed, frequently joined the fun.

An illusion that Sam introduced was titled "The Wizard," which we would play on an afternoon when Sam was not at Bobby's apartment but at his own. We would tell a newcomer that we knew a Wizard who could read minds over the phone: "Pick a card, any card, and the Wizard can read my mind and tell you what it is." I would make that pitch and then call Sam. My end of the conversation would go as follows:

"Hello, is the Wizard there?"
A brief pause.
"May I speak to him, please?"
Another longer pause.
"Hello, Wizard. I have someone here who would like to know the card I am holding."
I would then hand the phone to the newcomer, and Sam would correctly name the selected card.

How is that possible, you wonder? First of all, I had to know that Sam would be home and available to answer the phone. When asked if the Wizard was there, he would say, "Spades, Hearts…" and I would interrupt with, "May I speak to him, please?" as soon as he had named the right suit. Sam would then start enumerating the cards, "Ace, deuce, three…" Again, I would interrupt his recitation with "Hello Wizard," and he could then report the card as if he had read my mind. The illusion was dramatic, and the newcomer was always baffled.

Those were happy times. My courses were challenging and enjoyable, the war was over, and I fell deeply in love with Bobby. Our social life was busy and stimulating, as we spent time with my friends at the fraternity and their dates. I also volunteered to help with the book for an MIT musical comedy written largely by a Dutch friend, Art Van Stolk. It was called, *O Say Can You Si*, and it described the adventures of two MIT students in South America. To my great surprise, I see that the program from that 1949 production is reproduced in detail on the web today.[2] Many of the songs for the musical stand up well even now, and the comedy that Art and I wrote seemed funny at the time. Adding to my feeling of well-being, I had a car: a 1946 Mercury that I had purchased secondhand with money from my Aunt Katherine, plus my half of what we got from selling the Studie. In addition, the Boston music scene was full of life, and Bobby and I enjoyed all of it.

With the Mercury, it was possible for us to drive to New Jersey on some weekends to see her parents in Englewood, just north of the George Washington Bridge. Her mother, Eleanor, and stepfather, Oscar Lueders, lived in a one-story house just off East Palisade Avenue, not far from downtown Englewood. One lovely Sunday afternoon, I took Bobby to the Palisades Interstate Park overlooking the Hudson River, and in that dramatic setting I asked whether she would marry me. I was not at all sure what her answer would be, but to my delight she agreed to be my bride. We announced the decision to her parents, whereupon I received a good deal of harassment from her stepfather. He claimed that their daughter would quickly drive me into the poor house. I took it as good-natured kidding, but future events disclosed a hidden, more serious, concern. We drove back to Boston in good spirits and went ring-shopping

---

2   https://castalbums.org/recordings/O-Say-Can-You-Si-1949-Original-Cast/19041

the next week. The fall of 1951 seemed like a good date for a wedding.

Soon Bobby left MIT for a better job as secretary to Francis Rogers, dean of the Graduate School at Harvard. We could still meet for lunch in Harvard Square. Rogers was a hot-blooded boss, and Bobby was happy to get out of the office. Today, his behavior would be characterized as harassment, but many attractive women in the late 1940s had learned a bag of tricks to fend off such unpleasantries. However, the job with Rogers did not last long. In 1950, the idyllic postwar years came to end.

That September, Bobby's stepfather asked her to return to New Jersey to help take care of her mother, who had descended into a toxic mix of breast cancer and alcoholism. I think he hoped that the separation might dim our feelings for each other. So, Bobby dutifully pulled up stakes in Boston and moved to Hackensack, New Jersey, where her mother and stepfather then lived. I started the routine of driving to New Jersey on many Friday nights and returning to the fraternity on Sunday night. Bobby found a job on Wall Street as the secretary to the corporate secretary of Continental Oil, so she had to get up early to catch the bus that took her along State Route 4 and across the George Washington Bridge to the Eighth Avenue subway, which ran down the length of Manhattan to Wall Street. She did the same hour-long journey again after 5 p.m. At home in Hackensack, she made dinner, cleaned up afterwards, and tried to control the drinking.

One day at work on Wall Street, who should show up in her office but Dean Francis Rogers! He was eager to take Bobby to lunch. How he knew where she was working, or what his intentions were, are unknown. With some difficulty, Bobby fended off his advances and made it clear that the lunch she had in a brown paper bag was all she needed. Fortunately, Rogers took the dismissal gracefully and did not return.

Why had Oscar insisted on her return to New Jersey? It must have been a cry for help. She had agreed to spend a year at home, doing what she could, but it was a very trying time. Oscar was an enabler with regard to his wife's drinking, so there was little that Bobby could do beyond keeping the household safe and together as best she could. We set the marriage date for September 2, 1951, just a year after her move from Boston to New Jersey.

On occasional weekend trips to Boston, Bobby would work

on wedding arrangements. She chose Longfellow's Wayside Inn in Sudbury, Massachusetts, a fabled 300-year-old spot that had been restored by Henry Ford after his purchase of the Inn in 1923. Ford also built a fully working gristmill and a small, non-denominational church, the Martha Mary Chapel, both adjacent to the Inn. It was a popular spot for weddings and other gatherings just about 20 miles

Henry Ford had the Martha Mary Chapel built when he restored the Wayside Inn in 1923.

west of Boston along the Old Boston Post Road. The reception was to be dry to forestall any misbehavior by her mother. Since her parents were financially strapped, Bobby paid for the whole affair. We invited all our MIT and Katharine Gibbs friends and our parents. I also invited Doc Edgerton, who had been so important in my life and knew Bobby well from her days in the EE headquarters office. She invited her childhood friend, Lee Swartz, and Lee's father, a Presbyterian minister who was to officiate. My best man was Sam Mason, and Lee was Bobby's maid of honor.

The year at home was a trial for Bobby, but the fact that there was much planning to be done and a defined end in sight helped it pass by. On a trip east, my stepmother, Elrose, invited Bobby's mother to lunch in New York City, but it did not go well because liquor was available at the lunch table. It became necessary for me to reassure my parents that our marriage would be a good thing. For the honeymoon, I bought a new Chevrolet, black with no extras, which cost about $2,000 after the Mercury trade-in. *Holiday Magazine* wanted to do a feature on the Wayside Inn and the Martha Mary Chapel; they asked if we would be willing to have

The rain on our wedding day cancelled the carriage ride, but we carried on.

a photographer take pictures of our wedding. We agreed. With all of Bobby's careful planning, we hoped the event would go well.

It did, except for one small thing. It rained! The horse and open carriage ride we had planned between the Inn and the Martha Mary Chapel had to be called off. The *Holiday* photographer canceled, but a professional photographer we had hired, as well as Doc Edgerton, took pictures. It was a joyous occasion with so many of our friends, plus our parents, all present—and no alcoholic beverages to tempt Bobby's mother.

The reception was held in the second- floor ballroom at the Inn. Bobby's wedding dress was lovely. It was white with a high neckline, tiny buttons down the back and long lacy sleeves. I have a picture taken at the reception, now hanging in my bedroom, of my 9-year-old sister with such an admiring expression on her face as she looked up at Bobby in that wonderful dress. During the reception, Doc Edgerton asked Bobby whether she would be interested in becoming his secretary. She said we would talk about it

Bobby and I walk joyfully down the aisle at the Martha Mary Chapel in Sudbury, Massachusetts.

and call; we did talk, and it seemed right. So, we called from Niagara Falls, the first stop on our honeymoon trip, and Bobby happily accepted his offer. The trip wound its way through Pennsylvania, Virginia, North and South Carolina, to Sea Island, Georgia. We stayed there for a week at The Cloister Resort on the Atlantic Ocean, enjoying wonderful food and lying on the beach in the sun. On the return trip, we stopped in Annapolis to see Aunt Katherine and in New Jersey to see Bobby's parents. Bobby's mother was still abusing alcohol, but the situation had not deteriorated further, thankfully. All in all, it was a great trip that came off without a hitch.

Bobby, in her wedding finery, speaks with my nine-year-old sister, Candy, during the Wayside Inn reception.

Upon returning to Boston, we moved into a small apartment

The happy couple dancing in the second-floor ballroom of Longfellow's Wayside Inn, Sudbury, Massachusetts

I had rented at 94 Gainsborough Street just behind Symphony Hall. Bobby started work for Doc, and I returned to the Acoustics Lab. *Holiday Magazine* called saying they would like to do the photo feature anyway and could we pretend it was our wedding day? So, on a sunny day, Bobby and I took our wedding clothes to the Wayside Inn, ducked into a dressing room there, and came out in our wedding finery. We jumped into the waiting horse and carriage, posed for pictures, rode to the Martha Mary Chapel, posed again, and then went back to the Inn. It all took 20 minutes at most, and I am sure the bystanders at the Inn found the whole episode quite puzzling. *Holiday Magazine* got its photographic feature, and Bobby and I got a photo of the two of us in the carriage that hangs in our kitchen to this day.

But that is not the end of the story. I will jump ahead to September 2, 1991, our 40th wedding anniversary. Bobby and I thought it would be fitting to travel back to Sudbury and the Wayside Inn for an anniversary dinner. As we exited the inn after dinner, there was a horse and carriage waiting, just as there had been 40 years before. I asked the driver, an older man, if he was available for hire, and he was. Bobby and I climbed in, and as we plodded along toward the Martha Mary Chapel, we talked about our wedding and the delayed trip in the carriage. Our driver turned slowly around and, in a voice, straight out of the "Twilight Zone" television show, said, "I was your driver." It turned out that, in 1951, he was a young man hired by the nearby horse farm to drive the carriage. He enjoyed it so much that in retirement he had bought the horse farm, and he now drove the carriage at the Wayside Inn strictly for pleasure. What a wonderful nightcap to our anniversary dinner!

Back to our lives as newlyweds on Gainsborough Street in Boston. The apartment was a two-room affair with a kitchen/living room in front and a bedroom at the rear. The building was being renovated, and work on the first two floors had been completed, but the third floor was yet to be done. Just above us on the third floor lived a woman of indeterminate age, who told us not to be surprised if we saw men climbing the stairs to her apartment. She explained that she had an arrangement with the YMCA to take their overflow. She seemed nice—and we almost believed her.

We drove together in the honeymoon Chevrolet from our apartment in the Back Bay to Cambridge, where we worked on Vassar Street in Building 20 behind MIT. Doc Edgerton had his office on the second floor just two minutes' walk from the Acoustics Lab, so commuting was simple. We ate lunch together in the lab with a large group of graduate student friends. Working for Doc was a joy for Bobby. He was a wonderful boss and had many famous visitors who came because of his work with flash photography and underwater exploration: Gjon Mili, Jacques Cousteau, and more. Doc asked her to help with some of his photographic exploits. One in particular stands out. It is a multi-flash picture of Bobby skipping rope that has been published far and wide. The original now resides in the Smithsonian Museum and is available on the web.[3] The picture was shot in the lecture hall where I had gotten my introduction to MIT

This multi-flash picture of Bobby skipping rope, taken by Doc Edgerton, has been on display far and wide.

in 1943, Room 10-250. Bobby skipped barefoot across the top of two laboratory tables just in front of the large blackboard, with the only light that of the flash tube firing multiple times. It was important not to skip off the end of the tables.

There were other adventures, too. Bobby, Joy Reed, and I drove to the White Mountains one summer weekend to meet a party of fraternity brothers, whose plan was to hike up Little Haystack, then to Mount Lincoln, and across to Greenleaf Hut on Mount Lafayette. Joy, Bobby, and I were to be met by a few of the hikers at the Mount Lafayette parking lot on Saturday afternoon to carry food and supplies up to the hut for a grand Saturday night dinner. The three of us arrived at the parking lot on schedule, but no one from the hiking team showed up. We waited several hours until about 6 p.m. Still, no one had come down the mountain to meet us.

In that time before cell phones, there was no way to communicate with the hikers. The three of us assumed they had been delayed and

3   https://americanart.si.edu/artwork/moving-skip-rope-32686

that surely they were on their way down the side of Mount Lafayette to the parking lot and campground. We picked out the food that seemed lightest to provide a filling feast and started up the trail. The light was good because it was late June, and Bobby, Joy, and I made quick progress up Mount Lafayette, but we met no one on the trail. The sun went down, but we could still continue during the evening dusk. Finally, we gave up hope of reaching Greenleaf Hut or meeting our friends, and the three of us lay down on the trail. At first light, I got up and found the hut only a hundred yards from our makeshift camp, but there was still no sign of the hiking party.

Joy, Bobby, and I got to the hut, made a fire, and were relaxing when the hiking party showed up. There had been a medical emergency: One of my fraternity brothers, a diabetic, had developed the warning signs of hypoglycemia and had to be evacuated. The party managed to get him to medical care in time and then returned to the mountain, making their way to Mount Lafayette only about 12 hours late. We had a grand Sunday noon feast of steak and potatoes at the hut and then hiked down the mountain to the parking lot. We recovered our cars, and all went back to classes, graduate studies, or work on Monday, counting our blessings that we had somehow managed to avoid serious trouble.

On quieter weekends, the two of us could indulge my love of jazz in the many venues around Back Bay. One night stands out. My favorite singer then, Anita O'Day, came to the Hi-Hat Club in Boston's South End, just a few steps down Mass Ave from the Savoy Café. Bobby and I went and managed to get a table right in front of the bandstand. Anita's singing was great, and at the end of her first set, she chose to sit at our table. I expressed my admiration for her work, but Bobby observed afterwards that Anita had not made eye contact with her during the entire time she was at our table. My admiration for her singing endured, but not for her personality.

Those years were a delightful time for the two of us, and after the unpleasant year in New Jersey, they also came as a great relief. Bobby's friend Ann Page married her long-time boyfriend Dick Haggett and moved into an apartment similar to ours just next door on Gainsborough Street. Joy Reed moved to the Bay Area where she married Bobby's ex-fiancé, Keith Hunton. Dottie Chadwick had married Bill Richardson and they had found their own apartment on Commonwealth Avenue. The apartment on St. Botolph had broken up.

Then in 1952 came a big surprise: Bobby announced she was pregnant. Our two-room apartment would not do for three of us, yet our budget would not support a bigger place. What to do? I explained my quandary to Professor Beranek, who said that a possible solution had just been brought to his attention. Dr. Charles R. Williams, head of Loss Prevention Research at Liberty Mutual Insurance Company, had come to him looking for someone to help with the flood of industrial hearing-loss cases filed against Liberty's Workman's Compensation policyholders. It was something Williams did not know about, and Liberty's underwriters had set aside a \$3 billion reserve to cover what they figured was the company's liability. Did Leo know of anyone who might be able to work part-time to help?

When Leo told me about this opportunity, I was happy to interview. In my courses from Leo, I had learned how the human auditory system works, and that excessive noise could cause hearing loss. I was also familiar with noise measurements so was confident I could handle the scientific issues. I very much liked Williams, who insisted upon being called "Chuck." The deal was struck. I would work mornings at the Acoustics Lab on my dissertation, work afternoons at Liberty Mutual at 175 Berkeley Street in downtown Boston, and work after dinner at Leo's consulting firm—Bolt, Beranek and Newman (BBN)—at 16 Eliot Street near Harvard Square. It was a demanding schedule, but it allowed us to save money for the impending arrival. Bobby kept working for Doc Edgerton. He was a marvelous boss, looking the other way when she took an occasional afternoon nap in the lady's room near her office. We scouted out a lovely apartment in a development called Gardencrest which was located in Waltham, a westerly Boston suburb that was not an unreasonable commute. We arranged to move in slightly before Bobby's due date. Our finances were in good shape and I was doing well in my courses. What could go wrong?

Chapter 6
Doctoral Dissertation | 1952–1954

In late 1949, I had completed my Master of Science degree under Leo Beranek's supervision and had then been admitted to the doctoral program. I still had to pass the written qualifying exams, which covered material over the full range of electrical engineering subjects, but I studied hard for those exams and did well. I had also chosen my dissertation topic, but I needed to pass the final oral qualifying exam before I was admitted to full doctoral candidacy.

One of the courses that was added to my graduate program was taught by Professor Phil Morse. The course had no textbook, only mimeographed notes prepared by Morse. There were problem sets at the end of each chapter, but no one had ever worked them before. So, we students were charged with debugging Morse's problems. We teamed up, with Morse's permission, and spent entire days together working on them. Eventually, those notes, and the perfected problems became the two-volume set dreaded by many physics graduate students, *Methods of Theoretical Physics* by Morse and Feshbach.

It was a busy time for me. Leo had asked me to teach 6.35, the undergraduate course in acoustics. He had written the book on which the course was based, and I knew the material well. It dealt with microphones and loudspeakers, which I would also cover in my dissertation. In fact, I had already started making microphone measurements related to my dissertation in the large, two-story anechoic chamber in the lab. These were extremely precise measurements requiring accuracy of ±0.1 dB, or ±1%. In the afternoons, I went to the Loss Prevention Department at Liberty Mutual or to a nearby factory to make noise measurements that required an accuracy of ±1.0 dB, or ±12%. After dinner in the evening, I would often make my way to the BBN offices for a few hours, estimating the noise levels produced by jet engines that were yet to be built. In this case, we were pleased to be within ±10 dB or, ±316%, otherwise known as a "wag" (wild-ass guess). These estimates were associated with test cells BBN was designing for a new Air Force experimental facility in Tullahoma, Tennessee. Fortunately, as the days wore on, these increasing tolerances allowed me to dramatically reduce the care I had to take in my work.

I did not know how to study for the impending oral exam. The faculty could ask questions on any subject, and they wanted to see how the candidate performed under pressure. After it was over, I knew without being told that I had done poorly. Leo was considerate. He knew I had a heavy load, so he brushed the negative result aside and scheduled a second oral exam. Again, I tried to study, but hardly knowing where to begin and with little time available, I made only modest progress. When I got back from BBN to our apartment on Gainsborough Street, I would sit at the desk by our bed with the light directed away from Bobby, who was asleep, and spend a couple of hours reading material I hoped would help on the exam.

It didn't, and I failed the second exam, too. This time Leo suggested I take some tests that J.C.R. Licklider would select, to see if I had a personality defect that was hindering my performance on the oral exam. Licklider, known by all as "Lick," was an experimental psychologist who graduated with a triple major from Washington University (in psychology, mathematics, and physics) and then a doctorate in experimental psychology from the University of Rochester. During the war, Lick worked at Harvard in psychoacoustics; in 1950, he came to the MIT Acoustics Lab at Leo's urging. Lick's office was a couple of doors from mine, and he sat me down there to administer the tests. I never knew the results, but I was informed that there would be a third qualifying exam in January 1953. I don't know what those tests revealed but did know that I do not do well when I have to think quickly on my feet.

Bobby and I had moved into the two-story garden apartment at 8-9 Garden Circle that we had found in Waltham the previous fall. Ann Page Haggett and her husband Dick followed us from

Gainsborough Street, moving into an identical unit just two doors away in the same apartment building. Bobby's due date was February 1953, and I expected my exam to be over by then. We had made friends with the neighbors between our unit and the Haggetts place, and Ann's sister and her husband had moved into a building next to ours. It seemed this was going to be a wonderful place to live and raise our new baby. The only worry was my oral qualifying exam.

Professor Murray Gardner, Leo, Sam, and one other faculty member, whose name I cannot recall, were on my third exam committee. As I look back, I can see that Leo packed the committee in my favor, but I did not realize it at the time. Gardner was the registrar of graduate students and a feared taskmaster. Although I had done well in his famous course, "*Transients in Linear Systems*," that did not ease my mind. Also, my performance on the previous two exams gave me little confidence. The exam was set for January 21, 1953, and I fretted.

On the eve of the exam, Bobby told me she was having labor pains, and we had better go to the hospital, so we drove to Boston Lying-In Hospital, near the current location of Brigham and Women's Hospital. In the early hours of the morning, we received word that it was a false alarm, and we could return to Gardencrest, where I was able to get a couple of hours sleep. The following morning, I went off to the exam at MIT. I felt I did poorly. Sam asked me a very difficult question that I could not begin to answer. It seemed that, despite our carefully laid plans, our little ship was about to land on the rocks.

In the afternoon, word came that I had passed the exam and was authorized to continue work on my dissertation. Just then, Bobby called to say she needed to be taken to the hospital again and to please come pick her up. I did so, and after we arrived at the Lying-In, our OB told me it was going to be a while, so I might wish to get a bit of sleep to prepare for the long night ahead. In those days, the husband was not allowed near the expectant mother during labor, but instead was confined to the hospital waiting room. I gratefully took the doctor's advice, left the phone number of Dottie Chadwick's nearby apartment, and went there to catch a few winks on Dottie's couch.

I am embarrassed to say that my relief about the exam results, combined with my lack of sleep the previous night, led me to fall very soundly asleep. Early on the morning of the 22nd, the phone rang in Dottie's apartment, and I learned that we had a healthy baby girl. Mother and daughter were both doing fine, and I raced to the hospital to see them. We named the baby Nancy Jane Cox and soon brought her home to our apartment. Nancy was a name that Bobby liked, and Jane was intended to honor my mother. Thoughts of the possible shipwreck that our little family had avoided soon dissipated, and I settled back into my three half-time jobs that allowed Bobby to stay home with our new baby girl.

Paternity leave was unknown at the time, but I did briefly reduce my evening BBN consulting work. Instead, Bobby and I huddled in the apartment kitchen making baby formula. As beginners, we threw away several batches fearing that we had not done them exactly right. We even practiced putting fresh diapers on a pillow, trying to ensure that no safety pins would open inopportunely. Once, I spilled some hot tea on Nancy's arm and was miserable until she seemed to have forgotten all about it. Our pediatrician visited us in the apartment and pronounced that Nancy was doing fine. He was a kindly gentleman and told us he had once had Shirley Temple as a patient.

One morning, I ran into Sam Mason in Building 20 and said, "Sam why did you ask that tough question on the oral?" He said "Simple. If it had been an easy question, I might be accused of bias. If it had been an ordinary question, you might have flubbed it. Since it was a hard question, no one was surprised that you failed to get it." That was typical of Sam's reasoning, and I quickly forgave him.

The noise measurements I was making for Liberty Mutual were at the Continental Can plant in Malden, Massachusetts, just four miles northeast of MIT. The unfinished cans moved around the plant on a wire cable about a half inch in diameter; guard rails kept the cans from falling off the cable. Before the cans had their bottoms or tops affixed, they banged against the rails and slipped on the wire, making a great racket that exposed the workers to hazardous levels of noise. I recommended that the half-inch cable be coated with plastic to dull the noise, but management did not see any reason to make that expenditure at the time. Later, experiments by others showed that the plastic coating not only reduced noise mark-edly, but it also substantially extended the life of the cable. After that, management took notice and coated the cables.

Because I was spending a lot of time in noisy places while working halftime for Liberty Mutual, I had taken to carrying Flents with me on all factory visits. Flents are soft, disposable earplugs made of colored-foam plastic that can be molded to fit the ear canal, thus significantly reducing the noise that reaches the ear. We had employed a woman to help Bobby in the early days of motherhood by cleaning, doing laundry, and such. But we were brought up short when the Flents disappeared from my dresser, and the woman complained that those "candies" she had found did not taste very good.

My work at Liberty Mutual involved more than making noise measurements. Chuck Williams asked me to meet with their underwriters to review the calculations that had led the company to establish a reserve of $3 billion against hearing-loss claims. I discovered they had assumed that a hearing loss greater than the threshold of hearing should be compensated by their Workman's Compensation policies, when actually hearing loss up to 20 dB above the threshold of hearing is considered normal. This fact reduced Liberty's liability to about $1 billion. That $2 billion reduction, although only a paper gain, was clearly the most financially productive afternoon of my entire career.

In 1953, Chuck Williams and I published a paper jointly with Dick Mansur, a worker at the Maine Department of Health, and we titled it, "Noise and Audiometric Histories Resulting from Cotton Textile Operations." We had measured the hearing of two groups of employees at a weaving mill in Bangor, Maine. One included newly hired office workers, and the other newly hired weaving-room employees assigned to work sitting in front of an intensely noisy loom. A year later, we measured the hearing of the two groups and found that the office workers' hearing had changed insignificantly, but those in the weaving room had suffered significant and permanent hearing loss. This, I believe, was the first longitudinal study proving that industrial noise could be harmful to hearing. Scientists had speculated about it before, but a "before-and-after" study had not previously been done. Many other studies that followed firmly established the large Workmen's Compensation liability that the insurance industry faced in the mid 1950s. The mill did not worry about that liability since it was covered by Liberty Mutual's Workmen's Compensation policy. That was something for their insurance carrier to be concerned about.

That study probably led to my appointment to a National Bureau of Standards working group charged with setting standards for allowable industrial noise. The chair of that group was Hallowell Davis from the Central Institute for the Deaf in St. Louis—an impressive leader, who had been a professor in the neurology department at Harvard, president of the Acoustical Society, and president of the American Physiological Society. His honors and awards for government service during WWII were numerous. I was in awe.

We struggled with conflicting evidence involving many factors: the sound pressure level of the noise, the duration of exposure, peak-versus-average level of the noise, use of hearing protection, and hearing loss from other noise sources, such as hunting. All these factors affect a worker's hearing status. It occurred to me that an assault on hearing at just below what produces permanent damage was the cumulative noise exposure a mother receives by holding a series of six crying babies on her shoulder, one at a time, over a period of six years. The wisdom of Mother Nature emerged again.

At the Acoustics Lab, Walter Rosenblith had been recruited from Harvard and installed in an office next door to mine on the second floor. He began a lab of his own down the hall in Building 20 called the Communications Biophysics Lab (CBL), which was engaged in the study of the central nervous system using some of the electronic tools developed in the Acoustics Lab. Several of the graduate students in the Acoustics Lab decided to do their research at CBL. The mission of CBL intrigued Norbert Wiener, the famous mathematician who had coined the word and written the book *Cybernetics*.

Wiener was notorious around the Institute for his eccentric behavior and odd sayings. Everyone had a Wiener story. For example, he is said to have met a math department colleague who stopped him for a conversation halfway between Walker Memorial, the student union, and Building 2, where the math department was housed. They stood talking for a while and finally, at the end of the conversation, Wiener asked his colleague, "Which way was I headed when we met just now?" "Toward Building 2," was the reply. To which Wiener said, "Oh good, then I've had my lunch." He also is reported to have driven his car to Worcester Polytechnic Institute (WPI) for an appointment there and then taken the train back to Cambridge. Upon looking in his garage after his return, he was said to have called the police to tell them that his car had been stolen.

At the time, Wiener's interest was at the intersection of information theory, computers, and the operation of the brain. He was fond of stopping by CBL to discuss his abstract theories with anyone willing to listen. It was not long before the graduate students in CBL, tired of these conversations, established a DEWW line. To explain that acronym, it is necessary to review a bit of the history of the MIT Lincoln Laboratory, which was preceded by Project Lincoln, a 1951 study that found the nation needed a radar detection system to counter the threat of Russian bombers flying over the North Pole to drop atomic payloads on the U.S. A line of radar antennae, called the Distant Early Warning (DEW) line, was established in the frigid, distant reaches of Canada and Alaska to provide early warning about such an attack. Inspired by this history, the grad students coined the phrase Distant Early Wiener Warning or DEWW line. Anyone who saw Wiener approaching in the hall of Building 20 would sound the alarm so they could scatter to appropriate hiding places in time to avoid the seemingly endless conversations with Wiener.

Meanwhile, my dissertation was making progress in the mornings. My topic was how reciprocity can be used to calibrate microphones and speakers, most of which exhibit reciprocity. That is, a microphone can be used as a speaker and a speaker as a microphone. The sensitivity for the complementary function may be so low that its use for that function is impractical. However, the property of reciprocity can be used for the precise determination of the sensitivity of a microphone or speaker. Determination of a microphone's sensitivity, known as its calibration, is most often done with the reciprocity method because it does not require the maintenance of a standard microphone for comparison. Such a standard microphone is subject to change of its sensitivity due to aging, temperature changes, and mishandling.

My dissertation studied the fundamental physics of the reciprocity calibration process. I verified some of my conclusions through experiments in the Acoustics Lab anechoic chamber, a facility that has a wire-mesh floor and three-foot-long wcdgcs of sound-absorbing fiberglass placed on all six sides of the 20'x20'x20'-foot chamber cube. The chamber is completely quiet inside, and the absence of any echo can be disconcerting to a newcomer, but it was something with which I became completely comfortable.

In 1945, the property of reciprocity for lossless microphones and speakers had been proved from basic physics principles by Foldy and Primakoff. A lossless system operates without converting any of the acoustic or electrical energy into heat. Only theoretical systems are completely lossless, so the Foldy and Primakoff result could not be used with great precision on a real microphone. The amount of heat generated may be infinitesimal, but I felt the extension of reciprocity to such systems was an important advance. The extension to lossy (real) systems also piqued my curiosity about the relationship between Newtonian physics and the mechanism of heat production—something that results from quantum mechanical randomness.

Much like life itself, the reciprocity relationship is an intoxicating mixture of rules and randomness. Without rules, life would not be possible, but without randomness, life would not be interesting. In life, there are very few rules that cannot be broken, and most of these are the inexorable laws of physics that have been tested experimentally for a century or more. The rules imposed by governments, religions, societies, and families are fluid and transient. Very few examples of randomness are truly random at their root. Most events that are considered random are, in fact, explained by complexity, and assigning a stochastic explanation is only a matter of convenience.

In my dissertation, I analyzed and measured examples of microphones exhibiting lossy reciprocity. I showed how to deal with the calibration of real (lossy) microphones, but I could not completely understand the combination of classical theoretical physics and quantum mechanical uncertainty that lies beneath the surface of my results. Off and on throughout my life, I have returned to this question. It has occupied many odd hours and has been driven by curiosity. It is a nagging, unfinished job.

Bobby and I prepared my dissertation document using the hectograph technique, a long-since-discarded process involving a purple gel that served well then for short-run duplication. We had a manual typewriter at the apartment that Bobby operated masterfully, but equations and graphs had to be done by hand—and that was my job. The production of the dissertation took place on our dining room table, which was situated in a nook by the back door, adjacent to the kitchen. The table was a recovered antique that we had bought for $14 in 1951 at a used furniture store on Charles Circle in Boston. It was solid green, but Bobby saw potential in it. We stripped and varnished it at the Acoustics Lab shop and installed it in our living room on Gainsborough Street.

In its spot at Gardencrest, the table served well for my dissertation, though I had to press down so hard in writing the equations on the hectograph masters that I made marks on its pine surface, thus, adding to its distressed appearance. As the submission deadline of 11 January 1954 came closer, I recruited a couple of friends to help with the various production tasks. To my great relief and to the surprise of my helpers, it was finished the night before the deadline. But the next morning, Boston was covered with a deep snowfall. I fought my way over snow-covered streets to MIT—only to find that the graduate office was closed. Slipping a couple of copies through the mail slot in the door, I left, happy to have met the deadline.

My dissertation was accepted, my defense went well, and Chuck Williams offered me a full-time job at Liberty Mutual. I said goodbye to friends at the Acoustics Lab and started travelling the country, visiting Liberty Mutual policyholders with industrial noise problems, making measurements, and proposing noise-reduction alternatives. My experience with airline schedules, airports, and DC3 aircraft grew by leaps and bounds. Once, on a late-night flight to Dallas, I was the only passenger on the DC3. I asked the stewardess if the flight was always so lightly loaded. She said, "No, it's probably the tornado warnings." We landed safely, and I wondered whether the flight crew might not benefit from a bit of training regarding communication with their passengers.

Early in 1954, Chuck invited me to become the founding Director of the Liberty Mutual Research Center located near the start of the Boston Marathon in Hopkinton, Massachusetts, 26 miles from the home office at 175 Berkeley Street. The center was housed in a plain, one-story, concrete-block structure with only a single office and a large open area. There were just three employees: Murph, the machinist; Gladys, the secretary; and me. In addition, a sequence of Liberty Mutual loss-prevention engineers from the field would rotate in and out of the Center.

Our job was to investigate industrial noise, its sources, and its abatement. We had a complete set of noise-measuring instruments and several noise-making machines lent to us by interested policy-holders. One of them was a drop-hammer, an industrial metal-forming device that uses gravity to pound hot metal into a desired shape. But a drop-hammer is a notorious noise maker, and operators with any tenure are almost certain to be quite deaf. We concluded that the only way to protect them from deafness was for them to wear ear protection. But this was a hard sell to the grizzled operators, who saw deafness as a badge of honor.

On Fridays, Gladys, Murph, the currently visiting field engineer, and I would go out to lunch at a Hopkinton tavern. I introduced Murph to a gin martini at one of these lunches, and he liked it so much that he asked the bartender at his local saloon to make one. The South Boston bartender was unfamiliar with the drink but said that if Murph could tell him the ingredients, he would do his best. Murph obliged, and the martini arrived: a full water glass of gin topped off with plenty of red wine instead of just a touch of vermouth, plus four or five olives. Later, Murph returned to a single beer to adjust his mood so that upon reaching home he could deal pleasantly with his wife's many requests for conversation.

We soon fell into a pleasant routine. My commute from Waltham to Hopkinton was substantial, but I always liked to drive. Bobby thrived, making our homelife at Gardencrest warm and full of good cheer.

Nancy was an easy baby. Later on, when she was two, Nancy made friends with a boy her age, Charlie Duckworth, who lived in an apartment across the back yard. I can remember her standing on the back-stoop yelling loudly and repeatedly, "Charlie, Charlie Duckworth." I travelled to policyholders' factories, but not every week and never for long. Occasionally on a weekend, the three of us would travel to see Bobby's parents. Her mother's cancer prevented their travel to Boston, so they were delighted to see the three of us and behaved themselves. My salary at Liberty Mutual erased all financial concerns. It was a delightful time for our little family unit.

In the spring of 1954, Bobby, Nancy, and I were spending a restful Sunday at the apartment when the doorbell rang. It was Hal Davis and his wife Florence, who were visiting in Boston and said they hoped we did not mind them dropping in. We welcomed them, of course, and sat down for a chat. Eventually, Hal got around to the reason for their call: "Would you be interested in moving to St. Louis to take up the position of Director of the Electroacoustics Laboratory at the Central Institute for the Deaf?"

I made up my mind immediately but kept my reaction to myself, realizing there were many things to be worked out. Bobby was fond of saying, "I have never been west of the Hudson River." Thus, it would be a new adventure for her, but I did not know how she would take a move west. Further, Chuck Williams was counting on me to get the Research Center running smoothly. Moving a toddler halfway across the country would also be a challenge. We enjoyed the social life we had built up in the Boston area. Nevertheless, I was interested. I told Hal I would think about it.

Chapter 7
Central Institute for the Deaf | 1954–1961

Although my first impulse was to accept Hal Davis's offer of a job at Central Institute for the Deaf (CID) in St. Louis, I soon realized there was much to consider before making a firm decision. First and foremost, how did Bobby feel about moving almost half a continent away from her family and our Boston friends? She said she was willing to consider the adventure. We agreed that the move would be at least a year in the future, when Nancy would be a bit older and more able to travel; further, if we moved to St. Louis, it would only be for two years, three at most. I wanted to give plenty of notice to Liberty Mutual. Chuck Williams had shown great confidence in me, and I did not want to leave abruptly.

But why did I want to give up a challenging, well-paid job and leave the many friends we had made in Boston? The answer was Hal Davis. I instinctively preferred to work for someone I admired greatly. This decision was summed up in the phrase: Choose the boss, not the $$$. If Chuck Williams had still been my boss at Liberty Mutual, the decision would have been harder. Chuck remained as head of loss prevention research, and we were still close, but he was no longer my direct superior. After I took on the role of Director of the Hopkinton Research Center, I reported to a corporate VP, and it appeared to me I would be judged by corporate criteria— staying within budget and responding promptly to memos—rather than by how many problems we solved at the Center.

Clearly, it would be wise for me to visit CID to meet my potential colleagues and to be sure I would fit in. So, in the fall of 1954, I flew to St. Louis. It was a memorable visit on several counts. I was introduced to the research staff at CID: Ira Hirsh, who would be my new suitemate; and Art Niemoeller, who would be my graduate student. Next came research surgeon Don Eldredge, who assisted Hal Davis with surgeries on guinea pigs and chinchillas; these surgeries were expected to help in the quest for basic research results on hearing. Don *refused* to be introduced, saying, "No need to introduce me. I have known Jerry since he was less than five feet tall and a nuisance." That was true. Don came from South Bend and had dated Lisa Skillern. During their teen-aged capers, Lisa and Don had not wanted me and Scott, Lisa's younger brother, around. Don and his family had owned a cottage at Rosemary Beach a few hundred yards east of what had been our cottage on the lakefront.

Next, I spent some time with Ira Hirsh, the director of the Psychoacoustic Lab at CID. Like Hal, Ira was an impressive figure. He had trained at the Harvard Psycho-Acoustic Lab where Licklider and Rosenblith had been on staff before they moved to the MIT Acoustics Lab. Later, he had written the foundational text, *The Measurement of Hearing*, published in 1952, in which he defined the new field of audiology. He had a deep, resonant voice befitting a radio announcer. In fact, while earning a master's degree at the Northwestern School of Speech and Hearing, he had served as a staff announcer and dramatic actor on the CBS affiliate in Chicago. George Yak and I probably heard Ira during some of our high school summer days at Lake Michigan, when we were listening to WBBM radio.

Finally, I talked with Art Niemoeller, my potential graduate student. We hit it off well, and Art invited me to meet his lovely wife, Janne, that evening. She served the three of us a delicious dinner in their charming apartment located near Washington University. It was decorated in just the way Bobby might have done, and I guessed that Bobby and Janne would become good friends—and in fact, they *were* very good friends for more than 50 years. I also guessed that Art would be a great partner for some of the adventures that Hal was planning for me.

I returned to Waltham convinced that my initial instinct had been right. Bobby and I discussed the move, and she agreed to do it, so I accepted Hal Davis's offer. All that was needed was to find my replacement so I would not leave Liberty Mutual without a director of the Hopkinton Research Center. Allen Cudworth, a colleague of mine at the Acoustics Lab, had completed his doctorate shortly after I had, and he was now working at Lincoln Lab, the organization that resulted from the Project Lincoln recommendations regarding the DEW line. He confided to me that he was not happy there. A discussion with him about the Hopkinton Research Center directorship was positive, so I introduced Allen and his wife Cynthia to Liberty Mutual management. The negotiations took a while but were eventually successful, and Allen took over my job in September 1955. It must have been a good match because Al expanded the center's program dramatically, first into research on other industrial hazards and then into replacement limbs and safety. He remained the center's director until his retirement in 1990, a 35-year tenure.

In the fall of 1954, I received a letter from my father that began, "My goodness, we are all in a tizzy." The letter went on to say that Elrose was pregnant. This was surprising since my father was 60 years old and Elrose was 41. Anita Cox was born in March 1955 and would be the aunt of our daughter Nancy, though she was two years younger. My father seemed surprised but very pleased to have a fourth child. Bobby and I looked forward to a family reunion when we stopped by Bexley, Ohio, on our trip to St. Louis. They lived in a grand house in that Columbus suburb. The partnership that brought my father to Columbus had worked well for a few years, but after collecting a good number of his own clients, he had chosen to open his own office on a different floor of the 47-floor LeVeque Lincoln Tower in downtown Columbus. Things were going well.

Bobby, Nancy, and I prepared for the multi-day trip to Missouri. A moving company was to pick up our furniture and deliver it to us in St. Louis about 10 days after we arrived. I thought we would have no trouble finding an apartment to rent in that time, and Hal Davis had graciously arranged for us to stay temporarily in a little apartment on the second floor of the CID Research Building, just below the office suite that Ira and I would share.

We set off in the honeymoon Chevrolet, made the stop in Bexley where the two infants, Nancy and Anita, got acquainted, and the older members of the two families enjoyed a rousing game of Charades. The next day we began the final leg of the trip, and all went well until we crossed Illinois, where Bobby wailed, "It's so flat!" We arrived at CID on our fourth wedding anniversary, the

2nd of September 1955. We transferred the belongings in our car to the CID apartment and, after a good night's sleep, we set out to find a place for the three of us to live. Happily, we found there were rolling hills in the western St. Louis suburbs.

However, apartments to rent were surprisingly expensive. We had expected to find a rental for the same or less than we had paid for the Gardencrest apartment in Waltham. Our budget was tight because I had taken a $1,000 pay cut to accept the job at CID; Ira Hirsh told me that pay cut was the price I had to pay for the privilege of working there. My initial annual salary at CID was $7,000 per year, which seems tiny today but was not unusual then. Apartment after apartment proved unsatisfactory for one reason or another. In desperation, I called Jack Garrett, an acquaintance from prior Liberty Mutual trips. Monsanto headquarters were then in St. Louis, and Jack was an industrial hygienist at Monsanto charged with worker-safety matters, including industrial noise. We had crossed paths several times in the previous three years.

Immediately, Jack responded that there was a house for sale at a remarkably low price just two doors from his house. The address was 119 Couch Avenue, Kirkwood, Missouri, a pleasant St. Louis suburb. We had not considered buying but decided to take a look. The weeds in the yard were a foot high, there was a large hole punched in one of the bedroom walls, and it looked as though there might be termites. However, the mortgage payments would be less than our Waltham rental payments. With the bravado of youth, I said that the grass, wall, and termites could be fixed, and we signed the mortgage just in time for the moving van to deposit our furniture at our new ranch home in Kirkwood. We moved out of the CID apartment and spread out into five rooms and a bath.

I spent a weekend with a scythe and lawn mower to make the outside look passable. It only took a few hours to patch the hole in the wall—but the termites were another matter. Like most ranch houses, this one was built on a concrete slab and had no basement. The termites were in scraps of wood left under the concrete, and it was not practical to rip up the concrete to find them. Even drilling holes in a regular pattern was dangerous because it risked hitting the pipes that were buried in the concrete and provided the hot-water heat. Commercial estimates to exterminate the termites were well beyond our budget. What to do?

My experience in acoustics at MIT came to the rescue. From parts obtained in the CID lab, I assembled an underwater sound detector and connected it to the plumbing between the furnace and concrete floor. I then donned headphones on a long cord that allowed me to listen to the output of that detector as I used a rented jackhammer to drill holes in the floor. Whenever I heard the jackhammer sound grow suddenly louder, I knew I was near a pipe in the floor and would need to move to another spot. After successfully drilling many holes in the floor without hitting a single pipe, I was ready for the next step. With Jack Garrett's help, we concocted a poisonous brew, well suited to killing termites, and squirted it into all the holes. The evil bugs were eradicated at a trivial cost.

Bobby was thrilled to decorate our new home to suit her excellent taste. She installed the dining room table with my dissertation scribbles and many other antique New England touches in the large living room/dining room area. One of the three bedrooms became my study, a great luxury that allowed me to work late without bothering Nancy or Bobby. We were able to buy a used Plymouth so that Bobby was not marooned at home. She was so exuberant that, just to celebrate, she drove it around the house several times through our newly mowed back yard. Jack and Mabel Garrett introduced us to a half dozen of our new neighbor couples who shared with us and all the neighborhood children a large common area behind our houses.

At CID, I soon learned that Davis had two initial assignments for me. First, he had arranged for my part-time appointment as Assistant Professor of Electrical Engineering at Washington University, a short drive across Forest Park from the medical campus, where CID was located. This was a complete but pleasant surprise. I signed up to teach an undergraduate course in acoustics that would parallel MIT course 6.35 and use Leo's *Acoustics* book as a text. As the spring semester began, I learned the twists and turns of the quiet, winding routes through Forest Park that allowed me to avoid heavy traffic on the highways that border the park. All too often I needed that advantage to arrive at my late-afternoon class on time.

My second assignment was the development of equipment for project ANEHIN (Auditory and Non-auditory Effects of High-Intensity Noise), a multi-organizational contract with the Navy that had CID as its lead institution and Hal Davis as its Principal

Investigator (PI). Personnel aboard aircraft carriers were exhibiting hearing loss and also complaining of various real or imaginary medical problems that they blamed on flight-deck noise. In addition to hearing loss, these complaints included sleeplessness, headaches, erectile dysfunction, and a number of more ambiguous ailments. ANEHIN was a many-pronged project, whose goal was to track down which complaints were real and which were not.

Art Niemoeller and I put together a large, sound-treated trailer that could be used for the audiometric and psychophysiological testing of ten sailors at a time. It contained a semiautomatic audiometer that we had designed and built, as well as equipment requested by other members of the team. The Navy shipped it to Guantanamo Naval Base (known as "Gitmo"), located at the southeastern end of Cuba, on the east side of the bay that separates Gitmo from the city of Guantanamo.

Because of our class obligations at Washington University (WU), Art and I could not take advantage of the weekly Navy transport to Gitmo. Instead, we flew a commercial airline to Havana at the beginning of spring break, which gave us about 10 days before classes resumed. Cuba's dictator Fulgencia Batista was still in power in the spring of 1956, while Fidel Castro was in the hills of eastern Cuba brewing his revolution. In our three suitcases, we carried our clothes, but one of the three also had tools, measuring instruments, and last-minute things we forgot to send on ahead. Included was a sound-level meter, octave band filters, an FM radio system, screwdrivers, pliers, and a Weller soldering gun. The inspectors at the Havana airport immediately impounded that suitcase, apparently fearful that we were attempting to deliver a secret ray-gun to Castro. For those who have never seen a Weller soldering gun, it looks like a very fat, brown pistol with a menacing, heavy wire barrel. We were not allowed to take that third suitcase with us but were assured by the Cuban customs officers that it would follow on the next flight.

The flight across Cuba from Havana to Guantanamo city via Cubana airlines DC3 was more like a bus ride. We had many stops at "airports" whose only feature distinguishing them from a cottonfield was a windsock. Passengers would board with live chickens that had the run of the aisle. We made it to the airport at Guantanamo city and collected our two bags; an accommodating taxi driver said he would pick up the third bag when it arrived. He drove us to the Gitmo officers' club where we met our ANEHIN colleagues, all of whom had arrived earlier via Navy transport.

A day passed and no third suitcase appeared. The *U.S.S. Forrestal* was about to weigh anchor. The instrumented trailer was on board tethered on the hangar deck so our group could make audiometric and psychophysiological measurements, but we would not be able to make sound level measurements without our missing equipment. Reluctantly, we got on board, our hopes dashed that the taxi driver would make a last-minute arrival at the base with the third suitcase. That was not how it played out. After the *Forrestal* had weighed anchor, a tiny motorboat pulled up alongside the massive aircraft carrier. It was our taxi driver with the precious third bag! We tipped him what I hope was a handsome amount and were on our way to sea.

Soon we began our work. I had outfitted a helmet with two microphones and an FM transmitter. I expected that each member of the forward flight-deck crew would wear it in turn, which would allow the transmission of noise-level recordings to our equipment in the trailer. However, the crew chief did not want any of his men wearing this crazy helmet. So, I had to do it, wearing the helmet and shadowing each of the catapult crew in turn while Art recorded the noise level in the trailer. This was very exciting, particularly during night air ops when the flight deck was completely dark except for the afterburner on takeoff. There was no guardrail on the flight deck, so anyone who made a misstep could fall six stories down to the sea below. It is hard to convey in words the drama of a night takeoff from a carrier: The flight deck crew is gathered around the fighter jet making sure all is in order, the afterburner flames on, the catapult jolts forward, and the fighter is airborne off the carrier bow, but then it quickly sinks below the line of sight only to labor upward as its glowing exhaust comes back into view a quarter mile beyond the bow. The noise and drama are brief but intense. Shadowing each of the flight deck crew during night air ops was a once-in-a-lifetime experience for me.

Before the week was out, we returned to port at Gitmo and had a celebratory meeting at the Officers Club. Hal Davis and Dick Silverman had arrived on the weekly Navy flight and joined us. While at the club, Dick had made friends with a Navy corpsman whose job was to verify the good health of the ladies at the Guantanamo city brothel. He volunteered to give us a tour the next day.

We did not want to miss the opportunity to broaden our education, so the next morning we joined Dick and the corpsman. The ladies were busy cleaning their rooms, but we did learn from our guide that the women were all healthy, and those who did well in the Guantanamo city brothel could be promoted to Havana, where the pay was much better. One can't say that the Navy wasn't looking after the welfare of its sailors!

We all flew back together on a Navy aircraft to the naval base at Pensacola, Florida, and then on a commercial flight to St. Louis for those of us from CID. The analysis of the noise measurements and the audiometric data showed several things: that any intense noise was indeed very brief, occurring exclusively on takeoff; that threshold shifts were minor for the short length of time studied; but they were of sufficient concern that the Navy instituted requirements for the use of hearing protection by all flight deck personnel. As best as could be determined from the battery of psychophysiological tests, no measurable, non-auditory effects were found. The ANEHIN project concluded with the preparation of a substantial final report written by Hal Davis. Subsequent to ANEHIN, ear protection became mandatory on board the flight deck and was no longer "sissy stuff."

The adventures at Gitmo were my introduction to Dick Silverman. I learned that he had grown up in Brooklyn; gone to Cornell on a football scholarship, graduating in 1933; come to CID to work under its founder, Max Goldstein; received his doctorate in audiology at Washington University in 1942; and become the director of CID in 1947, while only in his mid-30s. He had a marvelous attitude toward life, a love for CID, a commanding presence, and a trove of fascinating stories. For example, in his youth he had sold candy in the aisles of a Brooklyn burlesque house and could still imitate the comics on stage, complete with the appropriate accent. As Director of CID, he had made the school an internationally known organization in the deaf world. So now I had gotten to know three of the leaders at CID—Hal, Ira, and Dick—and found each of them a wonderful validation of my decision to come to St. Louis.

Meanwhile, on the home front, Bobby was expecting our second child. We arranged for her mother to visit around the time the baby was due in order to help out—and we cleansed the house of any alcoholic beverages before she arrived. We had engaged an architect to design a large family room at the rear of the living room; its fireplace and high ceiling would make us feel we had a fine home that was less cramped even with a visitor and a new baby. Our son, Jerome Mills Cox, was born on 4 August 1956. This time, I waited anxiously in the hospital waiting room, as fathers did in those days. It was a great joy to see our new son and my wife together in her room in St. Louis Maternity Hospital.

After we returned from Cuba, Dick Silverman had asked whether I would be willing to assemble equipment for a new audiology lab to be set up at the Venezuelan Institute of Speech and Hearing in Caracas. I agreed to do that, and in late August, after Bobby and young Jerry were at home and it was clear that everything was going smoothly, I left St. Louis for a weeklong trip. Silverman, Hirsh, and

A horseback ride for young Jerry on his daddy's back

I flew to Caracas by way of Miami. The installation went smoothly, and I remember well the celebratory cocktail party held at the Hotel Tamanaco, with martinis on the patio and a marvelous view of the city against a fabulous mountain backdrop. When an afternoon rain shower interrupted the celebration, those of us who were visiting headed for cover inside the hotel—but I noticed that none of our hosts had moved. Instead, they merely put their hands on the top of their martini glasses to avoid any possible dilution and continued chatting in place. Sure enough, the rain shower stopped, and quickly we gringos rejoined our hosts on the patio. We learned that such brief afternoon showers were well known and no cause for a retreat.

Soon after our return from Venezuela, Hal Davis gave me my next assignment as director of the Electroacoustics Lab: setting up tests to assess the hearing safety of Audio Analgesia (AA), a recently introduced procedure designed to reduce the pain of certain dental work. The idea for AA had originated with my colleague J. C. R. Licklider, who was dreading a visit to his dentist, Dr. Wallace Gardner. He asked Gardner if he could bring some audio equipment to his next appointment thinking that listening to music would be soothing—but to his surprise, it was more than soothing. With the volume turned up high, the music clearly reduced the pain. As a scientist, Lick did some careful experiments and concluded that the effect was real both for music and white noise, so he and Gardner published a good paper and started a company to market AA to the public at large. A flurry of sales of AA equipment to dentists across the country ensued, but the American Dental Association was concerned there might be danger of hearing damage and commissioned CID to find out the seriousness of that concern.

Our tests were straightforward and showed there *was* danger of hearing damage with sound pressure levels up to 120 dB, well above the ASA standard we had previously set for industrial noise. Davis and I developed a proposal for a qualifying procedure for AA systems, but the concern about hearing damage—along with papers that failed to demonstrate, outside of a clinical setting, any effect of AA on the pain threshold—dimmed public enthusiasm for the procedure. Licklider and Gardner's company eventually failed. I never discussed with Lick our damaging results when I saw him subsequently.

Soon Hal introduced me to another adventure, this time an acoustic consulting job at the Chase Park Plaza in St. Louis. Apparently, Harold Koplar, owner of the hotel complex located just blocks from CID, was looking for an acoustic consultant to help with the construction of a large ballroom there. It would be called the Khorassan Room for the mythical Veiled Prophet, a central figure in the high-society Veiled Prophet Ball, and the room was to hold up to 1,000 diners. On Hal's recommendation, I showed up in Koplar's office one day in the late 1950s, and he showed me the design he had in mind, a hangar-shaped room. I told him that such a shape was a terrible idea acoustically and would have uncontrollable echoes because of its semicylindrical shape.

Koplar, who had studied architecture briefly at the University of Illinois, had his own ideas about the design of the room. He said he was going ahead with the shape no matter what, and he hoped that I could help with the acoustics. I said OK but warned that my solution would make the room very dead acoustically, and I asked him to promise that he would not have any serious music in the new Khorassan Room. Koplar agreed. So, Art Niemoeller and I set to work figuring out how to absorb conversational sound between 200 Hz (cycles per second) and 1,000 Hz. Above 1,000 Hz, the job was easy with acoustic tile and drapes, but sound absorption below 1,000 Hz was a well-known problem in a big room like this one (14,000 sq. ft.).

But Art and I came up with a novel solution: 20,000 acoustic resonators spaced out in a regular pattern over the ceiling. Since the ceiling had an area of about 20,000 sq. ft. because of its curved shape, the resonators would be placed on one-foot centers. These resonators were composed of the acoustic mass of air in each tube, coupled with the acoustic springiness (compliance) of four inches of fiberglass above the concrete ceiling, made of five inches of concrete reinforced by rebar. The fiberglass was to be laid on top of the concrete and then covered by a built-up roof. But how to make the many three-inch diameter holes through five inches of concrete?

The solution came to me from memories of my days at the Continental Can plant in Malden, Massachusetts. In addition, for Liberty Mutual I had visited an American Can plant that made cans for Anheuser Busch, the beer giant. They were just the right size—2.75" x 5"—for a 12 oz. can.

The contractor got to work. Plywood forms were put in place to support the wet concrete. Tennis balls were cut in half and nailed to the plywood forms on a one-foot grid; the cans were slipped in place over the tennis balls and then the concrete was poured and smoothed out level with the top of the cans. When the concrete had set, workers could crisscross the roof with a large can opener, quickly removing the can tops. As a finishing touch, they placed Christmas tree lights inside the cans before laying in place the four inches of fiberglass. Finally, the contractor installed roofing material on top of the fiberglass, and the arched ceiling of the Khorassan Room was finished.

When Art Niemoeller and I tested the reverberation time of the empty room, we found that it matched our calculations closely. It was time for the debut event. To my consternation, Koplar arranged for the St. Louis Symphony to perform that Sunday afternoon, and the *Post-Dispatch* music critic subsequently gave the acoustics a very unsatisfactory review. This did not come as a surprise to me because the room was much too dead acoustically for serious music. Lively reverberations are needed to brighten such music. I did not need to say, "I told you so" to Koplar. To his credit, he cancelled further symphony performances and substituted "Wrestling at the Chase," an attraction that endured there for more than two decades. The Khorassan Room still flourishes at the Chase. All the Christmas tree lights have burned out, and the fiberglass is getting matted, but the room has served the hotel well for 60 years, hosting large weddings, institutional dinners, and a wide variety of celebrations—even the Veiled Prophet Ball itself. The echoes that are characteristic of semi-cylindrical-shaped rooms continue to be absent from the Khorassan Room.

Hal Davis had certainly delivered on the interesting adventures that I had hoped would accompany my move to St. Louis, and he had done so in style, without compromising his principles. I looked forward to my next adventure, but I never expected it to be the life-changing experience that it had turned out to be. The next adventure began with a simple question from Hal, "Can you build an instrument to measure the hearing of an infant? I have an idea how to do it."

It had become clear to teachers of the deaf that early detection of hearing loss was key to the treatment of deaf children. The brain is so plastic in its early years that it sucks up everything going on in its environment. Hal reasoned that knowing a child was deaf as soon as possible after birth would allow a great deal to be done in teaching language—a much harder task after the deaf child was in grade school. I listened to his idea for an instrument and then eagerly set to work.

Chapter 8
Going Digital | 1961–1964

Hal Davis was in a hurry for the instrument he had asked me to develop, one that would determine whether an infant could hear. His idea was to record the electroencephalogram (brainwaves) from a baby's scalp and average the recordings that we made after exposing the baby to repetitions of a brief tone called a tone pip. We would record these brainwaves from an area of the scalp near the auditory cortex, a region of the brain above and behind the ears that analyzes all sounds. Anything we recorded from these scalp electrodes that was synchronized with the tone pip must have been "heard" by the infant, indicating to us that the child's cochlea was intact. The cochlea is the part of the mammalian hearing system that transforms sounds into neural impulses.

Our instrument's design should allow it to average the brain's response to many repeated tone pips. Brain-wave fluctuations that add repeatedly to the average must have been "heard" by the infant, while fluctuations caused by random brainwaves that are not related to the tone pips would tend to average out. This process is analogous to a group of people flipping coins labelled +1 and -1. The instrument can only see the total of the labelling on all the coins, a total that hovers near zero since +1 and -1 are equally likely. If person C (the cochlea) can hear the tone pip and ensure that its coin is always a +1 whenever the tone occurs, our instrument can detect the presence of C by summing the group responses to many tone-pip presentations. A single group response is not far from zero whether C is present or not. However, the more group responses to the tone pip that are added together, the easier it is to determine the presence or absence of C in the total. This is because, when C is present, its response stands out more and more clearly in the total as the number of tone pips mounts.

I knew that the timing of the recordings had to be precisely linked to the timing of the tone pips; otherwise, the indications of the infant's hearing would not add up properly and be distinguishable from other brain activity. But I also knew that achieving sufficient precision in our recordings would be difficult. First, I tried a circular loop of magnetic tape, hoping to get the same spot on the tape to always pass under the machine's recording head at the same time as the presentation of the next tone pip. However, I could not get the accuracy needed. So, I also tried several other schemes that recorded the electrical brainwaves directly as signals stored on magnetic tape, on the phosphor of an oscilloscope, or on photographic film. But none made what I considered to be a successful computation of the average; either the timing or the arithmetic computation itself was flawed. These experiments took many months, and Hal's impatience increased.

A new graduate student, Maynard Engebretson, arrived at the Central Institute for the Deaf and suggested we try using a digital computer. The digital approach allowed microsecond timing of the signal samples and unlimited accuracy of the computation of the average. The latter depended upon the number of bits (binary digits) in the digital representation of a brainwave sample.

Fortunately, there were digital modules just then becoming available from the Digital Equipment Corporation (DEC), a small, newly formed Massachusetts-based firm. The modules that DEC provided were the basic building blocks from which any kind of digital computing system could be built. From these building blocks, Maynard and I designed and assembled a special-purpose digital computer, which was limited to computing just three functions of its input data. By contrast, a general-purpose digital computer could make any computation on the input data and could be built from the same DEC building blocks. However, it would require many more modules at a higher total cost.

We named our machine the HAVOC (Histogram, AVerage, and Ogive Calculator). A histogram is a graph of the number of times a specific value is observed. The average is, of course, the sum of all values observed, divided by the number of values. The Ogive is a graph of the number of times a voltage *no greater* than a particular value is observed. We included this calculation in the design at my suggestion, more for the ability to pronounce the name, HAVOC, than for any expected use that would be made of the Ogive functionality. My fascination with acronyms that can be pronounced will appear in later chapters.

Maynard and I had to design and build our own analog-to-digital converter (ADC) in order to transform the recorded brainwaves to digital form. When the components were all assembled, the HAVOC worked well, and Hal made good use of it. With the assistance of Shirley Hirsh, Ira's wife, he established the new field of evoked response audiometry (ERA), the measurement of the hearing of an individual obtained from brainwaves evoked by the presentation of a series of tone pips. Not unexpectedly, Hal had no need for the ogive or histogram functionality but used the averaging capability extensively.

This new instrument was popular with Hal and others. Maynard and I had requests for copies of the HAVOC from three investigators in the now-burgeoning field of evoked response audiometry: Don Teas, University of Pittsburgh; Don Nielsen, Tracy Clinic; and Jim Satterfield, Washington University. All four machines worked reliably and produced data for many research papers. The HAVOC not only supported these research studies, but it also taught me an important lesson: A lot can be done with digital systems when applied to problems in biomedical research.

Hal Davis's original insight regarding the need to measure an infant's hearing had a salutary long-term impact. Prior to the publication of the Davis-Hirsh papers on evoked response audiometry, there was no reliable way to measure a baby's hearing. After all, a newborn can't be expected to raise its hand upon hearing a tone pip. Soon, the field of ERA matured from placing the electrodes near the auditory cortex to shifting to a spot near the brainstem because of the increased reliability of results in that area. Next, other investigators established a screening test that was less expensive and could be easily applied to all newborns. Called the test of Otoacoustic Emissions (OAE), it measures the acoustic echo in the ear canal that occurs only when infant's hearing is intact. Because this test sometimes indicates a hearing problem when there is none, newborns who fail the OAE test are retested with the more reliable but more expensive ERA. Slightly more than 98% of newborns in the U.S. now receive the OAE screening test. Only a small fraction of them fail the screening test and go on to be tested with ERA.

If these tests detect a hearing problem, then babies as young as nine months old can receive a kind of internal hearing aid known as a cochlear implant. With such an implant plus early training, the child can, by first grade, learn to hear and speak as well as his or her normally hearing peers. This early intervention has made an enormous demographic difference in the population of students at CID. Most students enter CID's Family Center at a year or two of age, and after their implant they leave to join their hearing peers when they are in the primary grades. By contrast, when I first came to CID in 1955, most students entered CID in the primary grades and stayed until they graduated from high school. Now, only those who lose their hearing to disease in later years or somehow missed the newborn test will enroll in the primary grades and stay through high school. Hal's insight and the contemporaneous development of the cochlear implant were signal events in this marvelous shift. Not only do children who are born deaf become able to hear much earlier, but they speak more clearly, with hardly a trace of "deaf speech." Maynard and I are pleased to have played a role in the early history of evoked response audiometry, a crucial measurement technology.

During the construction of HAVOC, events in New Jersey had reached a tragic end. In early 1961, Bobby's mother, Eleanor, had suffered a mortal cancer recurrence and was in the hospital near Ossining, New York, her family home. Bobby took the train to New York City while I minded the kids. It was only a short while later, in March of that year, that she passed away. Bobby and I arranged for an elderly Kirkwood couple to take care of our two kids, and we flew to the funeral in Ossining, followed by the burial in a

Portrait by Binder-Adelier Studio

In 1960, Bobby had a photographic portrait taken that turned out well.

family plot in the Bronx. Subsequently, Bobby's stepfather, who had been spending a lot of time in the hospital prior to Eleanor's death, joined the support group active in the hospital and from which he had benefitted. Perhaps it was an effort to pay back the debt he felt that he owed to this group. He moved to New York near the hospital and devoted his time to helping others through their illness or grief.

During these years, I was also involved in other research at CID. In the physiology lab, where Davis and Eldredge were trying to gain a fundamental understanding of the mechanism of hearing by doing experiments on small-animal cochleae, I saw new possibilities for digital computer technology. The same was true of Hirsh's Psychoacoustic Lab. However, it became clear to me that the size of memory used in the HAVOC was too small to meet the needs of either lab. Many bioelectric signals had to be recorded for extended periods of time instead of a single average evoked response. Larger random-access memories were then much too expensive. I had hopes that an inexpensive, small-drum memory could be used to store laboratory results for analysis months or even years later, but I needed to learn more about such a unit.

I discovered that the only small drum memory in use nearby was at the Defense Mapping Agency (DMA) location, now known as the National Geospatial-Intelligence Agency, just east of the Anheuser-Busch Brewery in downtown St. Louis. In 1962, DMA was less concerned about security than it is today, and the agency allowed me to visit carrying along my oscilloscope, which made it possible for me to understand the timing of signals to and from the drum memory. It took much longer for me to make the measurements than expected, but at least I saw that this unit was exactly what we needed in the labs at CID. It could store enough experimental results to accommodate the data that Hal, Ira, and others at CID were creating.

That day, the only problem was that I was clearly going to be late for dinner with Bobby and the kids. In those days, no outgoing calls were allowed from DMA, and cell phones were yet to be invented. I persevered with my measurements, expecting to be done at any moment. When I finally finished, my plan was to escape the walls of DMA and, as soon as possible, head home for dinner and order a drum memory for CID the next day. But when I finally found a pay phone and talked to Bobby, I realized that I was in serious trouble. She had become alarmed and called Ira, who did not know my whereabouts either and was also alarmed. They were about to call the police.

When I arrived home, Bobby severely chastised me, and I had to skip dinner, since we were already due at the Kirkwood Theatre Guild (KTG) tryouts that night. KTG was an organization that Bobby and I had joined in 1957, and this time the production being cast was *The Golden Fleecing*. By way of penance, I agreed to read for a part, though it had been a long time since I had set foot on stage. To my very great surprise, I got the lead, a part that Tom Poston had played on Broadway.

The whole thing was great fun because we were all amateurs. The play was a comedy with lots of laughs, both intended and unintended. I rehearsed my lines while driving back and forth to CID. The venue would be the tiny American Legion Hall in Kirkwood. The biggest laugh came on the last night when, during our final bows, the ancient curtain fell off its roller and landed in a pile at the feet of the bewildered cast.

Through the years, Bobby and I were faithful members of KTG. She served as historian and then two terms as president. We both were in other casts: *Blood Sweet and Stanley Poole* for me, a comedy in which I had the part of Stanley Poole, a part played on Broadway by Darren McGavin; *Twelve Angry Women* for Bobby, in which she played one of the 12 jurors.

The Guild was only one of several organizations that enlivened our social life in Kirkwood. The "Mr. and Mrs. Dance Club" met in a different venue every month but had the same live band and couples who enjoyed dancing and jitterbugging. We played bridge in a bridge group, and there were many parties. We drank too much, but that was the norm in the 1960s era. Fortunately, neither we nor any of our close friends suffered a serious auto accident.

One very close call did occur one day while Bobby was alone at home, Nancy and young Jerry were at school, and I was at CID. First, I got a hurried call from Bobby in which she said, "A man just tried to attack me, but the police are here, so I can't talk now." Click! I raced home in record time to find Bobby with the police, who were winding up their interrogation. A man with unusual yellowish hair had knocked at our door asking directions to a neighbor's house. Just as Bobby started to open the screen to point the way, she spotted a knife holstered under the man's arm and quickly clicked the screen's lock. This enraged the yellow-haired visitor, who pulled out his knife and started slashing at the screen. Fortunately, Bobby had time to close and lock the wooden front door and call the police. They arrived promptly, but the man had run away. Several weeks later, we heard that a man with the same head of hair and same M.O. had broken into a house in a neighboring suburb and raped the woman resident. But this crime was a unique occurrence. Overall, Kirkwood was a great choice for our early years in St. Louis. We had many good friends and an active social life. Some of those friends survive to this day, but most have passed away.

Our social life was orchestrated by Bobby. I was happy to join in, but her charm and good taste made for great times and great friends. No matter who she might be talking to—a titan of industry or the woman next door—she found a way to make that person enjoy the conversation. In fact, the long talk that Bobby and I had had in her dining room on our first date was the tip-off. As I told her on many occasions, this lovely, charming lady gave me a much-needed boost in confidence because she was willing to have me for a mate. We had a blessed and loving union. Perhaps because we were both only children, we had no need to entertain each other. The two of us worked out our respective responsibilities and found ways to negotiate instead of fight. Many of our friends found it strange that we never fought, but that was because of her skill at personal relationships—not because she was a martyr, or I was a saint.

Our plan to leave St. Louis after two years had long since evaporated. By mutual, unspoken consent, we stayed, openly commenting later that we had overstayed our two-year limit. For me, that was because of great leadership at CID, and for Bobby it was because of the social life we had in Kirkwood. That social life extended to parties among the CID research staff and their wives, especially the Silvermans, Hirshes, and Eldredges. Under my supervision, Art Niemoeller had finished his doctorate and, with Janne and their family, had moved on to work for Bill Lang, a colleague at the MIT Acoustics Lab, and Leo's consulting firm BBN, who had established a well-funded and respected acoustics lab at IBM.

At work, Dick Silverman kept the social interactions lively

through the daily Research Department lunch. About eight of us—with Dick, Hal, and Ira commanding the stage—had lunch in a small room on the second floor of the CID research building. All of us in that department were expected to participate in these daily discussions, which ranged over politics, science, engineering, national standards work, and local news. Everybody brought lunch in a brown bag or a lunch box. Dick had a famous Snoopy lunch box that his wife, Sally, packed daily for him.

One day, Sally decided to conduct an experiment. She felt that Dick was much more interested in the lunch conversations than in the lunch itself. To test that premise, she packed a lunch with a slice of bread for the sandwich filling instead of peanut butter or jam: that's right, three slices of bread in all. Until Sally asked him, Dick never said a word about the unusual sandwich, either in the lunchroom or at home. He had not noticed, but he got seriously roasted on the subject when he confessed at a subsequent CID lunch.

In 1962, I was busy at the CID Electroacoustic Lab with many different chores: I had a small National Science Foundation grant and a number of graduate students; I was getting acquainted with the Washington University IBM 650 computer; I was teaching a graduate class I had pioneered called "Random Signals and Noise"; and I was thinking about how to outfit the Davis-Eldredge physiology lab with digital instrumentation. The HAVOC experience had convinced me that a digital computer was what was needed. However, no laboratory digital computer was available in the marketplace, so the only thing to do was to build one myself. I wrote a proposal to the National Institutes of Health (NIH) to fund my hazy ideas, and to my great surprise it was quickly funded. Because I had a lot to learn, I headed off to DEC in Massachusetts, where we had purchased the digital modules for the HAVOC.

Although I had no appointment, I knew that Dick Best, a colleague from years before in the DU house, was now DEC's Chief Engineer. I expected no trouble getting in to see him, but when I walked into the DEC headquarters, located in an old mill building in downtown Maynard, Massachusetts, I was greeted with the information that Dick was out of town. However, I was then told, "Our CEO, Ken Olsen, has his morning free and can see you." What a break! I spent a couple of hours explaining my ideas to Ken, who finished our conversation with the advice, "You need to see Wes

Clark over at Lincoln Lab. I suggest you go there right away this afternoon."

So, I did that and met with Wes, along with his close friend and collaborator Charlie Molnar and the rest of the LINC team. The LINC was the "Laboratory Instrument Computer," designed for the very same job I had described in my proposal to the NIH. It had all the features I had planned and many, many more. In particular, the LINC tape was something I

Wes Clark and Charlie Molnar at the LINC in a classic photo

had not proposed, but it was an amazing innovation offering walk-away portable mass storage, which came on a small, convenient reel that you could carry in your pocket or store in your desk drawer. This mass storage system solved the data storage problem that I had tried to solve with the drum memory, and it predated floppy disks and USB flash-memories by many years.

Events then began to occur in rapid succession. I was invited to join the NIH Computer Study Section by Dr. Bruce Waxman, its executive secretary. In the summer of 1962, I was invited by Molly A.B. Brazier to give a few lectures at UCLA on biomedical signals and analog-to-digital conversion. Molly was a well-known figure in neuroscience, who had recently moved from Boston's Massachusetts General Hospital and from CBL, Rosenblith's Communications Biophysics Laboratory at MIT, to UCLA's newly formed Brain Research Institute.

So, during the summer of 1962, we packed the family up in a new Ford automobile and headed west, visiting the Grand Canyon, Boulder Dam, and Las Vegas, before landing in a rented apartment in Santa Monica. After one of my lectures, Molly suggested that I ought to consider starting a biomedical computer lab at Washington University. She called attention to the strong neuroscience faculty at the university and ventured the thought that the NIH might be receptive to a proposal. This had previously been suggested quite casually by Lee Lusted, a member of the NIH Computer Study Section, but this time it stuck in my brain. As I taught myself more about the LINC and computers in general, the thought of a computer lab at the School of Medicine took hold.

We returned via the Bay area, stopping to see Joy (Reed) Hunton and Bobby's ex-fiancé, Keith Hunton, who were happily married and living in Los Altos. Another stop on the return trip was to see Dr. Homer Warner, the chairman of the Computer Study Section living in Salt Lake City. Our families met in his back yard for barbecue, and the interaction of the two sets of children verged on a good-natured disaster.

When we returned to St. Louis in the fall of 1962, I began to give serious thought to Molly's suggestion. If I were to go ahead, I would need to leave CID and run the lab from the Washington University School of Medicine, and that would require the approval and support of its dean, Edward Dempsey. I asked for an appointment to see him and make my pitch. His secretary wished to know the subject of my visit and then said she would have to check with the dean. The response came back that he would not be able to see me for several weeks, which puzzled me, because he did not appear to be overly busy or travelling.

Eventually, I got a call that my appointment with Dempsey was set. When I arrived at his office, Dempsey was behind his desk, and another man was in the corner of the office, trying to look inconspicuous. Dempsey did not introduce us, which seemed strange. I made my pitch for a Biomedical Computer Laboratory at the School of Medicine and was told to expect a response in a week or so. After several weeks, I received the green light and began working with medical school faculty whose support would be critical for a successful proposal: Dave Goldring in pediatric cardiology, his brother Sid Goldring in neurosurgery, and Bill Powers in radiation oncology. Each of them had an idea for how they could use small computers in their areas of research. The proposal took time, but I made progress. However, it was many months before I learned what was behind the delays that Dempsey had imposed.

Meanwhile, through phone conversations, I discovered that Wes Clark had developed an Average Response Computer (ARC) for Walter Rosenblith's CBL that predated by several years the HAVOC that Maynard and I had built. We were mutually ignorant of the other's efforts with averaging computers, so the topic did not arise until those phone conversations. Like HAVOC, their ARC was capable of doing both averages and histograms, but it did not have the capability to calculate ogives—a trivial difference since none of the HAVOC users had found a need for the ogive calculation. It was also interesting to note that Don Teas had left CID for a post-doctoral year at CBL, where he must have become aware of the Clark machine; then, when he heard that Maynard and I were making copies of the HAVOC, he ordered one. Both the ARC and the HAVOC had the same basic functionality, but no copies of the ARC were yet being produced. We had already built a copy for Satterfield at WU at his request. Teas, like Nielsen and Satterfield, paid us for the construction of his HAVOC out of his grant equipment funds.

Let me take a moment to explain the very important difference between the LINC and both the HAVOC and the ARC. The LINC was a general-purpose computer similar to modern computers that run Windows, MacOS, or Linux. Given enough time and memory, it could compute anything computable, as Alan Turing proved in his ground-breaking 1936 paper on computability. However, the ARC and the HAVOC were special-purpose computers, which could only do specific functions; thus, they were far less expensive and required far less memory. The genius of the LINC computer was its tape, which broke the memory barrier and made possible the great leap in flexibility associated with a general-purpose computer.

By the fall of 1962, Wes, Charlie, and the LINC team were busy moving from a prototype to production. Although the team had excellent NIH funding, the Lincoln Lab management felt their mission was to support the Department of Defense, not the NIH. Therefore, they wanted the LINC team to abandon what they were doing and pursue goals clearly related to defense. Clark and team leader, Bill Papian, disagreed with Lincoln management and arranged for the entire team to move to Cambridge under the administrative umbrella of MIT, carrying with them their NIH support. Walter Rosenblith would be Director and Bill Papian Associate Director of the newly formed Center Development Office (CDO), which was to be located in Kendall Square, Cambridge, just a few blocks east of the MIT Acoustics Lab.

In January 1963, the NIH established the LINC Evaluation Program, which would distribute LINCs to a dozen groups in medical schools around the country. Bill Papian had arranged for NIH funds to be available for continued LINC development. That same month, I was appointed to the LINC Advisory Board, established by the NIH to oversee the LINC Evaluation Program—a position that afforded me good visibility into the progress that was being made by Wes and his team.

Included in the group that left Lincoln Lab were: Wes and Charlie; Bill Papian, who had also developed the first ferrite core memory; Tom Sandel, a psychologist who was named executive secretary of the LINC Advisory Board; Mary Allen Wilkes, designer of the LINC operating system; Severo Ornstein and Mishell Stucki, both logic designers with amazing talents well beyond logic design; and about a half dozen other dedicated individuals. The competition was then on to select a dozen teams from U.S. medical schools that would receive LINC computers during the summer of 1963. With less than six months to go, Wes and his team were under pressure to complete the construction of a dozen LINCs in time for the machines to meet their new owners.

It was a frenetic time at CDO, in which everyone felt obliged to work to the maximum of their ability. The scene was vividly described by one of the team members, who reported on an all-too-realistic dream: "Wes was driving a steam roller directly towards the edge of a precipice while Charlie was furiously attempting to attach wings. Bill Simon [another member of the crew] sat in the rear, speed-reading a book on aerodynamics![4]"

Back in St. Louis that spring, I encouraged Sid Goldring to apply for one of the 12 LINCs that would be awarded, and he did so with a proposal to use both the LINC and the evoked-response methodology. These tools would help identify those areas of the cortex that should be spared from ablation performed during neurosurgery to remove those brain areas that triggered drug-resistant epilepsy. This proposal was successful, so a number of us—Sid; his technician, Bud Simpson; Maynard; and I—all showed up at the CDO in early July 1963.

Maynard and I were there to help the LINC team, since I knew they were running well behind schedule. It would also be a great

---

4   Severo Ornstein, *"Computing in the Middle Ages: A View from the Trenches 1955-1983,"* 2002

opportunity for us to learn about the internal details of the LINC and about fixing an ailing machine. During our stay, Maynard and I developed expertise with the LINC memory, a recurring problem area at that time. The winners of the competition from the 12 institutions came in two groups, each attending one of the month-long sessions. Maynard and I stayed for the first session in July and a bit of the second in August, while Sid and Bud left after the first session.

The machines were not yet finished when the first session began. As programming classes for the participants quickly became tiresome, Wes had the clever idea of letting the teams assemble their own LINCs. In addition to finishing the machines, this had the salutary effect of removing the novice's natural fear of harming the machine. After all, if you knew how to assemble a machine from scratch, what could go wrong that you could not handle during routine use? The LINC team, including Maynard and I, were standing by, ready to assist with the initial assembly process. There was still another benefit to Wes's idea: When the one-month LINC training course was over, each LINC team could disassemble their machine for shipping and then reassemble it at their home institution. It was a brilliant idea born of necessity. However, it remained to be seen whether the dozen LINCs would be successfully woven into the fabric of their respective laboratory settings. That question would take a year and more to answer.

Next door to CDO was a well-known, short-order restaurant called the F&T, more properly known as Fox and Tishman. It is now gone, a victim of Kendall Square redevelopment, but it served as a refuge during the intense push to deliver LINCs to the 12 winning teams. We could relax, have a bite to eat, and talk about other things. Charlie was intrigued by the abbreviated orders shouted by the counterman to the cook in the back. Most were decipherable, but what about "Franks four" as Charlie interpreted the call, when only *two* frankfurters would emerge from the kitchen? Eventually, he had to ask, and he learned that it was really "Franks *for*," an abbreviation of "Two *franks* for a plate of franks and beans." The F&T is a fond memory of those hectic days.

In the late summer of 1963, Maynard and I returned to St. Louis full of enthusiasm for the LINC. I set to work developing a graduate course in computer design to be offered the following spring to students in the electrical engineering department at Washington University. That fall, three of us—Maynard; another graduate student, Don Glaeser; and I—started assembling the LINC for CID's physiology lab. We would assemble this machine from "spare parts" that CDO had in inventory and could ship in bits and pieces to St, Louis. This maneuver would repay CID for the help that Maynard and I had provided during the summer in Cambridge and provide the computer for the Davis lab promised in our original NIH proposal. The funds from that grant were used to support the several graduate students working for me and to partially reimburse CDO for the LINC parts they sent to us at CID. I was also finishing the NIH grant application for the establishment of the Biomedical Computer Laboratory (BCL) suggested to me by Molly Brazier and now authorized by Dean Dempsey.

Adding to the complexity of those days was the move made by our family of four to a new home in a recent development within the nearby town of Sunset Hills. That spring, Bobby had found her dream house there, and we had signed a contract to hold the house while we arranged to sell our ranch house in Kirkwood. The day that contract ran out, Bobby went to reassure the salesman, a tall, strapping ex-boxer, that we were ready to buy. He looked over his glasses at her with a serious expression and said, "I'm sorry, but I just sold it." At that, Bobby lost her customary composure and started beating him on the chest! His glasses fell off onto the floor. Just then the builder, Dick Berry, happened into the room; he turned on his heel, found a phone, and called me, saying, "I'll build you the same house on any lot you choose. Just tell your wife it will be OK!" It was, and we have lived happily in that house ever since.

Needless to say, it was a busy period, and I had little time at home. Late one Saturday afternoon, feeling guilty for my absence, I called Bobby to suggest that she might like to accompany me on a trip to the airport to pick up the latest shipment of parts for the CID LINC. With only a bit of hesitation, she said, "No, that would be like asking me to hold your pants while you visit your mistress." I was chastened and tried to moderate my schedule.

Somehow, we managed to assemble the LINC, I submitted the proposal—and my schedule eased a bit. In January 1964, I received word that my proposal to the NIH for establishing the Biomedical Computer Laboratory (BCL) at the medical school would be funded by the new NIH Division of Research Resources. I was to go to Bethesda to meet the new head of DRR, Fred Stone, and the grant monitor, Bill Raub. When I arrived at the DRR building and met Dr. Stone, the mystery of the delays in my interview with Dean Dempsey was finally solved. Fred Stone was the man in the corner of Dempsey's office. An old friend of Dempsey and the presumptive head of the new division, he had been covertly vetting me. The delay in my meeting with Dempsey had to do with Stone's schedule and not with Dempsey's procrastination. What a revelation!

With the funds for BCL due to arrive in the spring of 1964, I had much to do: arrange for my move from CID to the School of Medicine; find a place to site the lab; line up graduate students and technicians for BCL; hire administrative staff; have conversations with medical school researchers about potential projects; and describe it all to the university's new young provost, George Pake. It would be a hectic spring.

Chapter 9
Biomedical Computer Laboratory | 1964–1969

On 1 January 1964, the formal notice arrived from the NIH that our new Biomedical Computer Laboratory (BCL) would be funded. Immediately, we started looking for a site. The dean's office advised me that nothing was available on the medical campus, so I and a couple of my graduate students walked the neighborhoods to the north and south of the medical school. We selected an old garage building several blocks north at the corner of Laclede and Euclid avenues. The location was not ideal, but it was spacious, and we had begun negotiations with the owners. Just as I was about to sign a lease, we heard that part of the old Shriners Hospital was available to us. We explored and found that the two-story Shriners nurses' quarters just north of the abandoned hospital building seemed satisfactory. The paint was falling off the walls in great sheets, there was no air conditioning, and the floor plan was far from ideal. However, these flaws could be fixed, and the medical school was directly across McKinley Avenue to the north. Geographically, this was an ideal location. We extricated ourselves as gracefully as possible from the garage deal and began working with the medical school to renovate 700 South Euclid.

The graduate students who would move to BCL with me were Maynard Engebretson, Don Glaeser, and Floyd Nolle, all studying for their doctorates in electrical engineering. On 15 April 1964, BCL opened in its newly renovated quarters. I hired a secretary, Wanda Meek. We had ample funding and high spirits. Meanwhile, I had heard from Wes and Charlie that things were not going well at MIT despite the fact that, with the assistance of Walter Rosenblith,

Bill Papian and Wes had received an enormous grant from NIH to fund a new program: The New England Center for Computer Technology and Research in the Biomedical Sciences. The award was an unprecedented $35M over several years.

The sudden prospect of the New England Center had caught the MIT faculty by surprise. They wanted control, and after a faculty committee review, Provost Charles Townes laid down rules for the Center's governance. But these rules were very constraining, and Papian and Clark concluded that they would have to move to a more accommodating university environment. Such a move meant that they would also have to abandon the huge grant to MIT so that all the funds could be returned to the NIH.

I suggested to George Pake, the new Washington University provost, that he might drop by the Center Development Office (CDO) in Cambridge to discuss the possibility of having the LINC group move to Washington University. George did that, mentioning to Clark and Papian that his visit was to let them "kick his tires." As the negotiations with WU and other universities proceeded during spring 1964, George also promised faculty appointments and financial support from the university even if a replacement grant from the NIH failed to come through. That sealed the deal, and most of the LINC group that had moved to CDO just 15 months before agreed to move once again to Washington University.

Meanwhile, as I sat in my new office at BCL, I realized that a large team of more than a dozen people would be coming to St. Louis, and they would require substantial support. Despite Pake's pledge, that move would

I am standing in front of the blackboard in my BCL office. The equations are the real stuff, unlike so many movie shots.

surely place an uncomfortable strain on WU resources unless a grant for the LINC group came quickly from the NIH. Through my stay at CDO during the previous summer and my position on the LINC Advisory Board, I had gotten to know Wes and Charlie quite well. What I knew of their work habits did not fill me with confidence about their prompt submission of an application for NIH funding that would cover the team in St. Louis. Papian would do the administrative part of the application, but the scientific part would be up to Wes and Charlie.

As the weeks passed, that worry became a call for action, and I booked a flight to Boston, appearing unannounced in Wes and Charlie's CDO office. They were not working on the grant at all but rather arguing about whether 2,047 was a prime number. Let me remind the reader that a prime number must be divisible only by itself and the number one. Charlie argued that 2,047 was compound—that is, not prime—because it had other numbers that could be divided into it (factors). Wes had said OK, let's figure out the factors. He then picked up pencil and paper and started dividing all the possible primes into 2,047.

At that point, I walked into their office. Wes was sitting at his desk, placed against the interior wall and arranged back-to-back with Charlie's desk. Charlie was pacing in front of the second-floor windows that looked out onto Main Street in Cambridge, just a few blocks west of the Longfellow Bridge over the Charles River. Wes had just divided 2,047 by all the primes—2, 3, 5, 7, 11, 13, 17, 19, up to and including 23—and announced that none of them were factors. I quickly grasped that this was not getting the grant application written, so I declared they should get to work, while I went to the next room and determined whether or not 2047 was a prime number. Starting with 29, the next prime number after 23, I tried all the possibilities up to 43, the largest possible prime factor of 2047 before factors repeat. None of my results divided 2,047 evenly. I marched back into Wes and Charlie's office and declared, "It's prime!" Charlie shot out his hand and said, "Do you want to bet?" We shook hands and arranged the stakes: dinner for all three of us at the Three Fountains, a fine St. Louis restaurant in Gaslight Square.

It was at that moment that Wes, looking at his calculations, said, "Uh, oh!" He had made a mistake. The number 23 was indeed a factor of 2,047. In fact, 23 x 89 = 2,047, and therefore 2,047 has two factors and is not prime. Charlie had won the bet. Of course, I claimed that it was all a set up, and that I was the pigeon, like the mark in the famous Pigeon Drop scam. Consequently, we dubbed the episode: "The Prime Number Drop." I was delighted to agree to pay off with a celebratory dinner at the Three Fountains restaurant, but only after the proposal was completed, submitted to NIH, awarded, and the group had moved.

By July 1964, we had remodeled the second floor of 700 South Euclid, and the LINC team made it their St. Louis home. Wes Clark, Bill Papian, and Tom Sandel all got faculty appointments. Mary Allen did not make the move because she had suddenly inherited $1,000 from a distant acquaintance and was in the middle of a round-the-world trip that the money had made possible.

Charlie Molnar, a man of wonderfully broad interests, did not make the move either because he stayed behind to finish his doctoral dissertation on the application of computer techniques to neurophysiology. However, he did travel to St. Louis late that summer for our dinner at the Three Fountains, the payoff of our bet associated with the Prime Number Drop. The party included Wes, Charlie, Bobby, and me. It was a delightful affair.

In late August, Bobby and I packed up our new and fancier Chevrolet with multiple suitcases and our two kids, Nancy and Jerry, for a grand tour, including Washington DC and the 1964 World's Fair in Flushing, New York. We drove first to Columbus where my father and his daughter Anita (9), the one whose birth he had announced in his "we're all in a tizzy" letter, joined the party. Anita, Nancy's aunt, was just slightly more than two years younger than Nancy, her niece. We visited tourist sites in the nation's capital and then proceeded in a caravan of our Chevrolet and my father's VW driving north to the fair.

Jerry, who had just turned eight, got tired of all the walking at the fair and rode on my shoulders for the last few hours of our visit. We were in and out of the various pavilions when we realized that my father and Anita were nowhere to be seen. Since there were no cell phones then, the best we could do was file a missing person's report with the police. We amused our two kids by taking in a nearby movie. Eventually, my father and Anita turned up at our motel having spent the late afternoon visiting his relatives, the Glasses, in

Brooklyn. He thought he had made his plans clear, but none of the rest of us recalled him doing so. In any case, all was well, and we made our way back to Columbus and then to St. Louis before the fall semester began.

During the summer and fall of 1964, with the NIH funds awarded to BCL that were under my control and those to the new LINC group that were under Bill Papian's control, we were able to increase the staff of both labs substantially. Bill had been the group leader at Lincoln Lab and then at CDO, but in St. Louis, while he was head of the new Computer Systems Lab (CSL), a dispute arose. Wes wanted to strike out in an innovative new direction, more than simply supporting the 12 LINC groups awarded machines in the summer of 1963. Bill and Wes argued about what that new direction should be. In Forest Park, just west of the medical campus, I took many walks with Bill and also with Wes, trying to iron out their differences. As usual, Wes had a distant vision, while Bill wanted a more conventional path.

As backdrop to this dispute, let me describe the prior accomplishments of the two. Wes had earned a bachelor's degree in physics from the University of California at Berkeley in 1947. After a try at graduate school in physics, he moved to Hanford, Washington, and worked for the Hanford Nuclear Reservation, an extension of the Manhattan Project. While there, he saw an ad for an open position with the MIT Project Whirlwind, where the world's first truly interactive computer and great-grandfather of today's personal computers was developed. So, in 1952, he moved from Hanford to Whirlwind, where he worked for Jay Forrester, the project director and the inventor of the ferrite-core, random-access memory. Early on, Wes experienced the Memory Test Computer (MTC), the first computer to provide fast and reliable interactive graphics. It was an unforgettable time for him, and it demonstrated what a stunning user experience it could be to have an interactive computer at your command. That experience was known to only a few in 1954, but it is something we all take for granted today.

Meanwhile, Bill Papian was a master's-level graduate student in electrical engineering at Projcct Whirlwind, and he had been tasked by Forrester, his advisor, to implement the first ferrite-core memory. He completed that assignment, and the core memory was installed in the MTC, providing the first fast and reliable random-access memory. The much-larger Whirlwind computer originally had a cathode-ray-tube memory that was also random access, but far from reliable.

A story that illustrates the cathode ray tube's shortcoming comes from Bill. Graduate students eager to use the mammoth Whirlwind computer were relegated to the early morning hours. Their habit was to set their bedside alarm for 1 or 2 a.m. and, upon hearing the alarm, tune to 1,000 KHz, right in the middle of the AM radio dial. The Whirlwind clock frequency was 1,000 KHz and the huge machine, which filled a very large room, was big enough that radio frequency energy from its clock could be detected easily on radios for many blocks around the machine's home in the Barta Building on Mass Ave, just north of the MIT campus.

Why did grad students wish to monitor energy from the machine? If Whirlwind had no active user, it would endlessly run a test program that produced a clearly recognizable sound on the AM radio band. Moreover, if the test program was encountering errors, a frequent occurrence, Whirlwind emitted a different but also recognizable audible pattern on the AM radio dial. Only if Whirlwind had no active user and was performing well did one need to get dressed, go over to the Barta building, and get some work done in the wee hours of the morning.

While other computers of the day had only punch-card or line-printer output, the Whirlwind and the MTC both had a display-screen output. So much that we take for granted today was not possible on those other computers. Only with an on-line display could the user interact with and control the full power of a computer. Wes Clark's attitude about how a user should be able work with a computer was forever ingrained in his mind as a result of these MTC experiences. He felt the user should be the master, dictating on an immediate, moment-to-moment basis what the computer should do next, without any competition from other users or devices. This attitude put Wes at odds with almost all other computer designers and managers, who argued that the computer's resources were so precious that users should be in line for every instance of service they required. Wes knew that, with the advent of transistors, computers would get smaller and smaller, and he saw, through his experience with the MTC, the power of direct user interaction. This led him to foresee, before others, the advent of the personal computer.

Bill Papian was an incrementalist, who had managed the Advanced Development Group at the Lincoln Lab, the successor organization to the Whirlwind project at the Barta building. That Lincoln Lab group included Clark, Molnar, and the LINC team. The path forward was the TX-0, TX-2, and LINC, all designed by Clark. TX-0 was the first all-transistorized computer, and TX-2 was the first computer with over a million-bit random-access memory—but LINC was the first computer that made computing personal. Bill had been in tune with Wes at Lincoln Lab and at CDO because they were exploiting new developments in both computer architecture and computer technology. That all changed in St. Louis. Wes wanted to provide users with the ability to explore computer architectures that were best suited to their needs but used current semiconductor technology. Bill wanted to explore the rapidly evolving field of semiconductor technology and how these developments would impact conventional computer architectures.

At Lincoln Lab, the usage of these ground-breaking machines by the fortunate few bore out Clark's belief in full control by a single operator, as opposed to batch processing or time sharing among many users. Clark's colleagues and coworkers were stunned by the power that these machines brought to their fingertips. For example, Ivan Sutherland did his doctoral dissertation on TX-2, inventing the field of computer graphics and becoming a devotee of interactive computing. J. C. R. Licklider experienced the TX-2 and imagined an "intergalactic computer network," though he thought the only way to achieve that result was through the timesharing of large computers. Walter Rosenblith was on the side of interactive computing, but he could not convince the leaders of the timesharing contingent of the MIT faculty. This difference of opinion had also played out in the 1961 report of the MIT Long-Term Computation Study Group. Six members of the group agreed that timesharing was the answer, while the seventh member, Clark, remained steadfast against timesharing and staunchly in favor of single-user interactive computing.

On several occasions, Wes claimed colorfully that he had the unique distinction of having been "fired three times by MIT for insubordination." I believe that this committee vote was one of the events that Wes could caricature in that way. He never specified the three incidents, but I further believe that his move from Lincoln

Lab to CDO, followed by his move to Washington University, were the other two occasions.

At Washington University, the differing visions of Clark and Papian led to competing arguments for each alternative. The CSL team from MIT strongly preferred to follow Clark wherever he led. Papian felt he could win funding to pursue his vision, and I arranged a move for him to the engineering campus, where he joined forces with a young electrical engineering faculty member, Henry Guckel. Bill became director of the Computer Components Lab (CCL) specializing in advanced integrated circuits. In spring 1967, I formed the Washington University Computer Labs, an umbrella group that included BCL, CSL, and CCL. Unfortunately, Papian was not able to obtain significant funding, and a few years later he moved to the DC area to become a consultant, bringing an end to CCL. Guckel then moved to the University of Wisconsin and had a long, successful career in the burgeoning microelectronics field.

In 1964, the same year that the LINC group moved to WU, Ivan Sutherland replaced Licklider as the head of the Department of Defense Advanced Research Projects Agency (ARPA) Information Processing Office. Jumping on the opportunity that his friendship with Ivan provided, Wes secured a substantial ARPA grant to design

and build large computing systems; these systems, which were unlimited in size, grew from building blocks (macromodules) for which all the engineering problems were pre-solved—an extremely challenging computer-design effort. However, two

Wes and I discuss macromodules in his office

important people were missing from Wes's team: Mary Allen Wilkes was still touring the world, and Charlie Molnar was finishing his dissertation at MIT. Thus, the initial phases of the ARPA project fell to Wes, Mish, and Severo.

All the while, both the BCL and the CSL were growing rapidly.

At BCL, the number of research assistants had swelled from three to six, the full-time programmers and technicians had grown to nine, and medical school and CID collaborators had increased to more than 60. We had to expand into the second floor and basement of the nurses' quarters. Use of our small group of LINCs was also bustling. BCL offered classes in computer programming and helped many medical school faculty members apply a LINC to their biomedical problem; BCL staff were co-authors on more than a hundred academic papers.

As the 1965 spring semester began, I asked Wes whether he would join me in teaching the graduate Computer Design course that I had originated the year before. He said that he would be pleased to do that, but the only way to teach such a course was to design and build an actual computer. This response startled me, but if Wes thought it could be done, I was game. We scheduled the last four weeks of the spring semester for the actual construction of two machines by two student teams. This computer became known as the "Four-Week-Wonder," or in the fashion of a then-current TV show, "That Was the Week That Was (TW3)," we labelled each of these three machines the "4W2." Wes brought Mort Ruderman of DEC into the adventure, and he agreed to lend us the necessary DEC modules.

Severo and I try to help one of the 4W2 teams debug their machine.

During the early part of the course, we reviewed the prior designs of several machines, including the LINC. Logic drawings were an essential part of these lectures, and Wes was a master of white space artistry. He took as much care in managing the white space around the logic symbols as he did with the symbols themselves. Viewing his logic drawings, one could quickly grasp the overall functionality of a related cluster of symbols. That kind of layout skill is a lost art, I fear.

In the middle month of the course, the class laid out the instruction set, the registers, and control layout of the machine on paper. During the next few weeks, each team independently developed detailed logic drawings, DEC flip-chip module backplane layouts, and complete wiring tables; finally, when the DEC modules arrived, the students, using wire-wrap guns, wire-wrapped their backplanes. The wire-wrap guns, a new technology, had replaced the soldering guns that had gotten us into so much trouble on the trip to Cuba. The backplanes provided all the interconnections that are needed between the individual modules that DEC lent to us. Wire-wrapping was faster, more reliable, and could be unwrapped and rewrapped when necessary. We soon found that four weeks were not enough for one of the teams to complete the job even though both teams were working enthusiastically day and night. In the end, six weeks after the arrival of the modules, both teams had working machines.

It is hard to describe the joy that a computer engineer feels the moment that the "fetch-execute" cycle of the computer, built with that person's own brains and hands, begins to work. A successful fetch-execute cycle demonstrates the very first signs of life for a computer, and debugging the rest of the problems is increasingly easy. For most of the students in the class, this experience meant a change in the direction of their careers. In fact, most went on to significant jobs in computer engineering in St. Louis or on the west coast. Several were on or were recruited onto the staff of BCL or CSL.

One ingenious student, Bill Gerth, wrote a program for the 4W2 that carried out a demonstration of interactive radiation treatment planning. Computers had been used for treatment planning before, but these programs required stacks of cards that produced line printer output. The program that Bill wrote showed how treatment plans could be developed in a fraction of the time through graphic interaction with the 4W2 keyboard and oscilloscope screen. Both Bill Powers of Washington University's Radiation Oncology team and Bruce Waxman of the Division of Research Resources (DRR), our grant monitor, were dazzled. After Bill Raub had moved up in the ranks to Chief of the Special Resources Branch at DRR, his place as monitor of our BCL grant had been taken by Bruce, who had moved to DRR from his position as executive secretary of the NIH Computer Study Section. As a result of his fascination with the 4W2 demonstration, Bruce added about a half million dollars to our grant to turn the demonstration into a useful computer application.

I dug into the redesign of the 4W2 to make it fit the treatment-planning job. As a result, we added several new features: 4,096 12-bit words of memory (the original LINC had 1,024 12-bit words); a storage oscilloscope that simplified treatment-planning graphics; a graphic position sensor that facilitated the entry of drawings; a modem channel to provide communication over phone lines to a central computer; and an incremental plotter to produce hard copy of treatment plans.

These were all great additions to capabilities offered by the LINC, but I made one serious omission: the LINC tape. The complexity of the LINC tape control put me off, and my substitute for mass storage, magnetically stripped cards, never did work well. Maynard Engebretson had the job of trying to make these magnetic card readers work and eventually resorted to waving chicken bones, ones he kept in his toolbox, over the card reader, all to no avail. Nevertheless, we plunged ahead, renaming the 4W2 the "Programmed Console" or PC, thus recognizing its ability to work collaboratively with a mainframe computer. This may have been the first server-and-personal-computer system ever. More than a decade later, the IBM PC popularized this form of computing. In 1982, we briefly considered asking IBM for royalties for their use of the initials PC, but we thought better of it before calling in the attorneys.

In June 1966 Bobby, Nancy (13), Jerry (9), and I made a trip to Europe. We had been invited by Erling Dessau as a reprise of a brief visit that Mort Ruderman of DEC and I had made in November 1964. That earlier visit was to show Dessau a DEC version of the LINC. Dessau, representing a major Copenhagen hospital, was a possible DEC customer for the LINC. Unfortunately, the LINC arrived in a non-functional state, and I had to get out my toolbox. Mort found the repair episode quite unnerving since he had arranged for the LINC shipment and saw Dessau as a possible customer. Fortunately, all went well after a few tweaks of the memory timing.

During that same visit in June 1966, Erling and his wife Brigita invited our family for a visit to their lovely summer home at the northern tip of the Danish Jutland peninsula; we would arrive just before Midsummer Night's Eve. How could we refuse? We arranged a grand tour: London, Paris, and Copenhagen. In London, we all saw, *Hello Dolly*, and the changing of the guard at Buckingham Palace. Young Jerry did his best to upset the composure of the guard but without success. In Paris, we did the usual American tourist things: Arc de Triomphe, Champs-Elysées, Eiffel Tower, the Louvre, Notre Dame, and Montmartre.

We landed in Copenhagen, rented a car, and drove to Hirtshals, where Brigita and Erling were our hosts for a memorable night on the beach in front of their summer home. We could just barely see the bonfires on the Norwegian shore and witness the midnight sun at the horizon. Brigita was an arresting beauty and Erling an attractive continental charmer. We all felt privileged to have been invited to experience Midsummer Night's Eve with them. Brigita and Erling allowed us to return the favor a year later in the summer of 1967 when they visited BCL and the medical school. I fear it was not nearly so glamorous.

When we returned from the trip to Copenhagen in late June 1966, Lee Myers, my half-sister Candy's husband, had started work as a summer technical assistant at BCL. I had invited him to come to St. Louis between his first and second year of medical school in Guadalajara, Mexico. They rented a house in University City. Candy was pregnant with Chris, their first son. Lee's work at the lab didn't go well, so he was not invited back for the next summer. Sadly, this was a foreshadowing of things to come in their marriage. After their second son, Michael, was born in the early 1970s, they divorced, and Candy raised the two boys on her own while working as the event manager at the Lodge at Vail.

The summer of 1966 was a busy one. Beside the trip to Copenhagen and the visit of Candy and Lee to St. Louis, the Beatles made their only appearance in St. Louis. It was a rainy night at Busch stadium, but in spite of the rain, the stadium was packed with screaming young girls, including our daughter, Nancy, then 13, and me. That was the beginning of a life-long appreciation of their music for Nancy, and it was an unforgettable experience for me. I felt the music was really good, but it was the wild appreciation of the crowded stadium that blazed a trail in my memory.

A related experience happened in August 1967. Son Jerry and I drove to Cleveland to see my father, who was undergoing treatment at the Cleveland Clinic. As we listened to the car radio, the Beatles came on with their recording of *Eleanor Rigby*. I was taken with both the music and the lyrics and realized that the Fab Four would be more than a teenage flash-in-the-pop-music pan. I still enjoy much of their music.

The visit with my father was sobering. He had been diagnosed with bladder cancer and was being treated by a urologist there recommended by Dr. Penn G. Skillern, the eldest son of Dr. and Mrs. Skillern, our South Bend friends, and also head of the Department of Endocrinology at the clinic. My father had driven there for treatment and returned to Columbus on his own as he would continue to do for almost another decade thereafter.

In the fall of 1967, back at BCL, we asked Bruce Waxman of the NIH to provide funds that would support a PC Evaluation Program similar to the earlier LINC and HAVOC evaluation programs. Later that same year, we enrolled six institutions instead of the 12 we had in the LINC program and the four in the HAVOC program. The six were: MD Anderson, the National Cancer Institute, Ontario Cancer Institute, Temple University, the University of Maryland, and Washington University. All six were supplied with a PC built under contract by Spear Inc., of Waltham, Massachusetts, which was selected through a brief, competitive-bidding process that also included McDonnell Douglas and Scientific Data Systems. Spear's quote was half that of the other two bidders.

An interesting sidelight occurred six months after we distributed the machines. Bill Gerth and I noticed that the keyboards of several PCs we had at BCL were repeatedly failing— but only two keys on opposite sides of the keyboard were subject to this problem. A bit of detective work disclosed that these two keys were the firing keys for a covert game of space war that had spread like a virus throughout the PC community. One of the programmers, Joe Milan at the Ontario Cancer Institute, had written this game for the PC. Jack Cunningham, head of the highly respected radiation physics program there, had given his tacit approval to the illicit space-war effort. It was unknown to me and to leadership at the other five institutions that so many of our staff had been playing this addictive game. Bill and I soon realized there was something important going on. We calculated how much we would have to charge to put PCs into public places to recoup their cost, and it seemed we might barely get by if we charged $0.50 a play and had good traffic. However, in 1967 it seemed ridiculous that anyone would spend $0.50 to play a silly video game. We quickly abandoned the idea. What is it they say about hindsight?

The PCs in the six institutions were working well, and we were getting inquiries from other institutions around the country. It seemed there might be a commercial opportunity in the offing. I took a trip to Spear headquarters in Waltham, only to find that the company had been acquired by Becton Dickinson, now BD, which had no interest in building computers. Discouraged, I returned to St. Louis for a previously scheduled breakfast meeting the next morning with Arne Roestel and Ken Krippner of Artronix, a local firm that made equipment to measure the strength of radiation sources. I poured out my troubles to Arne and Ken, and to my surprise, Arne said, "We are going into the computer business!" I had my doubts, but I lent Bill Gerth to Artronix for six weeks to help them get started building computers. It all worked out, and Artronix developed a good business selling radiation treatment planning systems. They corrected my mistake and added a LINC tape unit, plus several other improvements. Eventually, the company changed hands, becoming Computerized Medical Systems (CMS), which still has radiation treatment planning software among its many offerings.

Jumping backward to late 1964, Mary Allen had returned from her world tour and was living with her parents in Baltimore. The LINC memory had been expanded to 2,048 12-bit words, which meant a rewrite of the LAP4 operating system to incorporate the expanded memory and other new features. Clark shipped a LINC off to Mary Allen in Baltimore where she famously used this computer to create a much-improved LINC Assembly Program (LAP6). Recently, the *New York Times*[5] did a feature on Mary Allen and recognized her living-room computer as the first-ever "home computer." Wes and Mary Allen married in Baltimore in 1967, and the happy couple moved into a house in the Central West End of St. Louis.

In 1965, Charlie Molnar had completed his dissertation at MIT and accepted an appointment in the Washington University Physiology Department as an associate professor, a rare offer to a fresh doctoral recipient. He established his physiology lab across

5   https://www.nytimes.com/2019/02/13/magazine/women-coding-computer-programming.html

the street from BCL/CSL, but he could not refrain from visiting to see what Wes, Severo, and Mish were up to. Charlie would stop by one of their offices wearing his brown full-length overcoat—but he did not sit down or take off his coat because that would indicate he meant to stay. Sometimes he oscillated in and out of the door several times, thinking to depart, and then turning to say one more thing. The pull of the project on macromodules was in competition with his experiments across the street on the cat auditory system. Charlie and I became very good friends, and after he and his wife Donna bought a house in Webster Groves, we would frequently carpool to the medical school.

Gradually, Charlie spent more and more of his time at CSL with Wes and less at his physiology lab. The first versions of macromodules were taking shape, and the resulting units were being applied to computational drug discovery. This system had a powerful graphic user interface. Its development was under the direction of Garland Marshall and C. David Barry. Results were very promising, and Marshall started a company, Tripos, to sell drug discovery equipment, while Dave Barry returned to his home in the UK to pursue graphical drug discovery there. Tripos was later acquired by Ivan Sutherland's company, Evans and Sutherland, then located in Salt Lake City, where Ivan had moved to take a faculty position at the University of Utah.

The LINC program was drawing to a close. A grand celebration titled "Convocation on the Mississippi" brought the dozen LINC awardee teams together one last time at Washington University in March 1965. In less than two years, the 12 teams had created many firsts in the application of computers to neurosurgery, neurophysiology, electrocardiography, operant conditioning of experimental animals, patient records, hospital laboratory automation, and much more.

At BCL we had used one of our LINCs to analyze electrocardiographic (ECG) rhythm disturbances. Floyd Nolle, Harry Fozzard, Charles Oliver, and I developed a preprocessing routine that dramatically reduced the number of bits required to describe an ECG. It was an early and maybe the first effective compression routine used in electrocardiography, and it is still, more than 50 years later, being referenced by a new paper every month or so. It was simple, yet it preserved well the important aspects of the waveform. The result looked like a string of varied Aztec temples so my acronym fetish that began with HAVOC came in handy. I invented the name "Amplitude-Zone Time-Epoch Coding" or AZTEC, which described the process quite well.

AZTEC was the front end to the monitoring system installed in the new Coronary Care Unit (CCU) located on the 8200 unit at Barnes Hospital. Actually, the complete system was written by Floyd Nolle and called ARGUS (for ARrythmia GUard System), another example of my fetish for pronounceable acronyms. My fetish may have substituted for a fair amount of scientific effort since it succinctly called attention to our work without the tedium of publishing a string of scientific papers.

To keep track of all the patients' ECGs, we placed a LINC that ran ARGUS in a central location within the CCU. ARGUS sounded an alarm if any patient went into ventricular fibrillation, a life-threatening cardiac rhythm that needed immediate attention. Late in the evening before the new CCU opened in 1969, I made one last check of the system and found the LINC to be unresponsive. After several frantic hours, I was unable to diagnose the problem myself and in desperation called Charlie at home. He asked a few questions, pondered, and then said, "Check the memory." When I pulled it out and turned it over for inspection, a sheet metal screw fell to the floor. There was an air vent directly above the LINC with a cowling around its circumference that was secured by six mounting screws. Clearly, the workman who installed the cowling during final touches to the CCU that afternoon had accidentally dropped a screw into the LINC memory. I do not know how Charlie made that diagnosis over the phone on the sparse information I gave him. However, Wes was fond of saying, "Charlie is on a first-name basis with every electron in the universe." That night I believed him.

The CCU opened the next day with fanfare. As far as I know, ARGUS was the first computer-based monitoring system in the world for cardiac arrythmias. Famed Artificial-Intelligence founding father, Marvin Minsky, had been dubious about its prospects. After I described our plans at an earlier meeting in Santa Monica, he had remarked to me, "You are never going to make that work!" Fortunately, Floyd Nolle and I persevered.

There were no LINC malfunctions, and all went well for a few days. Then the LINC signaled that one of the patients had developed ventricular tachycardia ("v-tach"), a life-threatening arrythmia. A nurse came running, only to find the patient happily eating his lunch and obviously in no danger. Floyd led the team that tried to unravel the mystery. The computer record clearly showed v-tach.

It took more than a week of intense investigation to find the culprit: the TV signal from the Channel 2 tower, then located across Forest Park from the CCU in Barnes 8200. The rebar in the concrete floor acted as a receiving antenna. There were metal fibers in the CCU rug just above the concrete floor so that when a nurse ran—not an unusual event in a CCU—it modulated the TV signal. This pulsating signal, which mimicked v-tach, was picked up by a nearby Mennen-Greatbatch Corp. monitoring system, whose lead-sensing circuit happened to be tuned to the Channel 2 frequency. Crosstalk with the channel reporting the patient's electrocardiogram then caused the trouble. This unlikely combination of events—the nearby TV tower, the nurses running, the lead-sensing-circuit sensitivity, and the crosstalk—could never have been predicted in advance. The whole episode demonstrated the importance of clinical trials and a watchful eye. Mennen-Greatbatch modified the circuitry to eliminate the possibility for crosstalk, and all was well.

Floyd Nolle deserves great credit for developing the ARGUS arrythmia monitoring program, which involved much more than the preprocessing program AZTEC. He worked on it tirelessly in the basement of BCL before its installation in the CCU. There were pigeons nesting in the basement, and Floyd adopted a couple of them as pets. In a moment of intense frustration, he declared it would be far easier to train one of his pigeons to detect errant heart beats than to write a computer program to do so.

Subsequently, with our permission, Mennen Greatbatch developed and sold a computer-based monitoring system based on AZTEC and ARGUS. We were happy to see our efforts reach beyond Barnes 8200 and did not patent the system or claim any royalties. Elements of AZTEC and ARGUS were adopted by many commercial digital monitoring systems and survive to this day. A paper that Floyd, Martin Arthur, and I wrote, "Digital Analysis of the Electroencephalogram, the Blood Pressure Wave and the Electrocardiogram," appeared in the *Proceedings of the IEEE* and was frequently referenced by others for many years. With cardiologist Charles Oliver, we did many studies of Holter recordings of the ambulatory ECGs, and they supported the conclusion that premature ventricular contractions (PVCs) do not predict myocardial infarctions (heart attacks).

In 1969, Don Glaeser had finished his doctorate, and with pediatric cardiologist Dr. Remsen Behrer, he developed methods for recovering the fetal electrocardiogram from surface electrodes that record a mixture of both the maternal and fetal ECGs. When famed cardiac surgeon Dr. Michael DeBakey, who had heard of our work, asked me for a postdoc he could recruit for Methodist Hospital in Houston, I suggested Don. He applied and was hired to oversee the hospital's ECG monitoring program for patients recovering from cardiac surgery in their Intensive Care Unit (ICU). Don applied ARGUS and other techniques learned at BCL and had a successful career with DeBakey, working with him until DeBakey's death at age 99 in 2008. Don passed away in 2016.

Floyd Nolle completed his doctorate in 1972 and moved to Creighton University, where he oversaw a remote ECG monitoring program using ARGUS for patients in many hospitals in the Omaha area. Floyd's life was tragically cut short in 1989 by throat cancer. Maynard Engebretson, the third doctoral student who moved with me from CID to BCL, received his DSc degree in 1970 and became a CID scientist working on many projects, including the pioneering development of digital hearing aids. Maynard and I have continued to collaborate through all the intervening years.

The next chapter for me and for BCL began in 1967 with a year-long visit from Dr. Roy Bentley, radiation physicist from the Royal Marsden Hospital in the United Kingdom. Roy, a British pioneer in the application of computers in medicine, had visited BCL briefly during the fall of 1966 and had hosted me for a lecture I gave at Cambridge University on radiation treatment planning with the PC. While at BCL, he took the lead in developing an interface between a gamma camera and the PC that enabled the dynamic study of the washout of radioactive tracer from the brain. This was a first—and it would lead us on a merry chase toward dynamic 3D imaging of the body's physiology.

Chapter 10
Positron Emission Tomography | 1969-1975

Roy Bentley's year at BCL (August 1968 to July 1969) initiated a new direction for the lab. At his suggestion and with his help, we connected a gamma camera to a LINC in Dr. Jim Potchen's nuclear medicine lab, an interface that enabled researchers to record dynamic images of the path of a radioactive tracer after it was injected into subjects' blood vessels. This tracer travelled to their brains and eventually was washed out by fresh blood. Previously, only static images obtained photographically could be saved. All gamma camera results were two-dimensional, so that photons emitted close to the camera's surface could register at the same spot on the camera image as those emitted from the far side of the head. The image produced was confusing to a layman but made sense to a trained radiologist. Our dynamic images were a breakthrough because the researchers could infer the regional tracer washout rate, which meant they could quickly identify any blood flow anomalies. However, our results were sometimes ambiguous.

This was an early version of what has become known as SPECT (Single Photon Emission Computed Tomography). Meanwhile, others were having the same idea. Unbeknownst to us, David Kuhl and Roy Edwards at the University of Pennsylvania were also building an instrument similar to ours. Subsequently, they added multiple views by moving the camera around the body, and the SPECT field blossomed.

Before all that happened, I wanted to show off our accomplishment, and one afternoon I brought George Pake, the young physicist and WU provost, to Potchen's lab. George was polite, but he made it clear that we really needed to find a way to present a dynamic, *three*-dimensional image—three spatial dimensions recorded over a period of time. If such a system was possible, it would remove the spatial ambiguities in the present gamma camera studies. I had no idea how to do images with three spatial dimensions but stored his comment in the back of my brain.

By very good fortune, a team was assembling at BCL that would be ready to take on this mathematical challenge when the time came: Joanne Markham, BA in mathematics; Maxine Rockoff, PhD in mathematics; and Don Snyder, ScD in electrical engineering. Several others had also joined BCL to strengthen our blossoming relationship with the Radiation Physics Laboratory, located in the Department of Radiology and directed by Michel Ter-Pogossian, PhD in physics. Ter-Pogossian was on our advisory committee from the start of the lab in 1964, and collaborations on multidetector data gathering from the brains of experimental subjects had already begun in 1965.

Our relationship with the Radiation Physics Laboratory led to the development of a number of projects at BCL that we grouped together under the heading, "regional tracer kinetics." They all involved the measurement of radioactivity obtained from multiple photodetectors. A book on regional tracer kinetics, edited by Ken Larson and me, was prompted by a 1971 symposium we hosted on the topic. Attending were leaders in the field from across the country.[6]

The new staff members at BCL helped us understand point processes, which are the random occurrences of single events, such as a photon arriving at a photodetector after being emitted during the decay of a radioactive substance. The mathematics we used also applied to the arrival of shoppers in a grocery store checkout line and many other such practical problems. The fundamental background of point processes was established in the early 1800s by the French mathematician Siméon Denis Poisson, though many modern mathematicians have made important contributions to the field, including two whom I had encountered along the way: J. D. C. Little, mentioned in Chapter Four in connection with *Voo Doo*, and Philip Morse, mentioned in Chapter Six, who taught the MIT graduate course in mathematical physics that I took in 1952. These

---

6   Larson, K. B. and Cox, J. R., editors, *"Computer Processing of Dynamic Images from an Anger Scintillation Camera,"* Society of Nuclear Medicine, Jan.1974.

scientists and many others had laid the groundwork for a team effort on point processes at BCL, an effort that was led by new staff member Don Snyder. Don came to Washington University from MIT in 1969, joining both the EE department and BCL. Thus, by 1970, BCL had quite a few staff members with the mathematical skills necessary to describe the random point processes encountered in radioactive tracer studies.

So, in these years, three independent threads fortuitously came together at BCL: the interface between the LINC and the gamma camera, which was motivated by Roy Bentley's yearlong visit; the mathematical skills available among the BCL staff; and the expertise developed at BCL in computed tomography (CT). This latter skill came about after the dramatic announcement of the first CT scan at the November 1972 meeting of the Radiological Society of North America (RSNA). An EMI electrical engineer, Godfrey Hounsfield, produced this ground-breaking result in October 1971. Yes, that is the same EMI in whose Abbey Road studios the Beatles recorded their hits. In fact, through an internal competition, the EMI revenue from those famous recordings helped to fund Hounsfield's CT scanner development. The first CT scan, taken that October day in 1971, was a human brain scanned under Hounsfield's direction at Atkinson Morley Hospital in Wimbledon, England.

Hounsfield computed the 3D radiographic images of the brain by means of an algebraic reconstruction process. A way to think about this, without mathematics, is to imagine a forest in winter with just a few bare trees. Assume that we cannot walk through the forest but must determine the location of the trees and their branches using pictures we take from the edge of the forest. If we take enough pictures (views), and there are only a few trees, we should be able to reconstruct the locations of all the trees and their branches.

As the number of trees in the forest grows, more and more views are required to get the detail needed to determine the location of all the trees and their branches. The complexity of the reconstruction process is proportional to the number of views times the number of pixels per view, a process that rapidly becomes more tedious as the forest gets denser. The same is true of the X-ray views of the brain that Hounsfield described. Don Snyder looked at his published results and to the best of my recollection said, "There must be a better way to do that reconstruction!"

Joseph Fourier was a French mathematician who, in the early 1800s, pioneered the Fourier transform, a procedure that decomposes a waveform into its frequency components. A chord played on the piano is a complex sound waveform, but it can be built up from the many pure tones contained in that chord. Fourier showed how to transform any sound into its frequency domain components (a set of pure tones) and then back again, without corruption to the original time domain signal. This process can be generalized so that it applies to any image or to the X-ray views that Hounsfield obtained.

When applied to a chord, a high-fi amplifier's electronic filter will attenuate some of the frequency components—but not all. The same idea can be applied to any sound and even to images. Don proceeded to show me how to use these Fourier Transform procedures and a high-pass filter to carry out "filtered backprojection" on the raw data to obtain the reconstructed images with much less computation than Hounsfield's algebraic reconstruction required. As Don explained to me, the filter attenuated the low-frequency components of the image, and the backprojection took the filtered result obtained at a particular angle and painted it all across the image being reconstructed at that angle. The result was a faithful image—as if taken by slicing the head with a laser beam, but without any blood or damage. Not only do the multiple filtered back-projected images require significantly less computation than algebraic reconstruction, but they also give a reconstruction that is a valid 3D presentation of the data.

With a bit of research into the literature, Don and I found that filtered backprojection was old news, having been introduced in 1956 by astrophysicist Ron Bracewell, who showed that the procedure could generate a 3D image of stars from many 2D views captured using a telescope. Subsequently, we also discovered that David Chesler at Massachusetts General Hospital had made the same observation about CT scans just before our independent observation.

Full of enthusiasm, Don and I developed a novel way to collect data that was well-suited to filtered backprojection, and we applied for a patent. Picker X-Ray Corporation of Cleveland, Ohio, became interested, and BCL negotiated a contract with them. That contract quickly led to an additional patent held by Don and me, along with two engineers from Picker. More patents followed over the next few years. Not only were several BCL staff members involved in the Picker contract, but so were Michel Ter-Pogossian and a new PhD chemical physicist in his lab, Michael Phelps.

Abruptly, everything changed. Ter-Pogossian and Phelps withdrew from the Picker contract. I was annoyed at Ter-Pogossian because he did not apologize or explain either to Don or me. However, Phelps apologized and was quite sympathetic. In a separate shock, we learned that Picker had decided to build their CT scanner without our patented technology. Instead, they would cross-license our patents to a competitor, General Electric (GE), which used our technology in their highly successful CT scanner. In turn, Picker would use some of GE's patented technology in their scanners. Thus, we received no royalties, a result that can be blamed on the university's inexperience in such matters. If we had been more experienced, we would have put a clause in the Picker contract banning cross-licensing without royalties to the university. We never considered the possibility that Picker would exchange patents with a competitor.

In these strained circumstances, it was hard to explain to Picker why Ter-Pogossian and Phelps had pulled out of the contract when even we at BCL did not know. Much later, I learned that Ter-Pogossian had done so at the insistence of Ron Evens, head of radiology. Evens saw an opportunity to be among the first in the nation to have an EMI CT scanner, and the association with Picker would have been a stumbling block.

We finished up the contract with Picker as best we could. Two of our engineers involved in the project—first Jim Pexa in 1973 and a year later Henry Huang—went to work for Picker to help them produce a line of CT scanners. During the years that followed, Picker experienced a series of corporate mergers and transitions and finally was forced to go out of the scanner business in 2000. In 1974, WU Radiology obtained one of the first EMI CT scanners in the nation and went on to pioneer its use in brain imaging. For BCL, it was a sobering incident, but it did give us the third thread of the experience we needed to help us solve the problem of producing the dynamic 3D images that George Pake had recommended.

Through all these tribulations, Mike Phelps and I had become good friends. We met late on Friday afternoons—sometimes in his office, sometimes in mine—just to kick ideas around. On one of those Friday afternoons in Mike's office, he said he had an idea of how to obtain 3D dynamic images of a radioactive tracer passing through the body's circulatory system: positron imaging. He explained how the annihilation of a positron-electron pair produces two photons that travel in opposite directions. By detecting the coincidence of arrival of the two photons at a surrounding ring of detectors, it is possible to infer the line through the body that the photons must have travelled and along which the point of disintegration of the positron must lie. Phelps's question to me was: Is that enough information to reconstruct a 3D image of the locations of the positron disintegrations as they occur during the passage of tracer through a section of the body? Phelps envisioned many research applications of this positron-imaging technology, since it could map physiological activity within the body. I am not sure he then anticipated the widespread clinical use that has recently blossomed.

We went to his blackboard, worked out the math together, and concluded that positron-image reconstruction is much the same as CT image reconstruction, and that filtered backprojection could be applied. It occurred to me that this was the answer to George Pake's criticism of the 2D gamma-camera images that Roy Bentley helped us develop. In addition, I realized that Mike Phelps's idea was going to be very important, so I began making plans to bring the resources of BCL to bear on this development. Those resources included the three major efforts: our experience with the camera-computer interface, our expertise in regional tracer kinetics, and the skills in computed tomography we had gained during our work with Picker that began in early 1973. Of course, none of these resources would have been available without the generous funding we had received from the NIH.

After our Friday afternoon blackboard discussion, Mike Phelps got to work on some preliminary experiments. The results were promising, and he showed them off to Ter-Pogossian, whose reaction was abrupt and disheartening. He asked that Phelps stop working on positron imaging and get back to the work on the CT studies he had been assigned. That did not sit well with Phelps.

The two came from vastly different backgrounds. Ter-Pogossian was a man born in Berlin and educated in Paris; Phelps had grown up among lumbermen in western Washington state, where the most ambitious career he could imagine was becoming a prize fighter. When he was 19, a serious auto accident ended his promising boxing career. He told me that he did not know what to do instead, since all the men he knew worked in the timber business, something that did not appeal to him. A distant cousin had gone to college, so that chance fact suggested to him the alternative of enrolling at Western Washington University. He did so and received a dual BS degree in chemistry and mathematics. Moving on to Washington University, he received his doctorate in 1970 and immediately joined the Ter-Pogossian lab at the medical school.

Phelps was not one to take unwelcome orders gracefully. During the workday, Phelps grudgingly went back to the CT assignment given him by Ter-Pogossian, but he pursued positron-imaging experiments clandestinely at night and on weekends. Soon, he had results showing clearly that a positron emission scanner was feasible. He again approached Ter-Pogossian, and this time his reaction was much different. Ter-Pogossian revised the assignments of most, if not all, of the people in his Radiation Physics Lab. Henceforth, they were asked to work on positron emission tomography (PET). Phelps, along with his post doc, Ed Hoffman, enthusiastically led the team.

Meanwhile, at BCL, I pulled together the three threads: computer interface electronics, regional tracer kinetics, and filtered backprojection. At times, there were about ten BCL staff members working on the development of successive versions of PET. Don Snyder, and I spent many Saturday mornings working on a paper that analyzed the fundamental limitations imposed by a finite number of views and specified the image resolution that could be obtained by backprojection. Those Saturdays were a joy to me, because I was able to dust off the Bessel function mathematics that I had learned in that wondrous course, "Methods of Theoretical Physics," taught by Phil Morse during my graduate days. These sessions were an additional pleasure because they gave me an intimate view of Don's deep understanding of backprojection and of the mathematics on which it is based.

Our work was published as the leadoff paper in a volume reporting on a workshop on reconstructive tomography that was held in San Juan, Puerto Rico, in December 1974. Bobby and I flew to the conference and enjoyed seeing the sights on the island. We did not enjoy our flight back to St. Louis, however, since we both came down with a nasty case of the flu. As a surprise, I had bought an oak, possum-belly baker's table with a hutch top as a Christmas gift for Bobby. It was just the kind of antique I knew she would enjoy. To maintain the surprise, I had it delivered to the Niemoellers' house. Art and Janne Niemoeller had returned to CID from IBM and purchased a house just a block away from us. In spite of my temperature from the flu, I was able, with Art's help, to transfer the antique into our living room to a spot where it still resides. As I had hoped, Bobby loved it and used it throughout her lifetime as her office.

By 1975, our team at BCL had for several years been working well with the team from Ter-Pogossian's Radiation Physics Lab. Prototypes PET I through PET IV had been built, human subjects had been scanned, and the results were promising. More than a dozen BCL staff members were working with Radiation Physics staff, and two BCL staff, Nizar Mullani and Carol Higgins (née Coble), had transitioned or would transition to full-time status with Radiation Physics to assist with the development of the successive PET prototypes.

The time had come to write the definitive paper. Ter-Pogossian, who was from the old school, believed the lab director should get credit for everything that happened in his lab. However, Phelps felt that was unfair—and he further believed that he had an ironclad case as the inventor of the PET scanner. Phelps and Hoffman wrote a manuscript describing their results and asked Ter-Pogossian to review it, which he did—but substituted his name as first author and made a few other grammatical changes. This caused a disagreement between the two Mikes. Phelps felt he clearly deserved to be first author and that Ter-Pogossian had contributed only equipment and laboratory space.

When Ter-Pogossian submitted the manuscript to the *Radiology* journal without the knowledge or consent of either Phelps or Hoffman, the disagreement grew into an intense feud. As a defensive maneuver, Hoffman, Phelps, and Mullani worked day and night to do more rigorous and extensive experiments. They wrote a manuscript describing these efforts and submitted it to the *Journal of Nuclear Medicine* with authors Hoffman, Phelps, Mullani, and Ter-Pogossian. Both papers came out in 1975.

Even though both papers appeared in the same year, many scientists gave credit to Ter-Pogossian for the invention of PET, probably because Ter-Pogossian was well known in radiology while Phelps was a young assistant professor. Thereafter, the relationship between the two deteriorated even further, and Phelps left Washington University, eventually becoming the founding chair of the Department of Molecular & Medical Pharmacology at UCLA. He has recently retired from that post after an extremely successful 44-year run there.

The work on PET at Washington University spawned three separate companies involving in turn Phelps, Ter-Pogossian, and Mullani, though in the long run only the first—CTI Molecular Imaging, involving Phelps—survived. It was eventually acquired by Siemens, which today is the leader in the PET market. Today, PET scans are frequently combined with CT or MRI scans, though the latter two are largely limited to providing anatomical information. PET, on the other hand, provides physiological information: that is, information on where and how rapidly certain biological processes are taking place within the body. Put another way, CT and MRI tell radiologists what exists anatomically in the body, while PET tells them what's happening physiologically in the body, both in health and disease.

During the past three decades, these PET scanners have emerged from a primarily research role into a clinical role worldwide. PET and PET/CT scans are particularly useful in cancer diagnosis and the assessment of therapeutic response. Exciting new applications are also appearing in the early diagnosis of Alzheimer's disease, as well as in the diagnosis of Parkinson's and cardiac maladies.

A recent dramatic development[7] is the completion of a Total-Body PET scanner. This scanner can image the kinetics of physiological processes throughout all cells of the body simultaneously with high spatial resolution and temporal sampling down to less than a second. Like the Davis idea for evoked-response audiology for infants, the Brownell/Phelps vision for positron imaging has taken a long time and the work of many scientists to mature. Don Snyder and I are grateful for the opportunity to have played a part in the early development of PET.

Whatever his role in PET development, Ter-Pogossian was

---

7   https://www.youtube.com/watch?v=YnvNot3vrCM

certainly a star in his own right as a pioneer in the use of nuclear physics in medicine. In 1963, he advocated the installation of a cyclotron for biomedical use, the first in the nation. Since it was onsite at the hospital, it had the ability to produce short-lived radio isotopes and deliver them to the patient in minutes. He received many awards and served many years as Director of the Division of Radiation Sciences in the Department of Radiology, retiring in 1990.

Nobel Prizes were awarded in 1979 to Hounsfield for the CT scanner and in 2003 to Paul Lauterbur and Peter Mansfield for the MRI scanner. Many people thought that Ter-Pogossian, Phelps, or both would receive the Nobel for PET. But it was not to be. On a vacation trip to Paris in 1996, Ter-Pogossian died from a heart attack while walking down the street. Nobel Prizes are awarded only to the living. The impact of PET is still growing in research and in the treatment of disease. Maybe the Nobel story is not yet over.

Before moving on to the next chapter, I need to cover a few things that had been going on in my life. In 1961, I was asked to head a search committee for the chair of electrical engineering at Washington University. The search was successful, and it recruited Bill Chang from Ohio State. Of course, Chang's offer would have to include tenure at WU, and Jim McKelvey, the newly appointed dean of engineering, asked whether I would be willing to head the tenure committee. Naïvely, I said, "Sure." Afterwards, someone must have noticed that I was a non-tenured associate professor— not the right credential for the chairmanship of a tenure committee. To my great surprise, a letter arrived at my CID office a few weeks later notifying me that I had been promoted to full professor with tenure! Obviously, Provost George Pake and Dean Jim McKelvey had worked some magic to make me eligible to chair the tenure committee. We then granted tenure to Chang, and he did a great job as chair of EE from 1965 to 1970. Certainly, such magic would not have been possible only a few years later, when detailed tenure documents were the norm. This episode signaled the start of my increasing involvement with the School of Engineering.

Through Charlie Molnar's good offices, other Washington University faculty were recruited from MIT, including Russ Pfeiffer in 1966 and Don Snyder in 1969, both of whom joined the EE department. Russ also joined Molnar's lab in the Department of Physiology and Don joined BCL, as mentioned above. Both Russ and Don made noteworthy contributions to the EE department, between them chairing it from 1971 to 1975 and 1976 to 1986 respectively. Another contribution from MIT to WU faculty leadership took place as a result of the arrival of the LINC team: the appointment of Tom Sandel, executive secretary of the LINC Evaluation Board, as chairman of the psychology department, a post he held from 1969 to 1983, the year of his death. All in all, if you count Wes, Bill, and me, there were six significant faculty leadership transplants from MIT.

All this did not escape the notice of Bill Danforth, the new Chancellor who arrived from the medical school in 1971. He had been Vice Chancellor for Medical Affairs since 1965 and served on the computer labs' (BCL and CSL) National Advisory Panel. I was impressed by Bill's leadership and welcomed his elevation to Chancellor.

Meanwhile, in our new Sunset Hills home, three of the four bedrooms were occupied by Nancy and young Jerry, with Bobby and me in the master bedroom. The fourth bedroom became my study. All four were decorated by Bobby with a delightful New England flair. The $14 table that had accompanied us from our first apartment in Boston looked a bit lonely in the larger dining room, so we purchased a bigger dining room table that could seat ten instead of four. We gave the smaller table, still with its equation scribbles, to the Gordon family next door—but that is not the end of its story.

The Gordons moved away, and we assumed they had taken the table with them. However, a year or so later, Bobby was shopping in an antique store in Kirkwood and spotted what looked like our table. Closer inspection revealed indentations from my dissertation equations, though they had faded a bit into the overall distressed appearance. The table had the same slightly faulty lever holding up one of the leaves. Although the proprietor of the shop insisted the table had come from a New England dealer, Bobby decided it must be our table and gladly paid the $400 asking price, an almost 30x markup from our original purchase price. Clearly, the table wanted to come home. We placed it in a new back room that Bobby had designed which we added to the rear of the house. There it sits happily to this day. We think Mrs. Gordon must have sold it to the Kirkwood antique shop when her family moved, but we never verified that.

The back room was not the only change at home. Bobby and I thought we were done with having children, but to our surprise she became pregnant in early 1965 at age 39. A good friend, Bee Hanson, insisted on a baby shower but did not announce the honoree to any of the attendees, and Bobby's slim figure did not give away the secret. All the women arrived, knowing that one of them had a late baby coming, but not knowing which of them would receive the gifts. At last, after they had exchanged many wild guesses, Bobby confessed. A wonderful time was had by all.

During the late summer of 1965 the family travelled to Wisconsin for a vacation. One of the stops was the McKelvey summer home on Star Lake, Wisconsin, almost at the border with northern Michigan. Both Edith, Dean McKelvey's wife, and Bobby were showing their pregnancies clearly. Jim suggested a speedboat ride for the two expectant ladies, and I held my breath as the three bounced across the lake. Fortunately, the two pregnancies came to term as expected in October. Both mothers were in St. Louis Maternity Hospital concurrently, almost side-by-side. James Morgan McKelvey Jr. (Jim) was born first on 19 October 1965. Our son Randall Allen Cox (Randy) arrived four days later on 23 October 1965. As you will see, Randy and young Jim encountered each other a number of times later in their lives.

The addition of Randy to our household, composed of Nancy (then 12), Jerry (then 9), Bobby, and mc--causcd me to lose my study for the third time. Randy was a very colicky kid and cried a lot during his first six months. I spent many a long hour rocking him in the rocker, purchased at Paine Furniture in Boston, which sits to this day in front of the window in what was Randy's bedroom and is now once again my study. However, I am happy to report that, after the first six months of his life, Randy grew to be a wonderful child and is now a happy adult with a great family, just like Nancy and Jerry. What a glorious blessing the three children are! There will be more about their families and careers in subsequent chapters.

At BCL, the annual progress report for July 1971 to June 1972 listed 57 staff and 118 research collaborators, many of them from 14 other institutions around the U.S. and Canada. We had 51 papers and oral presentations that year—not a bad record and typical of the lab's productivity. The topics covered were not only radiation therapy, electrocardiographic rhythm monitoring, and regional tracer kinetics, but also seven other areas, including patient databases created with MUMPS, the MGH (Massachusetts General Hospital) Utility Multiprogramming System.

Our activities at BCL were now receiving some welcome international notice. Not only Roy Bentley from the Royal Marsden in the UK and Jack Cunningham from the Ontario Cancer Institute, but also Paul Hugenholtz from Rotterdam had initiated collaborative activities with us. Paul invited me to the Netherlands to participate in a meeting on computer applications in cardiology, particularly in critical care, which brought together the few scientists worldwide in this nascent field. Paul, a charming and energetic colleague, had trained in the U.S. but returned to his native country to help establish the new Erasmus Medical Center in Rotterdam.

Bobby and I visited Rotterdam for that meeting, and at a dinner party afterward, we sat next to a U.S. attendee and his wife who had suddenly been called back home for a family emergency. They were extremely disappointed because they had to abandon a planned trip along the Rhine and through Switzerland. It sounded so wonderful that Bobby and I decided to change our plans on the spur of the moment and asked for instructions that we could follow. We got the most compact directions imaginable—telegraphic and handwritten on the back of an envelope: "Take morning train to Cologne; visit cathedral; train to Koblenz; take steamer to Rüdesheim, overnight there; train to Zurich; stay overnight; bus to Lucerne." Clearly, this was an adventure packed into a few words. We took up the challenge and left the next morning, holding the envelope tightly.

Indeed, it was exciting, since we did not know what would be next. For example, *which* train to Cologne? But it turned out there was only one morning train to Cologne. Next, how could we visit the cathedral without missing the train to Koblenz? The cathedral was magnificent—and right next to the railroad station in Cologne. Further, the stop in Cologne was long enough for us to visit the cathedral and return to the train before it left the station for Koblenz.

We were surprised that our train tickets worked on the Rhine River steamer. A band was playing on the upper deck, which was great fun since we could enjoy the music as we watched the lovely Rhine River scenery, rich with castles that decorated the river's small mountainsides. When we disembarked at Rüdesheim, a wine festival was in full swing. The streets were packed with revelers, but we managed to find one tiny room for the night. The next morning, we boarded a train and were in Zurich for dinner. Each line on the back of the envelope promised new excitement. How would it work out? What sights were in store? Would we lose our way with these extremely terse directions? At Zurich, we rented a car, made the roundtrip to lovely Lake Lucerne and then boarded a plane from Zurich for the return trip to the U.S. It was a memorable and exciting coda to our Rotterdam trip.

When we arrived in St. Louis, you would think I would have been happy. Instead, I had become restless. It must have been a touch of midlife crisis. After all, I was 46. It was certainly not the seven-year itch; Bobby and I had been happily married for 20 years. I did not need a new house. We had recently moved to our delightful house in Sunset Hills. The third possible remedy for a midlife crisis was a new car, by far the cheapest of the three traditional alternatives.

So, I went to the Toyota dealership in nearby Kirkwood, where the salesman gave me one look and turned away as if he did not want to waste his time with me. Maybe he knew my mind better than I did. Annoyed, I walked across the street to a small dealership that was selling a British import, the MGB GT, a sports car with a tiny back seat and a hatchback. It was a quick sale, and I walked out with a new car and a new attitude toward life. However, it soon became a love-hate relationship. The car required a lot of attention, yet it was also so much fun to drive! One of our neighbors also had an MGB GT, and we joked that neighborhood kids who found parts in the street routinely delivered them to one of us—but often to the wrong house. All too often, the car had battery troubles, and the neighbors frequently saw me running downhill beside the car, jumping in, popping the clutch, and driving away. But more about what happened to the MG in a later chapter.

While all this was happening with the MGB GT, work was proceeding at CSL on the Phase 1 version of macromodules.

Charlie was spending less time in his physiology lab and more time in his CSL office. Both staff and visitors had developed a variety of macromodular systems to rapidly scan electrocardiograms, execute LISP programs, solve partial differential equations, carry out drug design, and much more. Wes and colleagues published papers on the results. I felt that Wes was beginning to look for his next challenge.

In his ground-breaking 1936 paper, Alan Turing described a theoretical computing machine that could compute anything computable. But had anyone ever built a physical machine just like Turing had specified? Wes decided it was time to do so and set out to create "The Only Working Turing Machine That Ever Was,

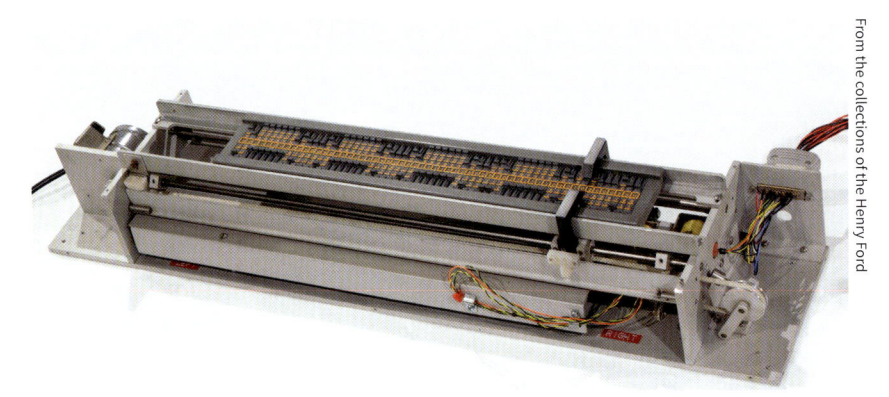

The TOWTMTEWP (The Only Working Turing Machine There Ever Was, Probably) was built by Clark and Arnzen. It is now retired at the Ford Museum in Detroit where it was featured in an episode of the video series, "Innovation Nation." (Available on YouTube here https://youtu.be/5_Hj5x6OWTM)

Probably," a job he did with the help of a CSL mechanical engineer, Bob Arnzen. The machine's name was shortened by Wes almost immediately to TOWTMTEWP, an acronym that he pronounced as "Too-tem-tewp." It worked, clattering along an extended row of slide switches that represented the machine's memory tape. It was an historical artifact, but it was not practical, since a computer, like the university's IBM 360 could simulate a Turing machine at least a thousand times faster than the TOWTMTEWP.

In 1972, Wes put the TOWTMTEWP aside, announced he was leaving Washington University, and said that Charlie had agreed to take over as the director of CSL. Mary Allen had decided she would like to fulfill a long-held dream of attending law school. But where to apply? Wes had not revealed where he planned to move, so she applied to ten law schools strategically located around the country at spots where Wes might land. I know this because I wrote letters of support for Mary Allen to every one of them. Unsurprisingly, because of her stellar qualifications, she was admitted to all ten, including Harvard Law. Wes, not wanting to be an impediment to Mary Allen's enrollment there, decided to move to Cambridge, thus ending an important chapter in Washington University's pioneering era in computing. Charlie and I would carry on, but it was not the same without Wes. I never could understand why Wes left St. Louis, but perhaps he thought that distance would insulate him from being drawn into the next, more routine, phase of the work on macromodules.

Chapter 11
An Adventure in Moscow | 1972

The Dramatis Personae for this chapter bear listing before we begin. They have all (except Natasha) appeared in the narrative before:

- **DAVE BARRY**, British co-developer of the CSL macromodular drug discovery system
- **JERRY COX**, founder, Washington University Biomedical Computer Laboratory
- **JACK CUNNINGHAM**, Chief Radiation Physicist, Ontario Cancer Institute
- **MICHAEL DEBAKEY, MD** and chair, Houston Methodist Heart & Vascular Center
- **PAUL HUGENHOLTZ, MD** and co-founder of Erasmus Medical Centre, Rotterdam
- **MGB GT**, unreliable British sports car
- **NATASHA**, Russian guide and translator
- **BILL RAUB**, Chief, Biotechnology Resources Branch, Research Resources, NIH

The above list should remind the reader of the affiliations of these characters. Each will play a role in this chapter.

In early 1972, I received an invitation asking me to organize a panel discussion on biomedical computing at a symposium on biomedical engineering to be held that August in Moscow. It sounded like a great adventure. All I had to do was select five panelists, in addition to myself, and arrange that we all show up in Moscow. The invitation recommended a travel director who would arrange a flight to transport us all from Copenhagen to Moscow and then a return flight to Helsinki. As requested by our Moscow hosts, I selected friends who would give the panel an international flavor: Dave Barry now from the UK, Jack Cunningham from Canada, Paul Hugenholtz from the Netherlands, Bill Raub from the U.S., and a Frenchman suggested by Paul whose name I have forgotten but will call Pierre. A total of six of us. That seemed satisfactory to the organizers in Moscow.

When I mentioned the trip to Dr. DeBakey, he insisted that during my visit I meet with several cardiac surgeons of his acquaintance. He pledged to make all the arrangements with them. Then, by phone and letter, I set up the topics and the order of speakers for our panel discussion. Travel arrangements were made for the six of us, and five of us converged on the Copenhagen airport. There, we met our travel director for the flight to Moscow, which turned out to be aboard an Aeroflot plane, the Russian airline. Bill Raub travelled separately because of other commitments.

Jack Cunningham and I occupied the two front righthand seats. To give you a taste of the Aeroflot plane's fittings, the drop-down tables that Jack and I each had unfolded from the bulkhead as usual. They were wooden but seemed to be individually hand-crafted—a quaint, but hardly reassuring, touch. The flight was relatively short, just a bit under three hours. When we touched down at the Sheremetyevo terminal, a converted military airbase, the ground crew placed a ramp at the front door so that we could exit the plane.

Jack quickly gathered his belongings and bounded down the ramp, but it took me a few moments longer to gather up my stuff. When I finally reached the bottom of the ramp, Jack was nowhere in sight. Soon the tour director came down the ramp, and when I told her what had happened, she became agitated and had a number of conversations with official-looking ground personnel. Eventually, she came back to me and said it was all OK, and I should not worry. Nevertheless, I worried.

Our group (minus Jack) got on a bus, were processed at the terminal building, and then were asked to board another bus that took us to downtown Moscow. We learned that we were staying at the enormous Hotel Rossyia, located just at the edge of Red Square. It was big enough to house more than 4,000 guests; until 1990, in fact, the Rossyia was the largest hotel in the world. As we walked into the grand lobby, there was Jack sitting with a gorgeous young lady whom he introduced to me as "Natasha." I asked what had happened at the airport. Jack said that when he reached the bottom of the ramp, Natasha was there, introduced herself as his guide and translator, and asked him to join her in a waiting limousine. He did, and they sped off directly to the Rossiya. No formalities were necessary at the terminal building.

Let me say a word or two about Natasha. She appeared to be in her late twenties, and not only did she have a lovely face and figure, but she also was dressed as though she had just stepped out of a Paris salon. This was in contrast to the other women we saw in the hotel or on the street. Her English was perfect and without a significant accent. She laughed and had a good sense of humor about my puzzlement at the airport. Other people in Moscow seemed monotone, without any spark or flair to their clothing or facial expressions.

We all checked in at the front desk and proceeded to the elevators. When I reached my floor, I was required to check in again with a woman at the floor desk. She examined my room key to verify my right to be on that floor and to make note of my location; that is, in or out of my room. My room was comfortable and not at all cramped. I sat down on the bed and wondered why Natasha had picked Jack for special treatment. Was it because he was the first down the ramp or did the authorities have a special interest in Jack? I never learned the answer, but later events suggested it was not accidental.

The panel discussion seemed to go well. Each of us on the panel described activities underway in our laboratories. There were few questions, perhaps because of the language barrier and the need for Russian translation, since those of us on the panel all spoke in English. Afterward, the five of us decided to have dinner together a few nights hence. We selected an Uzbek restaurant, and I agreed to make the reservations. I soon found that payment in advance was the custom, and I did so at the hotel courtesy desk where I received five dinner tickets.

When the day of the dinner came, we learned from Pierre that he had a conflicting engagement, so we now had an extra dinner ticket. Bill had to leave early but suggested that one of the other Americans at the symposium might wish to join us, so I went to the house phones in the lobby to reach someone who might be interested. As I dialed the first number, I became aware that Natasha was on the phone next to me, and an idea flashed into my head. The three other men in our group—Dave, Jack, and Paul—would likely be pleased to share in the cost of her dinner ticket. So, I turned to Natasha and inquired. To my delight, she agreed to join the four of us for dinner.

The appointed hour came and the four of us assembled in the hotel lobby. Natasha joined us and announced that she had arranged a limousine to take us all to the restaurant. It was a short ride, and as we walked up the steps, Pierre appeared, explaining that he had shifted his conflicting date. Now our party was six and not five, but Natasha declared that we should not worry. She spoke with the Uzbek restaurant management and made a sixth chair appear at our table.

At dinner, conversation flowed freely. Occasionally, Natasha had a side chat with Paul in German or with Pierre in French. By this time, most of us felt confirmed in our early suspicions that she must somehow be connected with Russian intelligence. Paul had spoken up first about it; then, during dinner, we realized that Natasha had smoothly managed to learn the locations of each of our institutions, what scientific efforts we were working on, and the size of our groups.

I did not see Natasha again for a few days, but shortly after I returned to my hotel room one afternoon, she knocked on my door. Clearly, she must have had access to how we all moved about to know exactly when I had returned. We sat on my bed, and she asked whether I would be willing to do her a favor. I cautiously agreed, and she pulled out an unsealed envelope. The message inside, to a music impresario in New York City, concerned one of his artists who was trying to arrange a trip to the U.S.S.R. but was having trouble with the Russian bureaucracy. Her instructions suggested alternatives to avoid these obstacles. It seemed a benign letter. In fact, Natasha said, "See, there is no hanky-panky!" Those were her words. She had been trained well.

Unwisely, I succumbed to her wiles and agreed to take the letter out of the U.S.S.R. and put it in the U.S. mail when I returned home. I calculated that, since it was written on the kind of ultra-thin paper that was used then for airmail, I could always eat it if worse came to worst. She left my room in good spirits after we exchanged a minor hug. However, the letter hung heavy in my suit jacket pocket.

Our group had lots to do during our stay in Moscow, but I will postpone that account in order to finish the Natasha story. For a time, I worried that Russian agents might be following me. In true Hollywood fashion, I would get on a subway train and jump off at the last minute to see if anyone else jumped off when I did. Soon that became tiresome. I realized that I was small fry and not likely to be of serious interest to the KGB. As I left the U.S.S.R., everything went smoothly at Customs. But immediately after I returned to St. Louis, I called the local CIA office, and an agent made a date to see me at BCL. When he arrived several days later, he asked to see the letter, which was still unsealed. He read it and then requested that I make a copy on our lab's Xerox machine. I did that, concerned that microdots are unlikely to reproduce well on a Xerox copy, but that did not seem to worry our CIA man, who took the copy and said he would get back to me. Further, he said I could go ahead and mail the original to the New York music impresario. I sealed up the envelope and dropped it on the outgoing mail.

Several weeks later, the CIA agent got back to me announcing that: "Yes, Natasha is a well-known KGB agent." She was called a spotter, and her job was to identify possible soft targets for the KGB to pursue further in the future. The only things that happened subsequently were Christmas cards that Natasha sent me annually for about five years. Later, I learned that Dave Barry had also gotten such cards. None of the other four of us, that I know of, seem to have been considered soft targets.

Back in Moscow in August 1972, the skies were getting darker. We learned that peat fires just outside the city were producing the heavy smoke, which became so dense that I could not see the end of the long Hotel Rossyia hallway from outside my door. Our Russian hosts did not seem to mind the dark skies, mentioning that this often happened in August.

We had several restaurant meals with Russian scientists in order to discuss topics of mutual interest. The conversation would always pause as the waiter approached the table. I asked why this wariness, since the waiter spoke no English? My Russian companion said cryptically, "You never know." No matter where we went for these meals, the food was not good. Veggies and fruit were scarce. In an effort to find a familiar diet, a few of us sought out a Chinese restaurant in hopes that it would be a more pleasant experience. It wasn't. We encountered the same monotone color and taste.

Our hosts wished to show off their latest supercomputer, and we were anxious to have a look since there had been much concern in Washington about Russian technological progress. This too was a disappointment, since the circuit boards showed no evidence of the level of integration common in the U.S. Also, the backplane connections were all soldered instead of being wire-wrapped. Even at CID, we had abandoned the unreliable soldered backplane connections during the 1960s. Advocates of the theory that the Russians were saving their advanced technology for military applications could not explain why they would hang on to such a mundane technology as soldered backplanes if wire-wrapped technology was available anywhere in the country.

Another field trip that led to a disclosure of Russian dependence on U.S. technology was to an image-processing lab located on the outskirts of Moscow. We entered a large, darkened laboratory where we were told that the lights were off to increase the visibility of the computer's display screen. However, I quickly realized that the computer generating the images was a Digital Equipment Corporation PDP-12, a machine that was a combination of a LINC and a DEC PDP-8. Wes Clark had helped DEC design this machine, which was introduced in 1969 and had sold a total of 750 units before being discontinued. Even in the dark, I could recognize it from the distinctive pattern of its console lights. Later I learned that a straw company in Sweden had purchased this machine from

DEC, shipped it to Poland, and finally sent it on to Moscow. To avoid causing embarrassment, I did not mention my observation to our hosts, who wished to convey an impression of Russian accomplishment.

Toward the end of my visit to Moscow came the lunch date with six Soviet heart surgeons that had been arranged by Dr. DeBakey. The chief surgeon was seated at the head of the lunch table, our translator/surgeon was to his right, and I was seated to the chief's left. The four junior surgeons were farther from the head of the table, two on each side. As the ceremony began, our host stood and offered a vodka toast to their "esteemed" visitor—me! Clearly, a response was required so I stood and offered a reciprocal toast to my host. Our translator obliged for both toasts, first from Russian to English and then from English to Russian. Then, the chief stood again and offered a second toast in Russian. This back and forth went on for several rounds, until I realized it was my duty to end the toasting. An almost-audible sigh of relief came from the translator, who I suspected must have had a surgery scheduled shortly. Lunch came, and I was glad not to be on any of my lunchmates' surgery schedules for the afternoon. Good fellowship, aided by the vodka, made the lunch conversation go well. I brought their greetings back to the U.S. for Dr. DeBakey.

This lunch was the last event on my schedule in Moscow. Our travel director assembled all the visitors from the West for a bus ride to Leningrad, named Saint Petersburg before 1924 and then again in 1991. The tourist sites there, including the Winter Palace and the Hermitage Museum, were glorious—and they were a stark contrast to the many dreary apartment buildings. Our return to the West was on an SAS flight to Helsinki. When the plane passed out of Russian air space, the pilot announced we were now over Finnish soil. As one, we all cheered and clapped our hands—largely because we no longer had the sense that surveillance was everywhere. After we landed, we had the added joy of the fresh and clean architecture that Helsinki offered, a delight after the drab surroundings in most of Moscow and Leningrad. From Helsinki, we went our separate ways to return to our home countries. Following an uneventful return flight, I was very glad to be back in St. Louis after my Moscow adventure.

That joy lasted until I went to the garage and found my MGB

with its engine in pieces on the floor. While I was away, Nancy, my then-19-year-old daughter, had regularly—with permission from me—driven the MGB to a life-guarding job at a pool in a north Saint Louis suburb. The fact that the oil gauge had dropped to mid-range did not alarm her since she assumed it was like the gas gauge, and she would not need to add oil until she got home. As seasoned drivers know, this is not the case, and immediate action is necessary to avoid serious engine damage. Nancy's boyfriend at the time, Bill Sullivan, said she should not worry. He could fix the burned-out bearings. So, he proceeded to take the engine apart, laying out the parts on a tarp placed on the garage floor. Once he had completed the disassembly, Bill realized that the job was more serious than he had thought.

After I assessed the situation, I scooped the parts into large bag, found a foreign car mechanic who would take on the job, and tried to convince myself that it was a good learning experience for both Nancy and Bill. The mechanic did a great job, and his bill was not hard to take. After the repair, it was great to get back behind the wheel of the MGB and even better to enjoy fresh veggies and fruits. Best of all was the opportunity to spend evenings and weekends with Bobby and our children.

Chapter 12
Computers in Cardiology | 1974-

Before describing the history of Computers in Cardiology (CiC), I would like to report on several events closer to home, family, friends, and BCL. In the summer of 1968, Randy was about to turn three years old, and we had planned a grand summer vacation at Chatham on Cape Cod. There, we had two memorable events. As a storm arose, Jerry and Nancy tipped over our rented sailboat in the saltwater inlet that our cottage shared with others, and Randy became friends with the live "mobster" that crawled around the cottage floor before our lobster dinner. Jerry and Nancy were rescued, and Randy enjoyed the lobster—but may not have associated it with the friend he had made on the cottage floor.

On our return drive, we stopped at off at the home of Ann and Dick Haggett, who were living in a lovely house in Wayland, a westerly Boston suburb. I had been in the unfortunate habit of accidentally leaving items of clothing behind on previous visits. Dick had patiently packed up and sent back the forgotten items. This time, Dick threatened to sell anything I left behind. Even so, I managed to leave my raincoat, and he followed through on his threat. Being a crusty old-timer from Maine, Dick often took pleasure in ignoring social norms, but this was beyond his usual mischief. It worked. I never left anything at the Haggett house again.

As we headed west, our family had dinner at the Wayside Inn before turning south toward New York City and a visit to Bobby's stepfather, Oscar Lueders, who had continued his work with terminally ill patients at the Westchester County hospital. In the early 1970s, he had moved in with one of those patients to help take care of her in her spacious Chappaqua home.

This visit to Chappaqua was the first of several we made over the next few years. Our final visit took place in the early 1980s when the owner of the house, his patient, passed away, and Oscar decided to live with us in Sunset Hills. We solved the problem of moving his furniture and belongings by packing it all up in a U-Haul van that Jerry and I drove from New York to Missouri. Between fathers and sons, long silences on a trip are no burden, in contrast to mothers and daughters placed in a similar situation. However, father-son discussions do take place that would be awkward in any other situation. This trip is a fond memory because of such discussions.

All of our kids went to Rott School, a small school with a single classroom for each of the first through fifth grades. The neighborhood children in those classes rode the bus to Rott. The school had a more than 100-year history, first in a log cabin on Rott Road and then in a small masonry building on Rott, about a mile farther south. In the 1930s, that building was enlarged as the school-age population grew. After the fifth grade, the kids went on to larger schools in the Lindbergh school district, but all the Rott alums looked back fondly on the good times there. I think this was because of the wonderful teachers at Rott, particularly Mrs. Janet Fendler, who, Randy said, gave individual instruction tailored to each student during class but could also pass a football like a great quarterback during recess.

In 1974, budget considerations were threatening to close Rott School just as Randy was about to enter Mrs. Fendler's 4th grade. Because we wanted him to have the same pleasant memories of the school that Nancy and Jerry had, Bobby and I joined with like-minded parents in an extensive door-to-door campaign, petitioning the school board to keep Rott open. We were successful for the 1974-75 school year, but in the following year budget pressures became too great, and the school closed. However, Randy was able to enjoy Rott through the 4th grade, as we had hoped. I felt a bit guilty that my motivation for door-to-door campaigning diminished markedly once Randy had finished his year with Mrs. Fendler.

In that same year, I learned from MIT friends that Sam Mason, my best man, had died of a cerebral hemorrhage on his 53rd birthday, New Year's Day 1974. He had become a full professor at MIT and was associate director of the Research Laboratory of Electronics, successor to the WWII-era Rad Lab. His textbooks were a treasure, and his reputation in the classroom was without parallel. Mason's Law of Feedback Control stands as an engineering tribute to him. Sam's death was a profound shock to me. How could such a wonderful, talented, and accomplished friend be taken away from us all at such a young age? I still think of Sam often, regretting that I failed to remain closer to him after moving to St. Louis.

Meanwhile, BCL was maturing. The number of projects that depended on medical databases had multiplied, and the use of MUMPS was growing rapidly. A separate laboratory focused on medical databases spun off under the direction of Simon Igielnik. Beyond the projects in radiation therapy, electrocardiography, and regional-tracer kinetics, many new areas had developed. Perhaps the most significant for the future of the lab was medical imaging, an area under the direction of Jim Blaine, a doctoral student of mine. Jim went on to become founding director of the new Electronic Radiology Laboratory at the WU School of Medicine, a national pioneer in the transition from radiological films to digital imagery.

Because of BCL's growing recognition for computer applications in electrocardiography, Paul Hugenholtz invited me to a second meeting in Rotterdam in 1973. While the number of attendees was small, Paul felt that interest in what computers could do for cardiologists and their patients was growing fast. We discussed the possibility of an annual international gathering, one that would meet in the U.S. in even-numbered years and in Europe in odd-numbered years. I agreed to ask Arnold W. (Scotty) Pratt to host the initial meeting at NIH in Bethesda, Maryland, in September 1974. Scotty was a good friend and director of the NIH Division of Computer Research and Technology (DCRT). Paul and I decided to call the meeting "Computers in Cardiology" (CIC) and to affiliate the meeting with the Institute of Electronic and Electrical Engineers (IEEE) for the publication of the meeting's annual proceedings.

Paul and I became co-chairs of this nascent international meeting, and Scotty agreed to host the first meeting at the NIH. He then recruited Ken Kempner and Harold Ostrow from DCRT, and I recruited Ken Ripley from BCL to help organize that initial meeting and review the papers that we hoped would be submitted. Indeed, a good number of papers were accepted, and attendance was modest but satisfactory. Ken Kempner and Harold served on the CiC board for many years thereafter. Ken Ripley helped with several subsequent meetings in the U.S., particularly the meeting two years hence in St. Louis.

The second meeting took place in September 1975, an odd-numbered year, and thus it was held in Europe. I decided it would be a grand adventure for 10-year-old Randy. We started off the trip with a stop in London, where I had booked tickets for the two of us to see a revival of *Arsenic and Old Lace*. As you may remember, it starts in the living room of the Brewster household, where the two old-maid Brewster sisters are sitting quietly. Randy whispered to me, "Why did you bring me to this dull play?" I told him to be

patient. Just then Teddy Brewster, who thinks he is Teddy Roosevelt, appears at the top of the stairs and races down yelling, "Charge!" Randy had no further complaints as the rollicking comedy proceeded to the final curtain. The next night, we had

Randy came along to Rotterdam with me for the Computers in Cardiology meeting.

tickets to the London production of *A Chorus Line*. I squirmed in my seat at some of the lines, but years later Randy said that he was not aware of anything awkward.

Paul, assisted by Cees Zeelenberg, hosted the next meeting, which was held in Rotterdam, and he stated forcefully that the social program was of equal importance to the scientific one. Generally, he said, these social programs should feature a bus, boat, or train ride with plenty of opportunities to sit next to someone you did not know and with time enough to explore mutual scientific interests. The program should be capped off in the evening by a lavish banquet offering more chances to make new friends. Then he proceeded to demonstrate, arranging a social program for the afternoon and a grand dinner for the evening of the first day. Randy attended both and remembers them well. So, in 1975, Paul had organized the first European meeting with flair, setting a high bar for future social programs. Further, the meeting was well attended and a grand success both socially and scientifically.

The third CiC meeting was held in St. Louis in September 1976. I was the host, but Ken Ripley did most of the work of planning the social program, which began with a boat ride on the Mississippi. In fact, we had two paddlewheel steamers, the *Becky Thatcher* and the *Tom Sawyer*; Paul was honorary captain of one and I of the other. After a cruise down the Mississippi, we raced back to the dock. Paul's boat won the race, a predetermined outcome and appropriate since he was the visitor. We docked and had dinner, which ran later than planned. Because we were marking the U.S. bicentennial, we had scheduled fireworks on the riverfront as the attendees disembarked. But as the rockets went off in the air, the police arrived, put a stop to the display, and looked around trying to find someone to arrest. They had undergone a shift change at 11 p.m., and the incoming shift knew nothing about riverfront fireworks that evening. We tried to explain that a permit was in place and the previous shift had been advised, but all our explanations were to no avail. The moment for the display soon passed, so we called it a night. Otherwise, from all the attendee reports, it was a great social program.

In 1977, the Computers in Cardiology meeting was again held in Rotterdam, where both the attendance and the scientific program grew in size. The social program continued the tradition of trying to outdo the previous year's program. Paul Hugenholtz was the host, of course, and he managed to rent a steam train to retrace the route of the World War II battle described in the book and movie, *A Bridge Too Far*. The train ran from Einthoven to Nijmegen, the last bridge of the Market Garden attack planned by Gen. Bernard Montgomery. Between 17 September 1944 and 25 September 1944, Allied ground forces fought their way north 100 miles along a narrow, elevated two-lane highway from Eindhoven to Arnhem. Our train ride roughly paralleled that route, which was named "Hell's Highway" by those GIs. The Market Garden goal was to link up with paratroopers who landed just west of Arnhem and north of

Nijmegen after the ground troops crossed the bridge there.

The timing failed. Only one out of five paratroopers was able to return to his unit; the vast majority were either killed, wounded, or captured. The quick victory Montgomery hoped for was not to be. Had the paratroopers' drop zone been one bridge further south, the war might have ended six months earlier. It was, as Gen. Frederick Browning said at the time, "A bridge too far."

On the trip to Nijmegen, Paul had arranged for an interpreter to explain what we were seeing. At the end of the ride north, Paul and I were invited to the locomotive, where we joyfully blew the whistle and took turns at the throttle. Then, on the return trip back to Einthoven, cocktails and dinner were served. Paul had succeeded in arranging a social program that had at least rivaled, and almost certainly exceeded, the excitement of the riverboat race in St. Louis.

I will not try to report on all the delightful CiC meetings. Some history, including a list of my esteemed colleagues, is on the Internet.[8] A few of the early meetings stand out for me: in particular, September 1979 when Randy again came along, and the scientific meeting was held in Geneva. The social program began in France with a hike traversing the side of Mont Blanc and reaching a chalet on the huge Bossons Glacier. After cocktails on the glacier, we descended by cable car and bus to have dinner at a castle near Chamonix, France. As our bus approached the castle, two trumpeters with long slender horns leaned out of two narrow top windows and tooted a welcome. It was a spectacular dinner, after which we wearily rode buses back to our Geneva hotel in Switzerland. Clearly, the social program was a grand success.

The 1981 European CiC meeting was held in Florence, Italy, and both Randy and Bobby made the trip with me. We flew to Frankfurt and rented a tiny Fiat, which we drove carefully with stops at Dachau, Munich, and Innsbruck. The next day we traveled over the Alps to Italy and finally to a hotel just outside of Venice. After a short boat ride into Venice, we gazed gravely at the Bridge of Sighs. Later, we took a gondola ride, but I confess to being too concerned about the way money was flowing out of my wallet and cut that ride short, to the great disappointment of Bobby and Randy. On the following day, we reached Florence, found our hotel, and quickly learned that the staff was on strike. We had to schlep our own bags

8   https://cinc.org/cinc-board-of-directors-history/

and make our beds, a minor inconvenience in the presence of the city's many beautiful spots. The social program featured a tour of a nearby monastery. The city's great art and architecture made up for any comparison to the adventures of the 1979 Geneva social program.

Next on our grand tour was the Leaning Tower of Pisa, then Monaco and Monte Carlo. We found a small hotel in La Turbie, a town just north of Monaco, where Randy came to our rescue. When we awoke hoping for an early start, there was no one at the hotel desk with any English. We were delighted when Randy, using his high-school French, seemed to converse easily with the clerk. Later, he confessed that all he said was, "Please speak more slowly," but that was repeated many times. Eventually, the bill was settled, and we were on our way via Geneva through Switzerland to Frankfurt in the tiny Fiat.

Bobby and I attended the 1983 meeting of Computing in Cardiology in Aachen, Germany, and decided to follow up with a side trip to Ireland. I had always wanted to visit Blarney Castle because my grandmother had told me stories that I wanted to explore. The Castle was easy to find just outside the city of Cork, and I kissed the Blarney Stone, an exercise more difficult to accomplish than I could have imagined. However, traces of my grandmother's Dunscombe family were even more difficult to find. At last, we located an elderly woman at the castle who gave us directions to nearby Mt. Desert, now a convent, but originally the Dunscombe estate.

The abbess there was friendly and confirmed that the nunnery had once been the Dunscombe family estate before the occupants, my ancestors, fled to England during the early-1920's conflict between England and Ireland. Additional exploration revealed that a branch of our Dunscombe family tree, the Colthursts, had indeed owned Blarney Castle. In fact, Sir Charles Colthurst still owns the castle and lives nearby in Blarney House. The close ties of the Dunscombes and Colthursts were demonstrated by the frequent use of each of those surnames as middle names in other family members, such as my mother's brother, Harold Colthurst Mills. What my grandmother told me at her knee was all true, and my adolescent doubts were all proven wrong.

I will not tell stories about the other meetings of CiC that Bobby and I attended annually until the one held in Durham, North Carolina, in September 1992. We made many good friends, most of whom are no longer involved, but the CiC meetings have continued; the most recent at this writing was held on site and remotely in September 2021 in Brno, Czech Republic—for a total of 48 years of continuous annual meetings. There have been many great social programs, and the format has held up remarkably over almost half a century. The name has been changed slightly to Computing in Cardiology, certainly a better match to the meeting's content. Long ago, Paul and I stepped down from our leadership roles, but CiC has been in good hands, as is clear from its longevity.

I must now shift back in time to just before the beginning of CiC. Russell R. Pfeiffer had arrived from MIT in 1966, having been recruited at least in part by Charlie Molnar. He was appointed chair of the EE department and also joined Charlie in the establishment of the Sensory Biophysics Laboratory at the School of Medicine. He was a charismatic figure who pulled the EE department together and created a strong program in Biomedical Engineering. Russ also liked to drive fast and loved his De Tomaso Pantera mid-engine sports car. Tragically, that enchantment led to his death in an auto accident in the spring of 1975. I remember clearly receiving the news while walking back from lunch at the Barnes Hospital cafeteria on a Saturday. It was a great loss to those of us who worked with Russ and were fond of him. The loss to the EE department was devastating.

In the mid-1960s, Dean McKelvey had established the Department of Applied Mathematics and Computer Science, which offered one of the first early computer science doctoral programs in the U.S. However, the small faculty did not get along with each other. The computer scientists and the applied mathematicians fought relentlessly about the curriculum. Eventually, McKelvey decided a divorce was the only solution and split the department in two, forming an Applied Mathematics department and a Computer Science department. He asked me to head a search committee to look for a chair of Computer Science. I agreed to do so, and we interviewed a number of strong candidates. Gordon Bell,

To kiss the Blarney Stone, it is necessary to lie on your back and lean over the edge of the castle.

Chief Engineer for DEC, came, but he was rejected by the committee because they claimed he could not finish a sentence. The words tumbled out of his mouth so fast that he could not be bothered with grammar. Of course, we all now know that Gordon became an international leader in computer science. Then there was Andy van Dam, an unknown PhD from the University of Pennsylvania, who was also rejected. We also now know that Andy went on to be the founding chair of what was to become, under his leadership, the top-flight Computer Science Department at Brown University.

I do not remember now how the committee's next step happened. I was asked to resign as chair of the committee, and then someone proposed that my name be entered into the search. I interviewed and was offered the position as chair of the new Computer Science department. If I accepted, I would be joining just three members of the new department. How my thinking evolved and the steps that were necessary for that to take place is the subject of the next chapter.

Chapter 13
Computer Science | 1975–1991

With the search committee's offer in hand, my mind was focused on whether I wanted to leave BCL and move to the Computer Science department. It would be a new challenge, of course, but it would also make the development of a medical database program much easier. I felt that this was the next big step in the application of computers to medicine. It was going to be difficult to recruit a team to create the kind of database management system which, it seemed to me, was needed for the anticipated applications in clinical medicine. At BCL, the pressures of satisfying application demands would be in conflict with fundamental database research, while that conflict would not exist in the Computer Science department.

However, I recognized that the direction of the department's research program would depend on whom we could recruit. During many site visits for NIH across the country, I was joined by and became friends with a rising star, Gio Wiederhold, who was doing his doctoral work at UCSF on the design of medical database systems. I thought we might be able to tempt him to come to WU when he finished his dissertation, and if we did, that would be a cornerstone hire for the new CS department.

Leaving BCL would be hard, but Lew Thomas had become the associate director in 1972, and I knew the lab would be in good hands with Lew as director. He was an MD who had practiced anesthesiology as a member of the medical school faculty before he was bitten by the computer bug; at first, he tried to use analog computers to solve problems in the modeling of respiration. He took one of our LINC programming courses, abandoned his quest of using analog computers, switched to digital computers, and never looked back. Starting in 1965, he worked with the lab parttime, becoming fulltime and then associate director in 1971.

I had no idea whether I could handle the bureaucratic chores associated with being chair of the CS department, but it was a new challenge and would take me away from several petty annoyances at the medical school. Dealing with Michel Ter-Pogossian had become a little difficult because of his unwillingness to explain his actions; I felt frustrated by my inability to make tenure-track faculty appointments; and it was hard to adjust to the changing leadership at the NIH Division of Research Resources. But the opportunity to make a fundamental contribution to medical informatics through the development of database technology carried the day. I said yes to the search committee's offer.

My move took place in the summer of 1975. We had a CS faculty of just four, including me, and only a few graduate students, so with the entire 4th and 5th floors of Bryan Hall to house the department, we had plenty of room. The staff that I inherited in Bryan 509 was not going to work out for me, so I called Merry Ambos, my secretary at BCL, who had resigned a half dozen years before because of her pregnancy. To my delight, Merry agreed that her young daughter, Nicole, could manage without her, and Merry came to CS to run the office. Some of the staff that Merry and I hired are still departmental stalwarts. In particular, a young Myrna Harbison has justified over and over again the confidence Merry placed in her. She has become office manager and continues as an essential member of the department. Merry's daughter Nicole is now managing director of the St. Louis Opera Theatre, so the workday absence of her mother when she was young seems not to have been a handicap. Merry and later Myrna made the office run like a fine watch, for which I am ever so grateful. After a few years, Merry moved on to an important role at Tripos, Garland Marshall's drug design company.

The initial CS faculty was composed of Bill Ball, Rich Dammkoehler, Sy Pollack, and me, a delightful quartet. On Wednesday at noon, we had regular faculty meetings at the conference table in my new office. Somehow, we decided that a glass of wine with our brownbag lunches would liven up the faculty meetings.

So, we obtained a corkscrew and passed it among us, in order to keep track of whose turn it was to bring a bottle of wine. In contrast to most faculty meetings, those were a great joy—but then reality set in. My conference table had its limits. Those who had a 1:00 p.m. class complained that their Wednesday afternoon lectures were occasionally a jumble. The coup de grâce came when one of the newer faculty members, on his turn, brought an Iowa wine that left too much to be desired. We shifted our meetings to 11 a.m. on Wednesdays and met in the large conference room adjacent to my office. Without wine, the faculty meetings became what any academic might expect. I missed the smaller meetings.

Recruiting new faculty each spring became the most painful part of my job. Typically, about ten candidates were invited to visit, perhaps three offers were extended, and one, occasionally two, agreed to join our faculty. It was a tiring routine for the faculty, staff, and me. When Gio Wiederhold received his doctorate in 1976, I tried to talk him into coming, but he had his heart set on an appointment to the Stanford faculty and declined. I was crestfallen. I approached a few other national leaders, but we were a tiny faculty at a then relatively unknown midwestern engineering school, and they politely declined my request to visit.

In an effort to begin the database work, I enlisted two faculty members who had recently joined the department: Dan Kimura and Will Gillette. At Dan's suggestion, we named our effort an "Abstract Database System (ADS)," which featured an arbitrary database structure that was defined within the database itself. It freed the user from the limiting constraints of a relational (table-based) structure that many medical workers have found confining. We built a prototype version in the C language and were able to demonstrate the concept of ADS, but this prototype revealed its heavy computation burden.[9] I'm sorry that ADS escaped the notice of the database community which, at the time, was focused on relational systems. Only since the turn of the century have the medical informatics leaders fully realized that medical databases are a poor fit to the tabular structure of a relational database. A combination of hierarchical and tabular is better, but a completely free and self-defining structure like ADS

---

9   Kimura, T. D., Gillett, W. D., Cox, J. R., "*A Design of a Data Model Based on Abstraction of Symbols,*" The Computer Journal, Vol. 28, No. 3, 1985.

would be best.

Maybe our timing for ADS was bad, maybe the lack of an advocate like Gio from the recognized database community hurt us, or maybe the ADS computational burden was too heavy. Whatever the problem, ADS was not a success, and that was a great disappointment to me and to the ADS team. The recent recognition that relational databases are a bad fit with medical data was a faint vindication.

I was the Computer Science Department's first named professor. My family gathered at a recognition event in Washington University's Whittemore House in 1989.

At my installation as the Welge Professor of Computer Science in 1989, I reflected on the use of computers for the establishment of medical databases, noting particularly the adoption of the automobile by physicians at the beginning of the 20th century. After the automobile became available, it took many years for an MD to travel easily between his office, the hospital, and the patient's home. Today, 30 years after my Welge address, we still have trouble making patient records travel electronically between those same destinations—as if the vendors of medical information systems cannot agree on which side of the road the records should travel or even on the width of the streets. How the information loads carried by the vehicles should be structured is also hotly debated. Furthermore, the payment systems in healthcare take priority over the delivery of information useful to the physician. Until these problems are resolved, I fear that each new medical information system (MIS) will be the nearest MIS yet.

Because of these problems and our inability to generate academic or commercial interest in ADS, the department and I moved on to other pursuits.

Almost directly across the hall from my office and our departmental headquarters in Bryan 509 was the men's room, which had just two stalls, the last one with a painted wall on its far side. This painted wall was frequently covered with obscene text and graphics that troubled me on my visits to that quiet spot. I had the wall repainted, but the same kind of rude ornamentation soon reappeared. While gazing at it one day, I had an idea: Install a blackboard complete with chalk and eraser. Using the eraser would be much easier than arranging for the wall to be repainted. It worked better than I had expected. Apparently, it was less fun to put offensive material on the blackboard, where it could be erased so easily.

The blackboard provided yet another opportunity. Hal Davis had taught me the joys of limericks in which the format, rhymes, and meter are all well-defined. The writer of a limerick must carefully observe these rules but also provide a punch in the last two of the five lines—and that punch should be somewhat, but not uncomfortably, off color. So, I announced a CS limerick contest on the blackboard. There was to be a prize, and I was to be the judge. To indicate the proper format and meter (five-lines and an AABBA rhyming pattern), I composed and posted on the blackboard the following two original limericks:

A kinky psych major named Jean
Had the hots for the faculty scene.
She engaged in coition
With a strange statistician,
Who was not only deviant but mean.

A CS grader and tutor
Wired his privates to a computer.
A synchronizer glitch
Gave his scrotum a twitch,
And he ended up totally neuter.

Unfortunately, there were only a few entries. The limericks submitted were not memorable, and the writers failed to follow the rhyming pattern, didn't pay attention to meter—or both. I reluctantly awarded a prize but did not renew the competition. When Bryan Hall was remodeled after CS left the building, the blackboard disappeared. However, it served its original purpose, if only indirectly, during our time there.

In 1976, a year after the CS department debuted, Don Snyder succeeded the late Russ Pfeiffer and became EE department chair. Because of our friendship at BCL, it was a joy to work together in the School of Engineering. We initiated a joint program in Computer Engineering, a field that was contentious at other universities because both departments felt they had the rights of ownership of the relevant material. Don's book, *Random Point Processes*, had been published in 1975 and rapidly became the go-to text for point processes in departments nationwide. I was proud of the role that BCL had played in its inception.

After Don stepped down as EE chair, the Computer Engineering program seemed to lose support from his department. Dean James McKelvey decided the program needed a single departmental home and moved it to CS. Our department received a name change and became the Computer Science and Engineering (CSE) department, a change that endures to this day. However, I still think a joint program is best. Maybe it will return someday.

In each of those early years, the department had about 25 graduates, and by 1980 the faculty had grown to 12. Bob Benson was director of the university's computing center, and he saw us as an important consumer of the services of the university's new IBM 360. I felt otherwise. Punch cards were, I believed, a thing of the past, and I managed to convince Dean McKelvey that we needed a DEC PDP 20. Of course, Bob saw this as a threat to the hegemony of the IBM 360, so he and I met frequently in my office, engaging in friendly, never bitter, discussions about the future of computing at WU. While Bob was a challenging debater, I felt I had the future on my side. It is hard now to imagine that there was any debate, but "Big Blue" was then synonymous with serious computing. The IBM PC was yet to come, and minicomputers were seen as mere laboratory tools—only toys when "real computing" was to be done. We outfitted a computer laboratory with remote terminals on the PDP 20, and our students were grateful that they rarely had to touch a punch card.

In August 1981, the world shifted when IBM introduced its PC. Subsequently, three of us—Sy Pollack; Tom Bugnitz, Bob Benson's righthand man; and I—took a trip to Boca Raton, Florida, where the IBM PC had been developed. In a closed-door meeting about the PC, one of the IBM attendees slipped by telling us more about the delivery schedules of the machine than he should have. The punishing stares from his superiors were enough to freeze his blood and chill ours. Sy and Tom were great companions on that trip. We rented a car in Orlando and drove to Boca Raton, finding as many locations as possible where we could sample my latest cocktail favorite, the Piña Colada. We gave each of the Piña Coladas a numerical score of 1 to 10, all across Florida. The scores varied widely, but our enjoyment of the trip and each other was an undiminished 10.

Back at WU, we ordered IBM PCs for the computer lab and completed the elimination of punch cards from all classes. The freshman students enjoyed assignments to interact with programs running on the IBM 360 through the PCs, including assignments on a Turing machine simulator that performed like Clark's TOWT-MTEWP but ran thousands of times faster. The debates between Bob Benson and me largely disappeared because students now had more assignments that used the IBM 360 remotely. Furthermore, it became clear that more and more computing would be moving to a network's endpoints.

From 1980 to 1983, there was an economic recession that caused the layoff of many engineers and the disappearance of some job opportunities. WU Board members concerned about the effect on the School of Engineering counseled Chancellor Bill Danforth to close the school and fold engineering classes into Arts & Sciences. I had an opportunity to discuss this matter with Bill, and fortunately he did not take the Board's advice. Otherwise, the flourishing school with its many biomedical engineering activities might have been stunted or at least delayed in its development.

While it is hard to believe now, many parents called on me then to reassure them that computer science was a worthwhile pursuit and a major course of study that would lead to jobs when their sons and daughters graduated. I felt sure their worries were misplaced and said so. At that time, I spoke to a conference of young St. Louis business leaders about the future of computer science. Naturally, I spoke glowingly in spite of the downturn in the hiring of engineers. One of these presumptive young leaders stood up in the back of the room and asked, "Isn't this activity we are seeing in 'Silicone Valley' [sic] just a flash in the pan?" I tried to convince the audience that Silicon Valley was here to stay, and that St. Louis should recognize that fact. Unfortunately, our leaders missed several significant opportunities. For example, the presence of an early silicon-wafer fabrication facility at Monsanto in Creve Coeur was never exploited and instead quietly closed in the late 1970s. The rationale given by Monsanto leadership was: "We don't produce anything that can't be shipped in carload quantities."

In the early years of the department, a bigger fraction of women had been attracted to computer science classes than to other engineering departments. As we moved into the late 1980s, that fraction decreased markedly. I tried to understand this trend, and talks I was asked to give to high school computing classes gave me some clues. Typically, these classes were filled with geeky boys, and the only female in the room was the teacher. The boys took great pleasure in demonstrating their superior knowledge of obscure corners of MSDOS, while showing little interest in the history, major directions, or underlying theory of computing and computers. The students even bullied the teacher, as they tried to outdo each other with their expertise in the arcane aspects of computing.

This environment would never attract girls to computing. It reinforced the movie characterization of the hacker as a loner speaking technical jargon and living in a world of machines, not people. Is it any wonder that young women looked elsewhere for their careers? Only recently has the fraction of women in computer science classes begun to recover to what it was in the late 1970s. In choosing a career, young women are beginning to see female mentors working on interesting computer science problems. For example: How should we teach computing to young children? Can computing provide answers to the problem of trafficking young girls? How best can we insure the privacy and security of our computing activities? The trend is in the right direction, but women are not yet close to parity in WU classes or in computer science classes nationally.

At home in 1975, Nancy had graduated from Drury University in Springfield, Missouri. She choose Drury for reasons she presented to us that seemed entirely logical: It was a liberal arts school, on Washington University's tuition exchange plan, and within driving distance from St. Louis. It sounded good to Bobby and me because we would have no tuition to pay. Nancy suggested that we check out her analysis, and sure enough we found there was only one school that met all her very reasonable criteria. Much later, we found that Drury was also where her high school boyfriend had enrolled, and only then did we realize the real reason for her choice.

After she arrived at Drury, that romance did not last long. Later, she fell in love with Craig Battersby, and they were married in Graham Chapel at Washington University in 1976, a year after she graduated with a teaching degree. Unfortunately, it was poor timing since there were no teaching jobs available that year. Fate stepped in, and she took a minor job at the YMCA, where she rose through the ranks while pioneering women's roles at the Y. She ended her career with the Y as director of both the Kirkwood and Webster Groves branches. There will be more to come later about Nancy's next career steps. On their home front, Nancy and Craig were blessed with two girls, Kim in 1980 and Erin in 1983.

All three of our children—Nancy, Jerry, and Randy— graduated from nearby Lindbergh High School in 1971, 1974, and 1984, respectively. Jerry was an art major at Westminster College in Fulton, Missouri, the *very same place*

Nancy and Craig's two happy youngsters, left to right, Erin and Kim

where Winston Churchill made his Iron Curtain speech in 1946. After graduation in 1978, Jerry arrived home and announced that he planned to be a sculptor. Bobby and I gulped, but he pulled it off and has made a good living, primarily carving and working with wood, his favorite medium, making fine furniture in a steady job at a local firm, NewSpace. Our house is rich with his pieces, which I enjoy every day.

Jerry's artistic talent did not suddenly burst forth while at Westminster. There had been many early indications. Left-handed and right-brained, he had needed help with reading. He painted huge and delightful murals on his bedroom walls. My maternal grandmother had won a County Cork, Ireland, watercolor contest as a girl in her twenties. The artistic gene had skipped three generations.

In 1969, I had taken Jerry to Chicago for the same aptitude testing my father had arranged for me in 1938. Both Jerry and I tested well on structural visualization, but I scored better on reading and math. While there, we visited the Museum of Science and Industry, a visit that has become a tradition for the boys in our family. Later, I took Randy and young Jimmy McKelvey there, when they were both 13 years old. They remember the trip well as one that provided a great stimulant to their interest in things mechanical and electrical. Jerry graduated from Westminster with an art degree in 1978, while Randy graduated from WU ten years later with a mechanical engineering degree.

On Randy's 20th birthday, Bobby hired a belly dancer to show up and perform at his fraternity, Sigma Phi Epsilon, which was also Jimmy McKelvey's fraternity. Because their birthdays were so close, the dancer was doing double duty. I think Randy's other fraternity brothers enjoyed the show more than Randy did. He did not enjoy being the center of the dancer's attention.

A few years before these events, Oscar Lueders—Bobby's stepfather, whom she called "O" —moved from Chappaqua, New York, into our house. His furniture was placed in the backroom, having arrived here inside that U-Haul Jerry and I had driven to St. Louis. O had many complaints: he missed the more beautiful Chappaqua scenery; he was not able to drive because of his failure to transfer his driver's license to Missouri; and he felt his space was limited in our back room. We found an apartment that was just a short walk from a large shopping center and not far from our house. O also asked us to help him get a Missouri driver's license, but on many successive tries he could not pass the written exam, which made him exceedingly frustrated. One night, while crossing the road to the shopping center, he was struck and killed by a motorist. She was not charged. I visited the county morgue to identify the body. Bobby and I wondered whether he had jeopardized his life purposely out of frustration or whether he was simply careless. We will never know. Ironically, he had campaigned unsuccessfully for a pedestrian traffic light at the location of the accident, and after his death, the county installed a pedestrian light on that very spot.

Bobby took on the task of settling O's estate, which was a jumble and caused her much frustration. It was a major relief when she completed the job after many weeks of puzzling over the scraps of records we found in his apartment. I do not recall that O had any surviving friends, certainly none in St. Louis, so there was no ceremony here. He was buried with a modest ceremony in the family plot in the Bronx. However, his death was an occasion to remember happier times for Bobby growing up in Tenafly, New Jersey, in the 1930s, where O managed the apartment building in which they lived. Also living there was the minister who married us: Rev. Allen Swartz; his family; and their daughter, Lee, who was Bobby's lifelong friend and maid of honor. Another fellow resident was bandleader Ozzie Nelson; his wife Harriet; their elder son, David; and the baby of the family, Ricky—all later to become stars of *The Adventures of Ozzie and Harriet*, a long-running TV show produced in Hollywood during the 1950s and 1960s.

With the hiring of new faculty, our departmental research branched out in several new directions. The Defense Mapping Agency (DMA), which had been entirely paper-based, was undergoing a digital revolution. I, along with others in the department, received security clearance to work on site at their office just east of the Anheuser-Busch brewery—the same spot where I had investigated the drum memory during my early digital days at CID. My secret-level clearance allowed me to travel unaccompanied throughout the building, visiting the sponsor of the contract we had with DMA in his office. On one of my visits, I was astonished when the Marine guard arrested me in the access cubicle to the secret area. The guard had me stand against the wall with my arms raised. Fortunately, a quick call by the guard to our sponsor resolved the issue. Unbeknownst to me, I had two badges: one was at the secret level, allowing me to travel throughout the building without an escort: and the other, a visitor badge that required an escort to enter any secret area. By mistake, I had been handed the visitor badge at the reception desk, and I was unaware of the oversight. Fortunately, a badge switch quickly resolved my problem.

The CSE faculty did good work for DMA, helping to train their staff, developing a 3D display system, and, perhaps most importantly, mentoring Annette Krygiel, a DMA employee and doctoral student of mine. She went on to become the Director of the Central Imagery Office within the National Geospatial-Intelligence Agency (NGA), the new name for DMA. In 2019, Annette won the NGA Lifetime Achievement Award, the first woman ever to do so. I am proud of having played a part in her education.

When Ivan Sutherland asked me to join his DMA external advisory committee, I was happy to do so both because of my familiarity with DMA and because my old friend Bruce Waxman had moved from the NIH to DMA. The Advisory Committee was made up of civilians who were charged with helping the general who was heading up DMA decide on ways to make a conversion: from analog data and paper maps to digital data and computer-based displays. At issue was the kind of electronic display to be used. There was no question about whether or not to go digital; that had to happen, but whose products to use was under debate.

After careful study we recommended that DMA purchase COTS displays; that is, "commercial off the shelf" displays. We determined these products were equal to, if not better than, what could be obtained by secret contracts with the big military vendors, and DMA could save millions of dollars. Our report was not received with the approval we expected. In fact, we were "fired," and our conclusions dismissed.

Much later, Bruce explained to me the commanding general's reasoning. Yes, a COTS purchase of displays would save money, but it would take precious time to pass through the DoD purchasing system—time that the general felt he did not have. In the late 1980s, the Soviet Union was thought to be an ominous and growing threat with great numerical superiority in both weapons and manpower. In an era of an all-volunteer military, we had to respond with more advanced technology, and better defense-mapping products were part of that effort. Hence, rapid delivery of specially built displays trumped the lower cost of COTS. The ways of Washington were once again a surprise to me. Later, Ivan received a request to reconstitute the civilian advisory committee and asked me to become its chair. I declined.

At the beginning of his senior year, Jon Turner transferred to our department from Oberlin as a dual degree student (BS and MS). All the faculty who had Jon in class were impressed by him; he was a standout in whatever he set his mind to. After finishing his two degrees at WU, he went on to earn his doctorate from North-western University, where he was in a joint program with Bell Labs working with leaders in networking. Upon graduating in 1982, he had offers from a number of schools, including Johns Hopkins and Washington University. His wife, Helen, whom he had met at Oberlin, announced that he should choose whichever of the two he wished, but if he chose Washington University, she would be glad to join him there. My sincere thanks go to her for changing the department's history.

In 1986, Jon published a groundbreaking paper titled "New Directions in Communications (or Which Way to the Information Age?)." Long before the notion had gained any credence elsewhere, his paper forecast the convergence of data, voice, and video traffic on digital networks. It won many awards and was featured in the 2002 50th anniversary issue of the *IEEE Communications Magazine* as a "landmark article." With Jon's leadership, Washington University became the place to go for advanced networking, but more about that in a later chapter.

By the beginning of the 1990s, the CS department had grown substantially from its four original faculty and 20 students in the introductory course to 24 faculty members with 100 or more students in that course. In 2020, the teaching faculty numbered 39, and there were more than 1,400 students in the introductory course, which is taken by 80% of all freshman in the university. All of this signaled remarkable growth in student interest in computer science over the past 45 years. In fact, CSE has replaced psychology as the most popular major, university-wide.

The course Wes Clark and I originated in computer design, CSE

560, had worked its way down in the curriculum from a graduate course to a junior-level course, CSE 360. In the process, because of its large enrollment, it had lost the unique feature of designing a real computer. Instead, I told the class that we were a company named Chips & Dips, which was charged with the task of designing a computer-based system of one kind or another. The class was divided into teams of four or five. It was fun for all, but never as much fun as designing the 4W2. There were often 30 or 40 students in the class and eight or 10 teams. I had a theater-style lecture hall with sloping aisles. One afternoon in the spring semester of 1988, I was surprised to see a gentleman roughly my age sit down in the back row about 30 minutes after I had started my hour-and-a-half lecture. He stayed for about 20 minutes and then got up abruptly, leaving as quickly as he came.

The following day was a Friday, and in the evening, we attended the rehearsal dinner for my son Jerry and his intended bride, Margaret Wolfe. It was my first opportunity to meet her mother and father. To my great surprise, Margaret's father, Paul Wolfe, was the mysterious visitor to my class the previous day. He was then the computer center director at the University of Kansas. Apparently, I passed muster, since the wedding the next day went off without a hitch.

That computer design course—originally CS 560, then CSE 360—is now CSE 260, a sophomore-level course, and is still being taught annually. I don't think it will ever become a freshman-level course, however.

Many of our graduates have gone on to national success. In addition to Annette Krygiel (DSc, 1980), there have been others. Mike Zyda (DSc, 1984) led the worldwide development of the field of computer games at USC. Jim McKelvey (BSc, 1987) founded the billion-dollar mobile-payment company, Square, Inc. Tony Apodaca (BS, 1987) was a member of the founding team and then became Director of Graphics Research & Development at Pixar, the pioneering motion picture animation company. Alex Gray (MS, 1981) worked for Steve Jobs at Next and then at Juniper Networks, where he recently retired as SVP and General Manager. There are many more, but these are a few of the department's most notable graduates who come immediately to my mind.

I turned 66 years old in May 1991, and after 16 years as chair felt it was time to retire. It was not that I wanted to stop doing interesting things, but rather it was time for the department to explore new ideas. In fact, the advice I had received many years before from Ira Hirsh was uppermost in my mind: "Retire as many

This is an unusual graduation in 1980, with three women receiving doctorates. Annette Krygiel is at the left.

times as you can." I happily swapped titles with Jon Turner and took over the directorship of the Applied Research Lab (ARL), which Jon had started a few years before, and Jon became department chair. The ARL mission was to develop advanced networking technology along the lines of his award-winning paper subtitled, "Which Way to the Information Age?"

Before describing some of ARL's activities, I will describe several other activities of mine that were concurrent with my departmental responsibilities: foreign trips and national committees.

Chapter 14
Two Thrilling Trips | 1973-1979

Toward the end of my time at BCL and during my term as chair of the Department of Computer Science, I was invited to travel to a number of interesting foreign spots. Two of these trips stand out as particularly exciting. Because my discussion of these trips might have interrupted the computer science story, I will report on them separately in this chapter. These reports will also include some personal events that tie into the trip reports.

So, let's go back to early 1973 when my friend Scotty Pratt, Director of the Division of Computer Research and Technology (DCRT) at the NIH, called and asked, "How would you like to go to Israel?" The Six-Day War that Israel had fought with Jordan, Syria, and Egypt had ended six years before his call, so conditions in this troubled land were tense but quiet. I asked for more details.

An Israeli government agency interested in biomedical research had asked Scotty to assemble a group to present a weeklong course in biomedical computing to interested Israeli scientists and physicians. The venue would be an Israeli resort hotel at Ein Bokek, which overlooked the southern end of the Dead Sea. Along with Scotty and me, the faculty for this course would be Judith Prewitt (Judi), a mathematician, who was then working on biomedical problems for Scotty as a staff member at DCRT. Coincidentally, Judi had been a great friend of Maxine Rockoff in the years when they were both pursuing their doctorates in math at the University of Pennsylvania. Scotty said that lectures were to run for a week, Monday through Friday, at the hotel. It sounded like a challenging but interesting assignment, and I agreed to go.

For scheduling reasons, I arrived in Athens a day and a half before Scotty and Judi. With this extra time, I decided to take in some sites in that storied metropolis so, after checking in at my hotel, I strode off toward Constitution Square and dinner. Halfway there, a friendly native with perfect English fell in step beside me telling me about the years he had spent working in Texas. We explored our shared musical tastes, and he suggested that I have dinner at his brother's establishment, where I could also enjoy great music to suit my taste. It sounded like just the ticket for the evening.

The restaurant was upstairs a block or two from Constitution Square. As we stepped inside the restaurant, my new friend disappeared, and I immediately noticed there was no live music. I was guided to a table where a bottle of champagne was waiting, and a friendly young lady sat down beside me. I realized that I had been duped. Immediately, I asked for the check (equivalent to about $30) and felt grateful to be on my way as cheaply as that. After a nice meal at a hotel on Constitution Square, I retired to my hotel. The next day, I visited the tourist sites—the Oracle at Delphi, the Acropolis, and the Parthenon—a very full day, but educational. Scotty and Judi showed up late that night, and early the next morning, we were all off to Israel, flying on El Al to Tel Aviv.

Our arrival at Tel Aviv's Ben Gurion Airport was dramatic. Two heavily armed Israeli troopers, with their machine guns drawn, suddenly appeared on our Boeing 747 just moments after the hatch opened. No one stirred until we were instructed to do so; then, in the terminal building, each of us had to undergo a thorough grilling. The three of us were then turned over to our host, a colonel in the Israel Defense Forces (IDF). Because he was able to take us anyplace we wished, we suspected he had Mossad connections.

After lunch in Bethlehem, we briefly visited Hebron, which was on the West Bank about 15 miles south of Bethlehem. Next came a drive in the Colonel's jeep to Mar Saba, a fifth-century Greek Orthodox monastery, located in the Negev desert and perched on cliffs overlooking the Dead Sea. Visitors still used a large bucket, lifted by ropes, to gain entrance to the monastery. As we gazed at this ancient structure, I noticed a shepherd minding his flock on a nearby grassy knoll. I said to Scotty and Judi, "It is as if we were transported back ten centuries." When we drew closer, we could see that the shepherd had a transistor radio and a receiver in his ear. I corrected myself and said, "No, it is never going to be the same."

Next, we were off to Ein Bokek, a spot on the shores of the Dead Sea about 15 miles from its southern tip. After checking in at the hotel there, Judi and I planned our week of lectures. We had

Despite the busy week at Ein Bokek, I managed to work in an easy float in the very dense, salty water of the Dead Sea.

learned that Scotty would take the quieter role of introducing us and occasionally stimulating discussion, so it would be an exhausting schedule for the two of us.

One night, the Colonel announced we were going to Masada, about 10 miles north of Ein Bokek. Masada sits on a high plateau facing the Dead Sea; it is also the site of a Roman siege against a Jewish splinter group, the Sicarli, who were encamped there in 73 A.D. The Sicarli had fled Jerusalem, attacking and defeating the Roman garrison at Masada. But the Roman governor then laid siege to Masada, building a huge ramp that allowed his troops to breach the wall of the Sicarli-occupied fortress. Legend has it that the Sicarli, when threatened by this attack, set fire to the buildings within the fortress, and then many of them killed themselves to avoid capture.

The evening we were there was declared to be the 1,900th anniversary of the Sicarli defeat, and a huge sound and light show was scheduled. The Colonel parked his jeep at a great viewing point near the base of the Roman ramp. The show was very impressive, and we felt privileged to be there at such an historic moment.

Our lectures concluded early on Friday afternoon. By then, Judi and I were exhausted, and we adjourned to the hotel cocktail lounge. After only two martinis, my memory completely failed, and I woke up the next morning, fully clothed, in my hotel room. It was reported to me that I had enjoyed the evening's company in the cocktail lounge and had left there under my own control, but I had no recollection of those events. As I awakened, I found an empty envelope in my pocket addressed to a person in Poland; the return address named a person in St. Louis. My comrades could offer no explanation. I packed the empty envelope away for the trip back to St. Louis.

Before catching our return flights to the U. S., the Colonel arranged a tour of Israel that included the Golan Heights, the Sea of Galilee, Jericho, and a visit to Jerusalem with its many tourist sites. This tour impressed upon us what a small country Israel is, but so rich in history. It was truly a thrilling trip.

After I settled back in St. Louis, I called Missouri Baptist University in St. Louis County and asked for the person whose return address was listed on the puzzling Ein Bokek envelope. When he answered and heard my story, he offered no explanation but said, "I don't want to talk about this. Do not call me again." The mystery of the empty envelope lingers.

❧

A few years later, in the late summer of 1978, I learned that my father was in a Columbus hospital because his bladder cancer had flared up, requiring him to be catheterized. I flew to Columbus and found him without serious pain and in relatively good spirits. He had his briefcase with him, filled with patent work, which he took pride in pursuing even in the hospital. However, he had not shaved in several days and looked quite shaggy. I found a razor and some shaving cream. and I lovingly gave him a shave. It was the last time

I saw him alive.

It seemed that my father had kept himself alive with his frequent trips for bladder cancer treatment at the Cleveland Clinic. In May 1977, Anita had graduated from Denison University in Granville, Ohio, and my father may have felt his job was done. Apparently, he, or his doctors, chose to have no more painful trips to Cleveland. Perhaps he knew his time had come, or perhaps he was ready to give up the fight. I don't know. He was 84 years old.

After that visit to the hospital, I was due in Bethesda at the NIH for a meeting of the DCRT External Advisory Committee, which I chaired. On 8 September 1978, I got a call from Elrose that my father had passed away, so I cut short the meeting and flew to Columbus. Elrose, her children, and I planned the funeral at the St. Alban's Episcopal Church in Bexley, Ohio. I remember sitting on his bed going through his things and crying, just as I am now.

The funeral took place, and the family—including Bobby, my three kids, Elrose, Randy, Candy, and Anita—all came. Elrose sold the house on Cassingham Road and moved into a nearby apartment in Bexley, using the proceeds to help fund her retirement.

My father, who had grown up as the grocer's son in Preston, Maryland, had come a long way. His early strictness with me may have been a reflection of the way his father treated him. As I have mentioned in Chapter Three, his tone with me shifted once I entered the Army. I was able to make my own decisions, and he supported them all. I think he liked his life in Columbus, was highly respected, and was viewed as an honorable man by the legal community.

A story that illustrates what his life in Columbus was like happened in the early 1960s. I was visiting Columbus by myself on a weekday and met him in his office. His law practice was going well, as evidenced by the busy workload of his secretary. He invited me to lunch at the Columbus Athletic Club, a few blocks east of his office. After lunch there, he suggested a game of pool and soundly trounced me. I swallowed but did not mention the stern warning he had given to me during my high school years: "Good pool is a sign of a wasted youth!" It would have taken the edge off his wish to display his successful office, exclusive club membership, and many service responsibilities for the Columbus Bar Association.

Upon my return from Bexley and the funeral, I had a routine

visit with my general practitioner, who told me I had high blood pressure. Maybe that should not have been surprising. I was 53 and had been through a lot during the summer and early fall. The hydrochlorothiazide he prescribed did the trick, but for the first time in my adult life I felt depressed. Gradually, things returned to normal, my spirits lifted, and I got back to my routine.

Nixon made his surprise visit to China in 1972. Shortly there-after, Severo, Wes, and several other noted computer scientists also paid a visit to China, and a reciprocal Chinese visit to CSL took place soon afterward. A little more than six years later, China was still working on opening to the West, during a time that had followed Mao's devastating Cultural Revolution. In March 1979, Stanley Spector, Chair of the Department of Chinese and Japanese Studies at Washington University, began organizing a July trip to China for selected faculty. Signing up were Spector himself; Lew Thomas and his wife, Jane; Bill Chang, past head of EE; Jim Davis, professor of Political Science and Associate Provost; Tom Sandel, then head of Psychology; and myself. Other faculty, WU board members, and some last-minute signups rounded out the group of 21 travelers. On the morning of 7 July 1979, we all boarded TWA flight 443 for Los Angeles, and Japan Airlines took us from there to Tokyo. After an overnight hotel stay, we boarded China People's Airline for the final leg of the trip, landing in Shanghai at 5:50 p.m. local time, two days after leaving home. The trip was to be three weeks long, a little too much time away from home for Bobby.

The trip began badly for me since my bags failed to arrive in Shanghai. Fortunately, Bill Chang was able to lend me clean under-wear while we waited for TWA to locate my luggage. After a few days, the bags were found in Los Angeles having never left the U.S. They quickly showed up in Shanghai, and all was well.

My host in Shanghai was Professor Chang (we never learned his first name), head of the fledgling computer science program at Jiao Tong University. Adding a bit of complexity to our introductions, Professor Chang's righthand assistant was faculty member Tony Chang. So, we had three professors named Chang in many of our meetings. Since Tony Chang's early education had been in an

English-speaking missionary school in Shanghai, he became my translator, traveling with us throughout the trip. But more about Tony later.

Our second night in Shanghai was crowned with an excellent Chinese dinner in a restaurant that had somehow survived the Cultural Revolution and included many, many dishes on a revolving turntable, as well as an ample supply of Chinese beer. We learned later that this dinner was quite unusual and a rare treat.

The next day, I gave my first lecture at Jiao Tong with Tony providing the translation. His English was excellent, and the only trouble arose when people in the audience were confused by the English habit of naming powers of 1,000, such as kilo, mega, giga, etc. Apparently, Chinese speakers name powers of 10, and since there are so many such names, it is not unusual for them to forget the order and feel bewildered. Tony did his best to help out the audience, but in talking about computer equipment, the powers of 1,000 arise frequently.

We were invited to observe a neurosurgery operation performed on a young woman who received initially only acupuncture as an anesthetic. She seemed to be free of pain and awake during all but the last minutes of the procedure when she received a dose of traditional anesthetic. When the surgery was complete she was in good spirits and came out to greet us.

The next day, we all assembled in a large conference room to discuss the main topic of our visit: faculty and graduate student exchanges between Jiao Tong University and Washington University. It was July, and the large conference room was without air-conditioning and quite hot. The windows were open wide, and we could see a storm moving in. When the front arrived, it burst into the room and blew over a large folding screen in the corner opposite the couches where our team was sitting. The downed screen revealed a short Chinese man who had been surreptitiously operating an ancient reel-to-reel tape recorder there. He scrambled to put the screen back in place. There was a stunned silence among all those in the meeting.

Jim Davis, our team leader, responded coolly and quickly. He reached into his jacket pocket, pulled out a small Japanese tape recorder, planted it firmly on the tea table in front of him, and with a flourish clicked it on. The meeting resumed as if nothing had happened. The feeling of great tension dissipated, and the discussion of who would pay for the expenses of exchange faculty and students continued. Face was saved.

In Shanghai, the streets were full of bicycles, pedestrians, and an occasional three-wheeled truck, with only a very rare passenger car. In the morning, many Chinese did their tai chi exercises on public display. These exercises are a component of martial art training, but they are slow and fluid, stressing balance and composure. It was not uncommon to see hundreds of Chinese along the sidewalks each morning carrying out their morning tai chi routines.

Our visit to Shanghai allowed us to explore the busy port and to watch the construction of modern skyscrapers using ancient methods. Apparently, the cranes used in the West were not available, so laborers pushed wheelbarrows filled with construction materials up temporary straw-and-bamboo ramps that spiraled round and around the rising structure. Today, modern construction methods have taken over, but my memory retains this fascinating blend of old and new.

We visited other universities in Nanjing and Beijing. Tony Chang accompanied our group as translator of the many talks that members of the WU team gave. He did an excellent job and also helped out when the Communist Party minders had trouble explaining the restrictions that followed us on our journey. Most areas we visited were restricted, which meant that a Party member had to be with us. In a few spots, such as the shopping area in Beijing, we were allowed to roam without a minder. Of course, we visited the Great Wall at Badaling, just 50 miles north of Beijing. Only a very short section (4.7 miles) of the wall had been reconstructed when our group visited, but more reconstruction is now underway of what was once a 1,500-mile wall.

One of our last stops in Beijing was a clean room, where we donned white suits and booties to see the efforts the Chinese were making toward integrated-circuit production. Remember, this was 1979, and our hosts were rapidly catching up with U.S. technology. The gap here seemed significantly smaller than the gap I had observed between us and the Russians when we visited there a half dozen years earlier.

Our final events in Beijing were a visit to the Forbidden City and a ceremonial dinner in the Great Hall of the People on Tiananmen

Our group and our hosts at the Great Hall of the People in Tiananmen Square

Square. We had speeches and Peking duck. The latter was terrific, a memorable finale to our trip.

The flight back to St. Louis from Beijing was long but uneventful. Shortly after arriving home, I decided to take Bobby to a nearby Chinese restaurant for Peking duck. The duck came, but without the obligatory plum sauce served with the dish in China. I repeatedly asked the waiter for our plum sauce before digging in, but it did not arrive. At last, in frustration, I rose from our table, pushed open the kitchen door, and demanded, "Where is our plum sauce?" It came with ample apologies, but nothing could compare with that last dinner at the Great Hall of the People.

There were two sequelae to the China trip that I will relate here. Professor Chang from Jiao Tong University had taken me aside and whispered that Tony Chang would very much appreciate an invitation to visit the Computer Science department at WU and that a request for him to travel to the U.S. would be favorably viewed. After my return, I wrote a formal invitation to Professor Chang for Tony to be a WU Visiting Professor. I worked with a St. Louis immigration attorney to help make this come to pass. Within a year it did, and Tony successfully taught courses in the department for several years.

During this period, Tony and I worked together with that attorney to apply for an immigrant visa that would allow him to become a

U.S. citizen. Meanwhile, he applied for a permanent position at various universities. By the time his visiting appointment at WU had concluded, he had an offer to become an assistant professor at the University of Rochester. He became a citizen, rose to the rank of full professor, married, and had two children. He has retired now and is living in Princeton, NJ. His two children are both employed at MIT, where one is a faculty member and the other, I believe, is on staff. I get a Christmas card from Tony every year expressing gratitude for his life in the U.S.

The other story requires a bit of background. After their move to Cambridge, Mary Allen graduated from Harvard Law and commenced a successful legal career in which she practiced as a public and then private trial attorney and taught in the Trial Advocacy Program at the Harvard Law School from 1983 to 2011. Meanwhile, Maxine Rockoff had left BCL to move with her husband David Rockoff to the Washington, DC area, where he became Chair of the Radiology Department at George Washington University School of Medicine; she worked for Bruce Waxman at the National Center for Health Services Research and Development, where she initiated a very early telemedicine program. Then David and Maxine divorced, and Maxine moved to New York City in 1980 to work for Merrill Lynch, where she proposed a novel broker workstation. She invited Wes and Ivan Sutherland to come to New York to convince the Merrill Lynch managers that the proposed workstation would be great for brokers. That meeting was the beginning of a romance between Maxine and Wes. After Wes was divorced, Wes and Maxine married. I remained close friends with all three, and I could also say that I was once the supervisor of two of the three Clark wives.

Here comes the China connection. Wes had had a deep interest in China since his trip there in 1972. He developed a computer terminal for the input of Chinese characters and, in the process, gained an appreciation for Chinese calligraphy. After he and Maxine married, Wes planned a wedding trip to China. As he told me later, they were in Shanghai and decided to take a bus trip to a village in the countryside. Late in the afternoon, to their astonishment, Maxine and Wes found that their bus had returned to Shanghai without them! No one there spoke English, and the Mandarin that Wes had learned was not up to the task of finding their way back to Shanghai.

Then Wes spotted a limousine, and he said to Maxine, "Our chances of finding someone who speaks English are better in the back of that limousine than on the street here." They approached, and sure enough the man in the back seat spoke good English and invited them to accompany him back to Shanghai. On the drive, he asked Wes what business he was in, and Wes replied, "Computers." "Ah," said their savior. "You don't happen to know Jerry Cox, do you?"

Now, I was not there, but I have a clear recollection of Wes telling me this story. It turned out that the passenger in the limousine was Professor Chang from Jiao Tong University, who had stayed in touch with Tony Chang and was a closet supporter of Tony's ambition to emigrate to the U.S. I have not tried to calculate the probability of this event taking place, nor even the conditional probability given my link to Professor Chang. It does make one wonder....

҂

In the fall of 1989, as was our custom, Bobby and I attended the 16th annual Computers in Cardiology (CiC) meeting. That year, it was held in Jerusalem, and the social program featured a trip to Masada. We climbed to the top of the mesa and saw the remnants of the fortifications left after the siege. It was an interesting visit, but it did not have the drama of my first visit to Israel.

There were other trips in addition to the annual CiC meetings—vacation trips to Hawaii and business trips to Rio de Janeiro and to Tokyo—but good stories are lacking. There was a trip to Cairo in the summer of 1976; however,

After the 1989 CiC, Bobby and I celebrated our traditional family Thanksgiving dinner. This event has always been held at the Hillsboro, Missouri, home of our son Jerry and his wife Margaret.

that became memorable even before boarding my flight. It was raining heavily, and on the way to the St. Louis airport on I-270, the MGB expired while approaching the Ladue Road exit. I felt the engine lose power and was able to glide to a stop in the breakdown lane at the bottom of the ramp. As I was looking under the hood, a kindly couple stopped and asked if they could help. I explained my predicament, and they volunteered to take me to the airport. It was a great stroke of luck, because otherwise I certainly would have missed my TWA flight to Athens and the connecting flight to Cairo. At the St. Louis airport, I called my mechanic and told him to tow the MGB away and sell it. I never wanted to see it again. He followed my instructions, and upon my return, I bought a much more reliable Toyota Camry.

Nothing can top the Israel and China stories, so I won't try. Onward to life after the chairmanship of the Department of Computer Science and Engineering.

Chapter 15
Electronic Radiology and Project Zeus | 1977-1997

Nearly all the projects reported in this chapter depend on high-speed networking done by the staff of the Applied Research Laboratory (ARL) in the CS department. The beginning of ARL at WU can be traced to Frank Starmer and Jon Turner. Frank was a friend and visiting professor in the department during the 1976-1977 academic year. A few years earlier, Frank and I had met while we were doing site visits for the NIH's National Heart, Lung, and Blood Institute. He was then an Assistant Professor of Medicine at Duke, but his doctoral training had been in bioengineering at the University of North Carolina. Frank had an insatiable curiosity about all things large and small, and I was delighted to have him, his wife Ellen, and their family visit our department that year.

One day, Frank observed that memory chips were doubling in capacity about every year, while other kinds of chips took more than a year and a half. The reason was that each memory chip was getting denser and also bigger. At that rate, as Frank pointed out, their capacity would increase by a thousandfold within a decade. Before long, it would be possible to store medical images on a few chips and transmit them over a high-speed computer network that linked the archive of these images to someone interested in viewing them.

So, I did what I do best: either help other people realize their ideas or just borrow those ideas, as was the case with Frank. It took almost two decades, but from the seed that Frank planted, WU became a national leader in electronic radiology. Then from Jon Turner's pioneering work in switching, WU became a national

leader in campus networking. In this chapter, I will trace the fortu-
itous events that propelled this transformation.

Back in 1977, only in science fiction could a high-resolution,
10-megapixel X-ray image have popped up on a physician's desktop
display. High-speed networks were then T1 lines over twisted pairs
of copper wires, which provided only 1.5 mb/s. In the mid-1980s,
fiber-optics had reached a stage of practical deployment, largely
as a result of research efforts by Corning Glass Works, GE, and
Bell Labs. The era of optical communication began when the Bell
operating companies replaced copper with fiber in their intercity
links and later in all their links except in the last mile, where copper
remained most cost effective. Jon Turner had prophesied this development in his 1986 paper subtitled, "Which Way to the Information Age?"

Optical communication and inexpensive semiconductor memory
replaced copper wires and ferrite-core memories at a such a rapid
pace that many people were taken by surprise. In 1986, inspired by
Frank's observation, several of us—Jim Blaine, Associate Director of
BCL; Gil Jost, Chief of Diagnostic Radiology in the Mallinckrodt
Institute of Radiology; and I—established the Electronic Radiology
Laboratory (ERL) with Jim as director, on the vacant third floor
of the Medical Center's newly acquired East Building. It was nick-
named the "Yeast Building" because of the smell that still lingered
from the previous occupant, a bread bakery. Under my direction,
Jim had recently completed his doctorate in high-speed digital
communications, and Gil saw the potential for computers in many
phases of radiology.

The problem was that the Ethernet was just then bursting on
the scene, and several companies were offering versions of it, all of
them slightly incompatible. This brings to mind a sardonic remark
I heard from Steve Wolff, Director of Networking at NSF: "The
wonderful thing about standards is that there are so many to
choose from." Almost every networked department on the WU
campus had chosen a different, and incompatible, standard and
vendor. These departments were fiercely independent and resisted
centralized control in such matters. However, in order to network

the medical and Hilltop (now Danforth) campuses, we needed a university-wide standard.

I realized that the cost of networking equipment would mean more to WU departments than taste in equipment selection. In a nationwide competition, the head of Medical Operations at DEC, Dick Corely, selected our proposal along with just two others from the many he had received, and that win gave us up to $25M in discounts for WU on all networking equipment. This discount program dramatically reduced the cost for any department that joined the program, and the arguments about which vendor to bless with a department's orders quickly melted away. Soon, we had a leading campus network and were able to establish the Office of the Network Coordinator (ONC), which was housed first in my office and then later in the same third-floor space as the ERL. Don Hirsh, Ira Hirsh's youngest son, followed me as ONC director. His instructions were to facilitate, but not direct, the internetworking of departments throughout the University.

One of the early ONC success stories was *wuarchive*, a collective that brought together in one place a variety of opensource software items and postings. It was initiated by a CSE student, Chris Myers, who started with a senior project and then proceeded to a role at ONC, reporting to Don Hirsh. Since there was essentially nothing like it on the web in the late 1980s, WU became, at times, the top destination for traffic in the world. I remember Chris coming to me to report that a complaint had been received about salacious material that had been posted on *wuarchive*. I organized a committee to look at it, and they quickly decided to take down the offending material. Perhaps Mark Zuckerberg should have used that same strategy more than three decades later. The *wuarchive* site survived on the web until 2010, a more than 30-year run.

Research collaborations between BCL and the School of Engineering, and between the School of Medicine and the Department of Biology, were already thriving, so it seemed important to have not only a network on each of the two campuses but also a broadband link between them. But such a university-wide network would take a substantial amount of money that we simply did not have. Jim Blaine and I applied to the NIH Shared Instrument Grant (SIG) Program declaring that the university-wide network we proposed would be a shared instrument. This was a stretch and not at all what the framers of the SIG program had in mind: They were thinking of shared large computers, shared mass spectrometers, and shared nuclear magnetic resonance instruments, all with price tags of more than a quarter million dollars. Yet Jim and I were able to convince the SIG program director that our dual campus network was indeed a shared instrument. The grant application succeeded, and I believe it was a unique award.

But we still needed a broadband link between the two campuses. Network routers, local twisted pair connections, and fiberoptic links between some departments were going in rapidly with the aid of the SIG grant and the DEC discount, but a broadband link between the two campuses required another solution. Trenching the four miles across Forest Park was beyond our budget and beyond our political skills. At that key point, Jim Blaine and several BCL staff members came to the rescue. They installed a microwave dish on the fourth-floor cupola at CID and on the roof of Lopata Hall, one of the taller engineering buildings. These dishes provided a 2.5-mile, 23 GHz link—and soon we were in business with a 10-megabit digital link between the two campuses. A decade later, the MetroLink tracks were extended from the medical center to Clayton, Missouri, a St. Louis suburb just west of the Hilltop campus. At that point, fiber was laid, connecting the two campuses along the tracks beside Forest Park, and the microwave system was then retired.

In 1986, Arun Kumar, an MS student of mine, built an inexpensive, high-speed frame buffer for radiographic images as his thesis topic. His work was a follow-on to the Chips & Dips project in my CS 360 class. Remember that Chips & Dips was the name of the pretend company set up in that class? His thesis made that class project a reality and demonstrated the emerging capabilities of semiconductor memory. The frame buffer contained 32 64-Kbit chips at $1.50 each, a total of $48 for a quarter of a megapixel buffer. That was less than 1/400th the cost of an equivalently sized core-memory buffer, and it signaled to me the end of the core-memory era.

We described this work toward radiological imaging on a campus network at the Society of Photo-Optical Instrumentation Engineers (SPIE) meeting, held annually in Newport Beach, California. Many attendees thought we were only dreaming about the need for high-bandwidth networks, but we felt the time had come to press for their broader availability.

The other meeting that Jim, Gil, and I attended regularly, reporting on progress at ERL, was the Radiological Society of North America (RSNA), which met every year in Chicago just after Thanksgiving. Another of my graduate students, Steve Moore, led the way in the development of DICOM (Digital Imaging and COmmunication in Medicine), now an international standard specifying how to manage medical-imaging information in medicine. Steve encountered many stumbling blocks along the way as individual companies tried to protect their own interests, but he persevered. Without his efforts, I doubt there would ever have been the widely accepted DICOM standard.

By 1990, Lew Thomas decided to retire as Director of BCL, and a search began for his successor. We recruited NIH scientist David States in 1992 to fill Lew's job, but he left for the University of Michigan when the renewal of the basic NIH grant failed, and BCL was then closed. I was sad to see BCL go, but its time was over. Small computers had penetrated almost all of the WU medical school laboratories, and their use had become so routine that the absence of BCL was not a jolt. I turned my attention to campus networking, ARL and ERL.

At ERL, we realized that many radiology images were much larger than a quarter of a megapixel or even larger than a megapixel. So, we began to investigate the performance of image-compression algorithms. I was invited to participate in a few Joint Photographic Experts Group (JPEG) meetings because our publications on psychophysical distortion metrics were useful in judging the quality of compression algorithms. After that, I was asked to consult for VTEL, a pioneer in videoconferencing located in Austin, Texas. VTEL was then a young startup, and it offered to pay me in stock, which I gladly accepted. I distributed the shares to my three children—and, happily, this stock paid the college tuition for at least a couple of my grandchildren.

Before traveling to VTEL in Texas, I learned that my half-brother, Randy, was living and working a few hours from Austin, and we arranged to meet at a halfway spot. I had a rental car, and Randy picked a restaurant for lunch. Soon, it became apparent that Randy was not happy in his job. He had married in 1968, and I was his best man. As we prepared for his 1968 wedding in Cleveland, he seemed to have doubts about married life. He nervously said to me, "If I am late tomorrow morning, please start without me." He wasn't late, and the wedding proceeded.

Their daughter, Allison, was born in 1973, but the marriage did not work out and ended in divorce in 1976. Subsequently, Randy finished his degree at Capitol University while living at home in Bexley and then in the basement of Elrose's apartment. At that time, Randy was working at Scioto Downs, a horse-racing track and casino just south of Columbus. His income was not steady, which may have led, at least in part, to his marital difficulties.

He loved the track and followed the horse-racing circuit, working in Fargo, North Dakota, and then in Texas at off-track betting establishments. Next, he moved to Erie, Pennsylvania, to work at the Downs at Erie, another off-track betting establishment, and things started to improve for him. Eventually, he was promoted to General Manager at the Downs. In 1985, Randy met and, a decade later, married Theresa Surovick, who was taking care of her mother in Girard, Pennsylvania, near Erie. In Theresa, Randy found his soulmate, with the same interests and offbeat sense of humor that he had. The twosome really enjoyed each other and had one of the happiest periods of their lives.

It is time to catch up on the other Randy, our second son. Like our other two kids, Nancy and Jerry, Randy went to Lindbergh High and did well. He then applied to Washington University and was admitted to the mechanical engineering program. In 1988, he graduated with a BS and took a job in St. Louis with Sverdrup and Parcel, designing HVAC systems. I thought he was happy there, but in 1990 he came home one day with a card that said, "I have decided to quit my job, travel the world, and wear live animals for hats." It showed a kid wearing a live beaver on his head. Inside the card he had written, "I am just kidding about the live animals." Nancy had found that hilarious card and given it to Randy for the

In spring 1992, Bobby and I took time off for a Caribbean cruise with Wes and Maxine aboard the Clipper Nitehawk.

occasion. She knew he was concerned about how to break the news to his parents, and it certainly was a wonderful way to do it. He still enjoyed designing air-conditioning systems at Sverdrup, but he simply could not pass up the adventure of being a travel director at Intrav, a St. Louis travel company founded by art collector Barney Ebsworth.

Indeed, Randy did travel the world, herding groups of retirees on that trip they had always wanted to take. In doing so, he had many adventures, and in only two years he was able to stick more pins in my big world map than I had in a lifetime: Alaska, Europe, Great Britain, Ireland, Russia, Japan, China, Australia, New Zealand, and many more. I had no idea that, when I brought him along on those CiC trips, I had helped to awaken a voracious travel appetite. I will not steal his stories; he can write his own book to reveal them. He has some marvelous tales that probably top mine.

One I can't resist, however, involves a trip that Randy took to New Zealand. Afterwards, he visited Bobby and me at home and presented us with a videotape to play. It was labelled "Bungee Jumping," and Bobby said, "Oh, Randy, you didn't!" To which he replied, "Only crazy people do that." We watched, and there he was, standing on a bridge over a deep canyon, waving and saying, "Hi, Mom! Hi, Dad!" We were glad to know that he was sitting in front of us, unharmed, as we watched him dip into the water at the end of the bungee cord more than a football field below.

Randy soon had another surprise: He had been accepted into the MBA program at the Cornell University Business School. He enrolled there in 1992 and graduated in 1994. Travelling back and forth to St. Louis, he frequently stopped off in Girard, Pennsylvania, to see our family's other Randy. Bobby and I went to Ithaca, New York, to see young Randy walk in the graduation exercise, which attracted a huge crowd that filled the football stadium.

That crowd was, I believe, slightly reduced in size by the absence of a few parents, who had accompanied us on our TWA commuter flight from LaGuardia. Our tiny aircraft could not land at Ithaca because a disabled aircraft blocked the single runway, so we were diverted to Corning, New York, about 35 miles away. TWA promised bus transportation to Ithaca, but when we deplaned, the single TWA staffer seemed surprised to see us. Since we only had a few hours to get to Ithaca for the ceremony, Bobby and I skipped the promised bus ride and rented the only car available at the only rental counter. We shared the rental with one other couple who had the same idea, and we quickly got on our way, arriving at the stadium in plenty of time. We doubt that the others on that diverted flight ever got their promised bus ride—or, if they did, it is unlikely that they got to the stadium in time.

In fall 1994, Randy took a job with Ernst & Young (EY) in Boston, as part of their business advisory services division. He had an apartment on Tremont Street in the South End, just a few blocks from where Bobby had lived with her roommates on St. Botolph Street. That fondly remembered spot was now paved over by I-90. His apartment was also not far from the Liberty Mutual headquarters that I had frequented nearly 40 years before. Soon, Randy was flying to Detroit regularly to work with EY automotive clients there. He met another EY staffer on those trips, but more about her later.

Before we get to that story, let's return to the campus network. Jon Turner and the ARL graduate students in the CSE department had built a chipset that carried out the high-speed routing of large network payloads—a step that was far faster than what Arun Kumar had done. We called it Fast Packet Switching. This chipset assumed that future networking would be done with a protocol endorsed by Bell Labs and called Asynchronous Transfer Mode (ATM). The chips were fabricated under the DoD Metal Oxide Semiconductor Implementation Service (MOSIS), a low-cost government program. Printed circuit boards were built and software developed at ARL under Jon's direction. Guru Parulkar, a recent faculty hire, and I helped out. Jon invited several dozen industry leaders to see what we had done. But we didn't yet have a working system, so there was a race to bring all pieces of the demonstration project together in time. The system only worked occasionally, but one of those occasions was the very time when our auditorium was filled with industry leaders. They were impressed. Large images and video were transmitted over our network to screens in the auditorium. This kind of event is an everyday experience today, but in the early 1990s, it was novel and very impressive—a glimpse into the future.

Jon Turner developed a partnership with SynOptics of Santa Clara, California, one of the visiting companies at our demonstration. SynOptics developed a hardware product, ATM Lattice Cell, based on the WU Fast Packet chipset, but they failed to develop adequate supporting software. As our next effort toward commercialization, Jon licensed the WU Fast Packet chipset to Nexion, a subdivision of Ascom-Timplex, located in Acton, Massachusetts. This time, the Nexen 8000 software was satisfactory, but the hardware was not. We were depressed. We had done our best to transfer our technology to eager industry partners but had struck out twice.

❧

The work with SynOptics gave me a chance to visit my half-sister Candy, who had moved to Monterey, California, from Vail, Colorado. She was sales manager for the Monterey Hotel, and her boys, Chris and Michael, had graduated from college. Candy had a knack for picking beautiful places to live: Big Sky, Vail, and Monterey. Since her divorce from her first husband, her life had been going well. She had met a wonderful gentleman, Michael Owen, who was just what she needed, and they soon married. Monterey was only an hour and a quarter south of SynOptics, so it was an easy drive—except in rush hour, which made it a multi-hour misery.

The Fast Packet chipset was the basis of our campus-wide network, which Jon named Project Zeus. We knew it worked well because it allowed us to transfer images rapidly and reliably between research projects located on the medical and Hilltop campuses. It also allowed us to demonstrate the Physician's Workstation, a futuristic system that displayed images and other medical data on the desktop with remarkable speed.

With the SynOptics and Ascom-Timeplex strikes against us, we figured we had one more swing at bat. Three of us—Jon Turner, Guru Parulkar, and I—assembled to talk about it over dinner one night at a favorite restaurant of mine. It was September 1997, and the weather was lovely as we sat at a sidewalk table in front of Dressel's Public House in St. Louis's Central West End. One of us made the suggestion, "Our two efforts at commercialization with established companies have failed, so the only thing left to do is start our own company." That will be the topic of Chapter 17. But first, I would like to report on some committee work that took place contemporaneously with the development of Project Zeus and will provide several interesting stories.

Chapter 16
Committee Work | 1982-1997

Two committees, one on brain mapping and the other on genome mapping, occupied a good bit of my time after my retirement as chair of the CSE department. However, my involvement with these committees had actually begun much earlier. Two people, Bob Livingston and Maynard Olson, each played important roles that I will explain first to set the scene before describing each of the committees.

Bob Livingston was Scientific Director of the National Institute of Neurological Diseases and Blindness when Wes and Charlie brought a prototype LINC to the NIH in 1963. In Arnold Starr's lab, they were able to demonstrate, on a living cat, the LINC's ability to carry out real-time analysis of neural firings. Livingston was there and later recalled, "It was such a triumph that we danced a jig right there around the equipment."[10] Shortly thereafter, Livingston left the NIH and founded the neuroscience department at the University of California, San Diego (UCSD).

Livingston approached Charlie in 1983 to help him evaluate a proposal by General Garrison Rapmund, MD, then the Assistant Surgeon General for R&D, who was stationed at the Fort Detrick, Maryland, home of the U.S. Army Medical Research & Development Command. He wanted to create a lavishly funded program in brain mapping, and Livingston was interested because of the support it would likely make available under contracts to his new department at UCSD. But Livingston was unsure as to whether the state of the nation's computer technology was ready for the job, so he recruited

10 https://history.nih.gov/display/history/Linc+02

Charlie Molnar. Then Charlie recruited me to travel with them to Fort Detrick to see what the General had in mind.

We learned that Rapmund wished to fund an ambitious program in which the brains of many cadavers would be cut into thin slices, scanned, and assembled into a large array of huge 3-dimensional (3D) images. Was this scientific curiosity on Rapmund's part or something else? We hoped to find out during our visit to Fort Detrick. Subsequently, Wes Clark suggested we add physicist Bruce McCormick from Texas A&M to our team. Bruce and Wes were old friends from the early days of computing, when Bruce was heavily involved in the design of the Illiac III at the University of Illinois. After the construction of Illiac III and until it was destroyed by fire in 1968, Bruce headed the budding Illinois computer science department and in his spare time wrote the Illiac III reference manuals. Later, in 1983, Bruce became head of the newly formed Department of Computer Science at Texas A&M and was just beginning his work on brain visualization.

After our visit to Fort Detrick, the team assembled for dinner and discussion at our house. The guests included Charlie, his wife Donna, Bruce, Livingston, Bobby, and me at our large dining room table. The discussion was lively, with Bobby and Livingston sparring about what constituted an acceptable age difference between a man and his mate. Bobby argued that the number of years of difference should be much smaller than Livingston wished to allow. As near as I could tell, the debate was a draw.

After dinner, we retired to our back room to discuss the potential for a productive brain-mapping program. My conclusion was that computer technology was not quite ready for the challenge because of the enormous memory requirements. Subsequently, a larger group, hosted by Bruce, met at Texas A&M in College Station. Memorably, there was a 2 a.m. fire alarm at our motel, and the guests all vacated their rooms; we sat around outside in the pleasant nighttime air, continuing the evening's discussion, while the firemen went about their urgent business inside.

So, did a major project develop and satisfy General Rapmund's request? The answer was influenced by two things: the eventual revelation of the General's covert motivation and the then-current state of memory technology. The General, we eventually learned, wanted the brain-mapping results so the army could automatically determine which assignment was appropriate for each incoming recruit—something that made us all more than a bit uncomfortable. Second, the sheer number of bits was daunting, and it took another decade for the needed storage to become available. Furthermore, the investigation Livingston and Rapmund had done focused only on anatomy, with no concern for physiological function. Overall, this sortie into brain mapping was useful in gauging the enormity of the problem but was otherwise too early.

I can't say that the Rapmund-Livingston project led directly to the next step, but it was in the background, at least for me. In 1989, when I was asked to join the National Academy of Sciences (NAS) Committee on a National Neural Circuitry Database, I quickly accepted. We met in the majestic, columned NAS headquarters on Constitution Avenue just northeast of the Lincoln Memorial. Our second-floor meeting room was big enough to seat the 15 committee members around a large table, with a dozen or so NAS staff members filling the chairs that lined the walls.

In retrospect, I am pleased to note that WU was well represented, with four of the 15 members having past, present, or future connections with our university. Those four were Max Cowan, who had recently departed from heading the medical school's Department of Anatomy to become Chief Scientific Officer of the Howard Hughes Medical Institute; Marcus Raichle, Professor of Radiology and an early LINC user in Ter-Pogossian's Radiation Sciences Lab; David Van Essen, soon to be head of the Department of Anatomy; and me. I knew others on the committee through computer science connections: Vint Cerf, co-developer, with Bob Kahn, of the Internet's internetworking protocol; James Kajiya, a student of Ivan Sutherland, who developed computer-graphic algorithms for displaying animal fur; and Diane C.P. Smith, Chief Scientist at Xerox Advanced Information Technology in Cambridge, who was a good friend of Wes Clark. Thus, I knew almost half of the committee in one way or another. Just because I knew these members did not make it a good committee, but it did ease my interactions during coffee breaks.

The committee chair, Joseph Martin, assembled four task forces, each one including several members of the committee plus several outside experts. These task forces met in the first quarter of 1990: two in Washington, DC, and two in Irvine, California. The committee report, which was published in 1991 as a 152-page book,[11] concluded that the time was right to begin a Human Brain Project with the goal "to achieve an integrated understanding of the brain's structure and functions." Furthermore, the report prophesied that emerging computer science research would lead to the necessary database and 3D visualization tools.

In retrospect, the committee's recommendations were not sufficiently focused to markedly change scientific progress. The various NIH institutes interested in the brain set up explicit programs that funded portions of the Human Brain Project. However, the scientific results obtained might have happened anyway. An overview of the Human Brain Project,[12] published in 1997, reports that more than 50 researchers were supported by it. My assessment is that results clearly attributable to the Human Brain Project were mostly in the realm of new computer science tools. I had the honor of being asked to write the foreword to this 1997 volume, but I dodged summarizing the results by tracing the history of the application of computers to neurophysiology from the early 1950s to just prior to the establishment of the NAS Committee. Perhaps this was a rather timid alternative to assessing results of the Human Brain Project, but it got me off the hook.

It is instructive to examine what has happened at WU in neuro-informatics during the three decades since the NAS Committee on a National Neural Circuitry Database concluded its work. Both Marcus Raichle and David Van Essen are still faculty members at the School of Medicine; Marc is Professor of Radiology, where he leads the Neuroimaging Laboratories; and David is now the past head of our Department of Anatomy and Neurobiology and runs an amazingly productive lab. Together, they have made remarkable progress toward the goals laid out in the 1991 NAS committee report. Graduate students from our CSE and EE departments have participated in the development of a large array of computational tools.

Through the development of imaging studies using PET and functional MRI scans, Marc and his laboratory colleagues have markedly improved our understanding of human brain function.

11   Pechura, C. M. and Martin, J. B, *"Mapping the Brain and its Functions,"* National Academy Press, 1991

12   Koslow, S. H. and Huerta, M.F, eds, *"Neuroinformatics,"* Lawrence Erlbaum Associates, 1997.

David's laboratory has led the Human Connectome Project, which endeavors to understand the structure, function, and evolution of the cerebral cortex from brain slices. Nearly four decades have elapsed since Rapmund and Livingston first proposed brain mapping to Charlie and me. During that time, the progress in neuroscience has been slow but steady and with many surprises. I do not think that the NAS committee report foresaw this protracted course of events.

Let me move on now to the second committee and the background for my involvement in it. One day in the late 1980s, Maynard Olson, Assistant Professor of Genetics at WU, came to my office. He was trying to sequence the yeast genome and realized he needed computational help, both in the development of algorithms and in the writing of programs. I asked Jon Turner to look at the algorithmic questions and Will Gillette to look at developing software. I also got interested on my own and found it was like putting together the top-edge pieces of a huge jigsaw puzzle—one with 12 million pieces across the top—for yeast. There were many partially assembled pieces from other copies of the same 12-million-piece puzzle edge, all overlapping with each other. Our goal was to generate a significant portion of the top edge of the puzzle in proper order. Each piece of the puzzle corresponded to a group of several DNA base pairs, each represented by letter pairs: AT, GC, TA, and CG. It was clearly a great computational challenge, and its exact solution fell in the class of highly difficult NP-complete computational problems. Jon Turner and his student Gwangsoo Rhee developed some approximate but useful solutions, and Will Gillette implemented software that was effective in assembling the pieces—so much so that Will eventually left our faculty in 1992 to join Olson, who by then had moved to the University of Washington.

To my surprise, in 1990 I got an invitation from the NIH to join its National Advisory Council for Human Genome Research, which was chaired by James Watson, the famed partner of Francis Crick in the discovery of the structure and function of DNA. That sounded pretty exciting, so I agreed. However, I did wonder how I was selected for this elite committee. Finally, I concluded that Maynard

Olson must have put my name into the hat when the NIH organizers of the Council realized that they needed at least a token computer scientist.

Indeed, I *was* a token. All the others on the Council were geneticists without a trace of computer experience. I felt on the spot when we reviewed the very rare application that had a few mathematical equations. They would all turn to me and say, "Jerry, does this make sense?" I bravely soldiered on as best I could, assuming the committee would identify and reject any genetic nonsense.

The Council had been formed by the director of the NIH to monitor the program charged with mapping the human genome—all 3 billion base pairs of it—roughly 250 times the difficulty of mapping the yeast genome. Optimistically, the organizers, principally Watson, thought that goal could be attained in a decade or so, but as the years went by without significant progress, our anxieties rose. Watson was not a good chair, allowing the committee members to divide between a strategy of giving a few big grants and, alternatively, letting a hundred small flowers bloom. He also frequently failed to take note of committee opinions that did not align with his own, sometimes stating clearly biased views.

Francis Collins, a geneticist from the University of Michigan, was brought in to replace Watson, who retired to his Cold Spring Harbor Lab on the north shore of Long Island, where he had been director since 1968. He remained director of CSHL until 2007, when he was relieved of all administrative duties. His titles of Professor Emeritus and Honorary Trustee were also revoked for offensive statements concerning race, genetics, and intelligence. From his behavior as Council chair, I must say I was not surprised

Collins was a breath of fresh air. The Council settled down to the business of getting the human genome mapped. At one of the meetings in 1995, Bob Waterston, chair of genetics at Washington University, made a presentation in which he described how he and his partner, John Sulston at the Laboratory of Molecular Biology in Cambridge, England, had mapped the worm genome and then described how they would do the same for the human genome. The Council was elated. After all the struggle of the past years, they could see the end of the quest. In fact, many of the Council members were so relieved that they stood and clapped. I had been on dozens of councils and committees at NIH, but never had I experienced that kind of overt emotion. It was wonderful.

Francis Collins later became head of the National Human Genome Institute and then in 2009 became Director of the entire NIH, where he just concluded more than a dozen years of service, all with great distinction. I rotated off the Council in 1995, and Waterston and Sulston completed the human genome in 2003, just 50 years after Watson and Crick's seminal publication of the structure of the human genome. It was a breath-taking adventure for me to be a fly on that historic wall.

Meanwhile, back in St. Louis, Ira Hirsh had come out of his third retirement (chair of the WU Psychology Department, Dean of the WU Arts & Sciences Faculty, and Director of Research at CID) to become Director of CID. This was expected to be a short-term assignment, just long enough to have a search committee appointed and do its work. The previous director had departed suddenly, and in 1992 Ira was asked to fill the gap. Ira asked me to join the CID Board of Directors. I accepted and am still on the board.

Soon, I found myself on the search committee for the new director of CID. The leading candidate, Don Nielsen, accepted and took over as Director in 1994. Ira retired for the fourth time. Unfortunately, Nielsen got into an unnecessary dispute with a popular teacher; he fired that teacher and two others, much to the distress of many other teachers and students, He also misused the funds he had raised for new buildings by investing them in the market just as the dotcom bust sent prices tumbling. Bob Clark, CEO of Clayco and a board member, took over the directorship from Nielsen in 2002. Pulling a rabbit out of a hat, Bob sold the new CID buildings to WU, which leased them back to CID. The cash obtained from this transaction allowed CID to pay off its building loans and avoid bankruptcy. To this day, I wonder if things would have turned out differently if, early in the search, I had contacted a friend of mine who had been a co-worker of Nielsen's. The guilt from my delay still lingers.

In 2003, Bob went back to running Clayco, a very successful construction firm, and he recommended Robin Feder as the replacement director. Robin had been successful at CID as the chief development officer, and Bob's recommendation was wise. Robin led CID from 2003 until her retirement in 2021, managing well the huge demographic shift caused by the development of auditory testing of infants and the cochlear implant. This shift in school population to younger-age children was triggered in part by Hal Davis's evoked-response results.

For many years, my position on the board at CID required me to report to the full board on progress made by the Program in Audiology and Communication Sciences (PACS), headed by Bill Clark. Bill and I had known each other for two decades before my appointment to the board. One twist of fate between the two of us involved a chapter in the series, *Industrial Hygiene and Toxicology* by F. A. Patty. In 1958, I had written the chapter titled "Industrial Noise and the Conservation of Hearing," for the 2nd edition of Patty, published in 1960. Bill completely rewrote the same chapter in the edition published in 2000. He then discovered the coincidence, and when he updated the chapter for the 2010 edition, he graciously added my name as coauthor. What a kind tribute!

Switching topics, let me provide an update as to how Elrose was doing after my father's death. The apartment in Bexley pleased her. My brother Randy had moved out of the basement, and she was living alone, which suited her. She was active in the St. Alban's Episcopal Church and got to know the priest well. He led a "low church" service that retained fewer of the rituals, such as swinging incense pots and frequent bell ringing, than were familiar to both Elrose and me from our South Bend church, St. James Episcopal. One Sunday, during communion at St. Alban's, Elrose accidentally hit the heavy wine chalice with her ring as the priest tipped it to her mouth. It rang with a proper bell-like peal throughout the entire church. Elrose whispered to the priest, "I just wanted to give you a touch of high church." He could not contain a robust laugh— breaking the solemnity of the deeply religious occasion.

I visited Bexley whenever I could, and Elrose would always take me to her favorite restaurant, a spot on Main Street not far from her apartment. I noticed that she was increasingly frail; so did Candy, her elder daughter, who frequently visited from Marina, California.

We learned that Elrose was no longer able to climb or descend the stairs in her apartment but went up or down on her bottom. We felt that something had to be done.

We agreed on a kind of kidnapping, since Elrose insisted upon staying in her Bexley apartment. We persuaded her to visit Candy on the pretext of a short stay, and while she was there, a team— including my son Jerry, his wife Margaret, my half-sister Anita, and I—cleaned out her apartment, sending her clothes and all keepsakes on to California. After Candy found a single-floor apartment near her home in Marina, California, Elrose accepted her fate and had a few happy years in her own place within a few blocks of her daughter. Eventually, Elrose became too frail to live alone and was moved to a small retirement home in lovely Carmel, California, where she passed away peacefully in 2001.

Chapter 17
Growth Networks | 1997-2000

Before describing the Growth Networks adventure, I would like to say a bit more about our family life. Since these stories span several decades, there is no one place in the memoir where it is just right to recount them all. However, they deserve to be told without being divided into small bits.

Over the four decades that Bobby and I lived in the young town of Sunset Hills, our social life prospered. Bobby loved to entertain and made it look easy. Occasionally, guests would offer to help, but she would always say, "Thanks, but this is a one-cook kitchen." Sometimes, after dinner, we would play bridge; we also had treasure hunts with clues hidden in obscure spots around our neighborhood and nearby towns. Each clue had to be deciphered before our guests searched for the next one.

Many of our friends were from the Kirkwood Theatre Guild, and they enjoyed the party games we played in that group, though acting out charades or drawing them were favorites. The latter game featured teams in separate rooms at the house of the host, who would stand in the hall at a point equally accessible to all the teams. He would whisper the title of a book, play, or TV program to the next team representative who approached him. That person would run back to the table and try to draw the title on paper or on a small blackboard without using any alphabetical letters or giving verbal clues. The team that finished first by correctly guessing the greatest number of the ten titles won the game.

In doing all of this, drawing skill was not required. In fact, it could be a detriment, since a careful drawing took time. Conveying the idea with the smallest number of pen or chalk strokes was the key when it came your turn to draw. The combination of the team's wild guesses, the drawing player's monosyllabic shouts of yes or no, the dashes to the host with the team's guess and then back with the next title, made for much excitement and laughter. Not a very cerebral game—but lots of fun.

On our 45th wedding anniversary in 1996, we gathered some 60 of our family and friends at the Washington University Faculty Club. Our three kids arranged the program, but I composed a limerick for the occasion:

> I had hoped to find something clever
> To proclaim our true love; however,
> My search for a gimmick,
> Gave only this limerick,
> Which, unlike our love, won't last forever.

Bobby narrated a set of slides that garnered many laughs, while our kids arranged a parody on the classic TV program *Let's Make a Deal*, complete with a rubber chicken quickly slipped behind the door that Bobby and I picked. Craig recorded a video of the whole affair that the rest of us review with smiles and tears every year or so to this day.

Sunset Hills was incorporated in 1957, just six years before our move from Kirkwood. In 1965, a friend asked me to join him as a member of the Police Review Board. The duty was uneventful since the city had hardly any crime, but it gave me the satisfaction of doing my civic duty, something my father had instilled in me as a teenager. That all changed when the chief demoted a sergeant for failing to work a dispatcher's announcement of a robbery in progress.

After an investigation, it turned out that the sergeant and the dispatcher were having a turbulent affair. He claimed it was unfair for the dispatcher to expect him to work this crime, since it came at the time of a shift change. The chief rightly felt that a crime in progress took precedence over any personal disagreement, or any technicality related to a shift change. Therefore, the sergeant should be disciplined and demoted.

Then the sergeant sued the city over the chief's action, and the city attorney settled the case out of court, allowing the sergeant's failure to respond to the notification of a crime in progress to be expunged from his record. The city attorney advised me he had made a business decision that saved the city considerable money, but I was distressed and resigned from the police board in protest. The sergeant went on to serve in another St. Louis suburb with a raise in pay. My protest and resignation changed no minds at City Hall, but it gave me insight into how "bad cops" can move through the system unscathed by their bad performance—an even more pressing problem today than it was in the 1960s.

In 1970, my family also had our own encounter with the police. One night at about 2 a.m. the phone rang, and a voice said, "This is the police, and we have your son." I quickly slipped on some clothes and headed for the police station. As I left the neighborhood, I noticed there were four other cars making the same trip.

When we all arrived at the station, we discovered that our sons, who were supposed to be at a sleep-over at a neighbor's house. had strayed to a nearby all-night restaurant. They were all 13 or 14 and had been arrested for violation of curfew. The police were pleasant and left further discipline to the five grumpy fathers who had been unpleasantly aroused from their slumbers. I don't think I was as severe about this escapade as my father was about my high school misbehavior, but that may depend upon which side of the infraction you were on.

A decade or so later. I was asked by the mayor to become a member of the Board of Adjustment, the committee that grants exceptions to the city's ordinances. I accepted and served on the committee for nearly 35 years, including more than a decade as its chair. It was a pleasant way to discharge my civic responsibility with only occasional outbursts of emotion or tears from disappointed applicants.

By 1984, Randy—our youngest—was off to WU, and Bobby began looking around for something to do outside our home. She tried a number of jobs, but enjoyed her time with her company, *First on the Agenda*, the most. Bobby and Merry Ambos, my former secretary, established this company themselves to arrange and supervise corporate events. Its services included selecting the venue, choosing the menu, hiring the caterer, seeing that all went well, and overcoming the inevitable glitch or two. It was quite successful and had a good run through the 1980s.

❧

Allow me now to return to September 1997 and that fateful dinner on the sidewalk in front of Dressel's Public House. With two strikes against us, Jon, Guru, and I thought we had just one more swing at bat to make a profitable product out of the fast-packet chipset. This

Washington University Photographic Services Collection, Julian Edison Department of Special Collections, Washington University Libraries

In 1997, I received the Eliot Society's Search Award. Left to right are Chancellor Mark Wrighton, me, Bobby, and emeritus Chancellor Bill Danforth.

time we would start our own company. After that dinner, I found a couple of rooms we could rent in the White Building on Brentwood Boulevard, not too far west of WU. There were six of us then: three faculty (Jon, Guru, and me) and three graduate students (Andy Fingerhut, Zubin Dittia, and Will Eatherton). Jon selected the name Growth Networks, Inc (GNI), which suggested the ability of the chipset to scale up capacity without logical limit, although certain practical considerations, related to power and size, were likely to arise for systems above the terabit level (10^{12} bps).

In late 1997, we prepared a slide deck and set out on the first of many trips to Sand Hill Road in California. On this spot, Palo Alto borders Menlo Park, and many of the West Coast venture capitalists are lined up next to each other, like ducks in a row, just north of the Stanford campus. Over the next spring and summer, each visit revealed another weakness in our slide deck—which we would dutifully repair before the next visit. It was discouraging. We thought we had the makings of a great product, but the repeated rejections forced us to question our convictions.

One summer afternoon, Jon had a long phone conversation with a Cisco engineer. He seemed seriously interested, and we invited him to visit St. Louis, where we presented the slide deck and showed him a working demo. His enthusiasm restored ours, and we set up another Sand Hill Road trip in the early fall of 1998. The first stop was New Enterprise Associates (NEA), a well-established venture firm with offices both there and on the East Coast.

When we met with Rob Coneybeer, we asked whether he would prefer to see slides projected on his screen or look over paper copies. He said "paper" and flipped through them rapidly with an occasional grunt. My heart sank in anticipation of another rejection. Instead, as he reached the last slide, he said, "Let's set up a date with our attorneys to work on Articles of Incorporation." It turned out that their attorneys' offices were conveniently located only a few blocks away at the western end of Sand Hill Road.

Jubilantly, we decided that we must have finally gotten the slide deck right, but later our more sober thought recognized that information leakage around Silicon Valley is abundant. More likely, NEA had somehow learned of Cisco's interest in our fast-packet chipset, and this more probably led to Rob's quick decision than anything we did to our slides.

Rob also said they would like to introduce us to a CEO candidate, Ron Bernal. To facilitate that meeting, Ron came to St. Louis for a mutual checkout. We liked him. He had been President of MIPS, the microprocessor subsidiary of Silicon Graphics, Inc., and was now an engineer-in-residence at NEA. By October 1998, Silicon Graphics veteran, Dan Lenoski, had been added to the company as VP of Engineering; various documents had been signed; the financial pie had been sliced; a "cap table" (capitalization table, the list of all the owners of a company's stock and the number of shares they own) had been produced—and GNI was in business.

Our investors at NEA made it clear that the company had to be headquartered in the Bay Area. None of the three of us really wanted to move to California, but Guru volunteered to do so, and I agreed to spend every other week there. Since Jon was teaching, he

The Growth Networks team from left to right: Lenoski, Parulkar, Turner, Cox, and Bernal

could only fly west for board meetings. Fortunately, TWA then had convenient direct, nonstop flights from St. Louis to San Jose. We insisted that the three graduate students—Andy Fingerhut, Zubin Dittia, and Will Eatherton—finish their degrees: the DSc, DSc, and MS, respectively. They were able to do so before their moves west in early 1999.

The GNI office was set up in a building just east of US 101 in Palo Alto. There, the staff grew rapidly with engineers that Dan Lenoski knew, plus Guru, Andy, Zubin, Will, and me from St. Louis. In less than a year, we outgrew the Palo Alto location and moved the GNI office to Mountain View.

The growth of the GNI staff bore no relation at all to successful sales of our chipset. The chipset network format had to be redesigned from the Asynchronous Transfer Mode (ATM) standard that we had used at WU. Of course, AT&T would have liked to have had their ATM network format become the industry standard, but that was not to be. By 1999, the computer industry was solidly wedded to the Internet Protocol (IP). We, and AT&T, had to swallow hard and make the change.

Our NEA investors were expecting a contract from Cisco, but after we got started with the chipset redesign, Cisco cancelled its plans to purchase chipsets from GNI. Cisco had decided to build its own chipset with its inhouse staff. So, there we were, with dozens of engineers on the payroll, and not a customer in sight. No one but Cisco had plans for a router that required a hugely scalable design like ours. It was a grim time. Board meetings were civil, but it was hard to ask for more financial runway, something we clearly needed.

By the end of 1999, we had more than 50 engineers in the company and still no customers. The initial investment had been augmented by another round of investment for a total of about $21M. Our CEO, Ron Bernal, kept an upbeat attitude for the benefit of the staff, but those of us on the Board of Directors knew that the $21M investment from NEA and a follow-on investor would not last forever. Then, in January 2000, everything changed. Ron's mood brightened, and we soon learned that the Cisco inhouse effort to build the chipset for their top-of-the-line product, the CRS-1, had faltered.

The CRS-1, short for the Cisco Carrier Routing System, had been informally announced by Cisco with the internal code name "BFR" in 1999. It was to be sold to large content providers and enterprises needing to handle network traffic that could reach almost 10^{14} bits per second. But the inhouse team was not a happy group, and many had decamped to other companies, thus dooming their chipset effort. Cisco was in a spot and came back to GNI to see whether we could help. On 16 February 2000, the deal was announced, and on 23 March 2000, Cisco officially acquired GNI for $355 M in stock. Within a few days, a cardboard slipcover over our pedestal sign had been put in place in front of our offices in Mountain View, and Cisco's acquisition team was on site dealing with such personnel issues as whether our employee-purchased espresso machine would be allowed within a Cisco building. The answer was "no," which almost led to a mutiny by our espresso zealots.

Within a month, 53 of us had moved out of our Mountain View location to one of the many Cisco buildings on West Tasman Drive in San Jose. Jon Turner remained in St. Louis and did not plan to move. While I had my doubts about working fulltime, as Cisco requested, Guru joined the crowd on West Tasman. My decision cost me a significant number of shares, but I neither wanted to move my family from St. Louis nor did I want to be separated from them. The Cisco stock the three of us finally acquired was locked up for six months. By that time, the Cisco stock price had fallen from an all-time high of $80 to about $50 per share. It ended its slide at $8.60 per share in October 2002 and has recently climbed to just above $50 per share. The peak at $80 was caused by a foolish belief that Cisco would be the first company to attain a trillion-dollar valuation. When the dot-com bust hit in 2000, it was hard to stop the slide.

Acting upon good advice from our Sand Hill Road attorneys, I had given shares in GNI to each of my kids before the sale. Because of the appreciation in those shares, Nancy and her husband had enough to help them buy a lovely new house even after the share value had dropped to about $50 each. Jerry and Randy have used their shares over the years to invest in their houses and play the market. As for the NEA, they cleared 22 times their investment in just 16 months—which produced broad smiles among their partners. I still have some Cisco shares, though not as many as you might think. The share that Jon, Guru, and I received was significantly diluted by the NEA investment and by shares that went to many others. Bobby and I did express our new-found prosperity by installing a lovely and somewhat ostentatious brick driveway and by basking in a more comfortable view of our retirement finances.

Washington University did all right, too, retaining the original Turner patents on the fast-packet chipset and licensing them to GNI. Upon the acquisition of the company by Cisco, those rights were transferred to Cisco for a tidy sum that was paid directly to WU.

After the company moved from St. Louis to the Bay Area, we wished to file additional patents. Ron Bernal, our CEO, asked me to work with a highly recommended Palo Alto patent attorney, but each time he completed a new section of a patent specification, I sat with him for hours correcting his technical errors. It was very inefficient. Ron suggested I find a new attorney. In poking around, I found a familiar name: Kirk Williams. He had been a networking student of mine, gone off to work for Bell Labs, felt the call to go to law school, and had then become a patent attorney. Kirk lived in Denver but was affiliated with a Bay Area firm. When I called him up, he said he was happy to do work for GNI. It was wonderful to have an attorney who could turn out technically correct patents on the first try. When GNI was acquired by Cisco, their chief patent counsel recognized Kirk's skills and retained him. Even today, the better part of Kirk's patent law practice is still with Cisco.

☙

A few months after Cisco acquired GNI, Ron Bernal announced we were going to take a victory lap, and in June 2000, the founders, executives, and their respective spouses embarked on a Hawaii trip. We rendezvoused at the Grand Wailea Resort on Maui where we sailed, swam, sunned, and explored the island. The only note that marred an otherwise delightful visit to the islands occurred one afternoon when Bobby and I were exploring Maui's north shore. After lunch, she felt a sudden sharp pain in her back. We sat together for a while, and it went away. We tried to convince each other that it was just indigestion, and that explanation seemed satisfactory, since the pain did not return during the remainder of the trip.

In the summer of 2000 at Cisco, the GNI team dug into developing the CRS-1 hardware. Dan Lenoski led the effort with the three WU graduates—Andy, Zubin, and Will—playing crucial roles. After four years of development, the CRS-1 was made available to customers. From then until it was retired in 2021, the CRS-1 was responsible for more than $3.5 billion in income to the company, more than 15 times the cost of the acquisition of GNI.

So, Jon Turner's fast-packet technology was a winner for everyone: Cisco; NEA; Washington University; all the stockholders, including the three founders; Kirk Williams; my three children; and the pavers who laid the brinks in our driveway—roughly in the size order of the respective jackpots. In addition, Bobby and I gave funds to the Computer Science and Engineering Department to support the Barbara J. and Jerome R. Cox, Jr. Chair, which Jon Turner was the first to occupy. Since Jon's retirement, Professor Raj Jain has held it.

While the Growth Networks saga was going on, a lot was happening with our kids. Remember the E & Y employee whom Randy met on his trips to Detroit? Her name was Patty Buczek; they fell in love and married in 1999. Their three amazing children—Noah, Adam, and Eleonor—were born in 2000, 2002, and 2005. Son Jerry and his wife Margaret also had three children: Sarah born in 1998 and twin boys (Michael and Daniel) born in 2000. They are equally amazing grandchildren. As reported in Chapter Thirteen, Nancy and Craig Battersby had two girls, Kim and Erin, born in 1980 and 1983.

Randy and Patty on their wedding day in a fabled Detroit mansion

By the turn of the century, these last two had matured into remarkable young women. Kim and Troy Spenard had met as teens in Nancy's YMCA Youth Leaders Club. They fell in love but observed Nancy and Craig's wish that they wait to marry until Kim graduated from Rhodes College in Memphis, where she was majoring in psychology. They did wait. In fact, just to see Kim, Troy often drove the 2000-mile weekend roundtrip between Wyoming Tech and St. Louis, during Kim's high school years. Troy also drove to see Kim on weekends during her college years, but the drive from his home in northern Illinois was much shorter. Kim graduated from Rhodes in 2002, and they were married at Graham Chapel on the Washington University campus in that same year. They now have two children, Paige and Payton, born in 2004 and 2009.

My next granddaughter, Erin Battersby, seems to have inherited the math gene. When she was six, she could make change faster than her mother. Nancy enrolled Erin in Kumon, a home-based math program imported from Japan to St. Louis by Dan Kimura, the professor who led the database effort in the CSE department during the late 1970s. Kumon flourished and is still going strong throughout the

Son Jerry and me on Father's Day ready to go fly a kite

St. Louis area. Erin enjoyed and did well in the program and also in school, all the way through grade school, high school, and college, graduating from Mizzou in 2005 with a joint major in math and engineering. Erin met Chris Rau at Mizzou and they were married in 2007.

After we had both retired from our posts at WU, former chancellor Bill Danforth and I became closer. He was interested in how the Growth Networks deal came to pass and why it was necessary to move the company to the Bay Area. We talked about his interest in increasing technology activity in St. Louis.

I remember a meeting that included Dick Fleming, chair of the St. Louis Regional Commerce and Growth Association; John Danforth, recently retired U.S. senator from Missouri; Bill; and me. Our discussion focused on a report from consultants who recommended that St. Louis invest strongly either in biotechnology or in computer technology. I felt that St. Louis had a strong head start in biotechnology, though a long way to go to become a player in computer technology. In 1998, Bill had already invested in plant science by taking the first steps toward the Donald Danforth Plant Science Center, then a small research organization named after his father, who had grown Ralston Purina into one of the 75 largest companies in the U.S.

I think Bill had very nearly made up his mind, but he was eager to hear my opinion. His subsequent support of the Plant Science Center has proven to be wise. The center has been a remarkable success, making St. Louis a worldwide hub in plant biotechnology. Over the following two decades, St. Louis, through the development of the Cortex Innovation Community district, has improved its position in computer technology, but it still has far to go to equal its commanding position worldwide in plant science.

Bobby's back pain on the Hawaii trip, along with a similar occurrence on a 1999 trip to Detroit to see Randy and his intended, was not simple indigestion. There will be more about that in the next chapter.

Chapter 18

Bobby's Last Days | 2000-2006

Bobby had other back-pain episodes after the one in Detroit and the second in Hawaii. At first, we did not know what they were because the pain went away within an hour or two, much like indigestion. Later, there were various scans that warned of possible cardiovascular problems that would continue to be aggravated by her smoking. After many tries, she gave up the habit, but it was not soon enough.

On Saturday, 1 May 2004, we learned that those many years of smoking were likely the root cause of the back pain. On that Saturday, a memorial service for George Pake was due to bring Wes Clark and me together to speak at Washington University's Ann W. Olin Women's Building. Maxine and Wes flew in from NYC on the previous Friday night, and Bobby and I waited at the St. Louis airport for them to arrive. Bobby felt uncomfortable, but it was nothing that she had not endured before. She had been seeing our primary care doctor, who diagnosed her head tremor as an "essential tremor," inherited from an aunt, and her back pain as cardiovascular in origin, something to investigate further.

While we waited at the airport, I reminded Bobby of the important role that George Pake had played in Wes's life, in my life, and, indeed, in the future world of computing. As I mentioned in Chapter Nine, George made important promises to Wes and his team that helped to lure them all to WU. Then, as WU provost, he provided sage advice and crucial help to the computer labs. In particular, CSL reported to George, which allowed Wes to make requests directly to him, bypassing the deans of both the medical and engineering schools.

After George left WU in 1970, he joined Xerox to create the Palo Alto Research Center (PARC). During the following decade and under George's leadership, PARC developed most of today's endpoint computing. Wes travelled there often to provide advice on whom to hire and how to proceed. As is now well known, PARC computer technology was largely ignored by corporate Xerox decision-makers in Rochester, NY, and later in Connecticut— but not by Steve Jobs who, after a covert tour of PARC, used their technology as a guide in the design of the Apple Macintosh. So many things that we all take for granted today were created at PARC: windows, ethernet, laser printing, and the many conveniences of modern endpoint computing. Both Wes and I owed a great deal to George and were eager to express that debt at his memorial service.

Wes and Maxine planned to stay with us in Sunset Hills that Friday night and then return to NYC late Saturday afternoon after the memorial service and a lunch together. They arrived as expected, and we retrieved my car from the parking garage. As the three of us drove south on Interstate 270 toward Sunset Hills, Bobby suddenly felt a severe pain in her back, much worse than anything she had endured before. I diverted to the Barnes West County Medical Center, where I knew there was an emergency department.

I was sitting with her in the ED as the attending physician began his examination. He was alarmed by Bobby's electrocardiogram and wanted to apply the paddles to her chest to arrest what he thought was atrial fibrillation. However, I had seen enough ECGs in our research work at BCL to know that that was not the case. Instead, the essential tremor she suffered from was producing muscle signals that masked her heart's P-wave. I asked that the physician call our cardiologist, Dr. Mitch Faddis, before applying the defibrillator. I thought the ED doc would not pay attention to a civilian in such a medical matter. But Mitch did return the call, blessedly interrupting his social evening, telling the ED doc to look again for the P-wave amid the electrical noise produced by her tremor. Mitch was also my cardiologist and had served us both well. In fact, Mitch asked for permission later on to present Bobby's ECG as an example of his dictum: "Always look ever so carefully for the P-wave."

Next came a CT scan and a long waiting period for it to be read, as the four of us sat quietly in the ED. By then, Bobby's pain had mostly subsided, and there was nothing else to do as we stood by for the results. Eventually, the ED doc appeared, announced it was an attack of pleurisy, and said we should all go on home. With great relief, we climbed into the car and made our way to Sunset Hills. At home, we prepared to retire and went to bed. In the morning, I felt Bobby should stay home—but not alone. After a phone call, daughter Nancy arrived to help out while the three of us—Maxine, Wes, and I—made our way to the Women's Building, just two buildings west of Bryan Hall, where the CSE department was located.

During the ceremony, Wes, Maxine, and I turned off our phones. But after Wes and I had spoken, the three of us began walking to the parking garage and turned the phones back on—and were deluged with messages from Nancy. She had been trying to reach us because there had been a call from a radiologist who had read the CT scan in the morning and realized the situation was much graver than we had heard the night before. He advised that Bobby should come to the Barnes Emergency Department immediately. As soon as we picked up the messages, the three of us rushed to join Bobby and Nancy at the Barnes ED.

There, doctors told us that Bobby had an enlarged aortic aneurysm and needed immediate surgery. She was admitted while the cardiac surgeon, Dr. Marc Moon, waited to receive an appropriate stent. Just the right stent had to be constructed by specialists elsewhere. A stent is a fabric-covered wire-mesh sleeve used to reinforce the blood-vessel wall where the aneurysm had weakened it. It took several days for the stent to arrive, while Bobby waited in her hospital room. The aneurysm was so close to her aortic valve that stenting would be difficult. But the surgery went well, and the stent was expected to reduce the recurrence of the severe pain she had experienced on Friday night.

Following Bobby's discharge three weeks after her admission, she felt reasonably well except that she needed supplemental oxygen, provided by a portable tank and a tube to her nose. I returned to work on the St. Louis Internet Access Collaborative (SLIAC), an organization I had started a few years before to provide direct access to the 100 Mbps Internet being organized by NSF and called "Internet 2" or simply "I2." At that point, network speeds of 100 Mbps were rare, and our access provider was not yet up to the job. I arranged to have WU, Saint Louis University, and the Danforth Plant Science Center join forces to lease private lines from each campus to downtown St. Louis and then to Indianapolis and I2. It all worked well, and SLIAC is still providing high-speed access to the three partners.

So, in the summer and early fall of 2004, Bobby had been comfortable and went about her normal activities: shopping, cooking, and attending lunches with friends. The only inconvenience was the supplemental oxygen tank, which made her feel very embarrassed. During the winter, Bobby began to have back pain again. That December, I had a biopsy of my prostate, and discovered that I had a choice to make. Should I have surgery to remove my cancerous prostate or radiation treatment to halt its progress? Surgery would put me out of commission for many weeks, while radiation required six weeks of treatment during which I could continue to support Bobby for all but a few hours each week. The prognosis for surgery could be complete cancer remission, but it could also, in a few cases, lead to a recurrence. The prognosis for radiation was, at that time, eight years symptom free—but no guarantees thereafter. Neither choice was perfect. I chose radiation.

By the spring, Bobby's aneurysm had grown to involve the aortic arch above the stent. This meant that the damage to that large blood vessel had moved closer to the branch point of the carotid artery, which feeds blood to the neck and brain. An extension of the stent was required.

My memory of those days is a patchwork. In the spring of 2005, Bobby had another surgery to extend the stent. She lost her voice as a result of damage to the recurrent laryngeal nerve that wraps around the aorta. Until the nerve recovered many months later, she had to whisper. She also fell, tripping in the back room and breaking her arm. We jointly signed up for physical therapy at St. Joseph's Hospital, which was then nearby. It did us both much good.

In the fall of 2005 at the Piper Palm House in Tower Grove Park, the engineering school held a celebration of our arrival in St. Louis 50 years earlier. Several of our friends spoke, and our children attended. Because of the oxygen equipment, Bobby was not comfortable at such an affair, but she was a trooper and attended. Only once did she show fear of what the future might hold: She lay on the couch in our living room and sobbed as I tried to comfort her. Otherwise, she seemed to accept her fate, whatever it might be. Dr. Moon said later that she was a brave lady. Bobby herself said that she would rather pass away than be a cripple or fat. She was very proud of her trim figure.

At this point, there was nothing else that could be done medically or surgically. Because the aneurysm was so close to the heart, it was just a matter of time before the aneurysm burst, but we did not know that. I thought mistakenly that, if there was more trouble, another stent could be inserted. My family and I did not realize how close to the end of the road Bobby was.

In May of 2006, WU honored us for the gift of the Barbara J. and Jerome R. Cox Chair in Computer Science and Engineering. I was so glad that those festivities occurred while she was able to enjoy them. In that same month, she insisted that I purchase a new car, and we picked a Lexus sedan, which has served me without trouble ever since. Bobby was doing well, considering what she had been through, cooking meals in our kitchen and enjoying visits from our children.

Then, one night in August 2006, she was sitting in a chair near the television when she suddenly cried out in pain. Immediately, I took her to the Barnes emergency room where she was admitted to a bed in 8200, the Coronary Care Unit (CCU)—the same place I had spent so many days and nights with Floyd Nolle during the development of Argus. Nancy, Jerry, and Randy came, and Nancy and I took 12-hour shifts of being with her, changing places at 6 p.m. and 6 a.m. The two of us alternated, sleeping in a room at the nearby Parkway Hotel just a few minutes' walk from 8200.

Within a few days, Bobby was transferred out of 8200 to an intermediate-care room on the second floor of Barnes. Nancy and I continued our 12-hour shifts. The plan was to see whether Bobby stabilized and could be sent home. Jerry and Randy went back to their homes. A few days later, on 28 August 2006, I came on shift at 6 a.m., relieving Nancy, who then took a break. I was holding Bobby's hand, she was sitting on the edge of the bed, and we were talking pleasantly, when she said, "Oh my goodness, the room is spinning." Then, she was gone. The aortic aneurysm had burst. Her death was almost instantaneous.

As Bobby had wished, her body was cremated. Both of us shared an agnostic view of life, and death and cremation seemed right for us. But more about that later. We found a two-compartment urn that we believe she would have loved. The urn was placed in her sunny plant window within our back room, its second compartment awaiting my ashes.

The family assembled. Jerry and his wife, Margaret, came to our house in Sunset Hills. Randy and his wife, Patty, also came from Detroit. We made plans that, in retrospect, worked out well. First, there was a reception at the Faculty Club with relatives and guests from St. Louis and others flying in from distant locations. Following that, a funeral ceremony with even more in attendance took place at a Kirkwood funeral home. Several family members spoke, and somehow we got through it all. It helped to have so many of her friends there from near and far. Our 55th wedding anniversary would have been a few days later on 2 September 2006. After the funeral, the family assembled at our house and cried a lot. She had been a wonderful and caring wife, mother, grandmother, sister-in-law, and friend. It is hard to believe that it has been more than 16 years since Bobby left us. I still think of her every day.

Chapter 19
Blendics | 2004-

The story of my company, Blendics, really began on 26 March 2004, several years before it was incorporated. That day, I had organized a symposium titled, "Clockless Computing: Coordinating Billions of Transistors," one of many events associated with the 150th anniversary of the founding of Washington University. The symposium brought together international leaders in asynchronous computing who would celebrate the university's sesquicentennial, as well as the 40th anniversary of the project on Macromodular Computer Design, a major clockless system design that Wes Clark had begun at WU in 1964. Wes, Ivan Sutherland, and a half dozen others spoke at that symposium, and during their talks, I started to wonder why clockless computing had not been widely recognized by industry as the next frontier.

One key thing seemed clear to me then: Computer chips that depended on a single clock were reaching the end of their road. An analogy is a billion-member dance band in which the players are all seated well apart and depend on hearing the rhythm section to make beautiful music. The rhythm section controls the beat, but once the distance between band members and the rhythm section grows too great, it becomes impossible for all of them to stay on the beat, and the result is a jumble of discordant notes.

The problem with modern clocked computer chips is similar in that delivering the clock signal to all portions of the chip simultaneously leads to greater difficulty as the chip becomes more complex and the clock rate grows faster in frequency. The clock tells each group of transistors when it should change state. It was understood by all of us at the Clockless Computing symposium that the billions of transistors anticipated on future chips, as well as the ever-increasing clock rates to be employed, had to undergo a significant paradigm shift. As one, we felt that clockless computing was the answer. Otherwise, within the next decade or two these enormous silicon dance bands would do nothing but hit off-beat sour notes. Unfortunately, we were all wrong.

Worldwide, the electronic design automation (EDA) industry is presently valued at about $12 B, and it is continuing to grow in value at about 10% annually. A fundamental change in direction for that business sector is much more difficult than changing the direction of a huge ocean liner. I don't think any of us realized how thoroughly all these design tools depended upon the clock. Like the maestro's baton, the clock keeps all parts of the chip working together. Not only that, but the clock is also built into all the design rules in a fundamental way, just as the beat is built into the music on the musicians' stands. My colleagues and I at the WU symposium, with the possible exception of Ivan, were not aware of this fundamental dependence within the tools.

Within a few months after the symposium, Bobby's health deteriorated, and I gave little thought to clockless computing. However, by the spring of 2007, my CSE colleague Dave Zar and SIUE EE Professor George Engel had begun discussing with me a paper I had written in 1988 titled, "Can a Crystal Clock Be Started and Stopped?" If such a clock were practical, it might prove to be useful in the struggle to make multi-clocked systems that coordinate the action of the billions of transistors, a problem the symposium had foreseen. George, Dave, and I designed such a stoppable clock and had it fabricated through MOSIS, the DoD chip design service for research universities. The stoppable clock worked well!

In the summer of 2007, nearly a year after Bobby's death, I found myself unsettled and wishing to touch base with times long past. I arranged a driving trip with Nancy to explore the properties at Rosemary Beach and nearby locations. I had in mind buying a lakefront lot with the hope of recapturing the youthful joy I remembered at Lake Michigan. We engaged a real estate agent, looked at properties she suggested, and also explored on our own.

To the south of Rosemary Beach was the new Cook Nuclear Power Plant that had opened in 1975. Bobby and I had learned about it much earlier, however. In 1960, a gentleman rang the door-bell of our Couch Avenue residence in Kirkwood. He was tall but round, wearing bib overalls. He said he was from a small town in Michigan just east of Crestview Beach, a new development located next to Rosemary Beach. My grandmother had purchased a lakefront lot there and willed it to me upon her death.

Our visitor said that he wished to build a lakefront cottage for his daughter, and in pursuing property opportunities, he had visited the courthouse in nearby Stevensville, Michigan, where he found that I was the owner of that lot. Since Bobby and I were living far away, he wondered whether we might be willing to sell the lot to him for cash. We should have been suspicious, but we had not then heard of the proposal to build a power plant there.

Our visitor offered a few thousand dollars, and we agreed to sell. Only later did we discover that he was an agent for a company commissioned to buy the land for the proposed Cook Nuclear Plant and that his story, overalls, and straw in his mouth were all a ruse. Needless to say, his company was successful, the necessary property was acquired, and the nuclear plant was built just south of Rosemary Beach. It began operation in 1975, lowering the property values at Rosemary Beach due to the plant's continuous rumble, the occasional announcements on the plant's public address system, and the dead fish found in the plant's effluent into Lake Michigan.

As a result, Nancy and I looked at properties north of Rosemary Beach. We trudged around on back roads, explored at the borders of the Grand Mere State Park and at Stevensville Beach. The prices for lakefront lots were then startlingly high, a million dollars and up, but it was fun scouting out the territory so near and dear to the days of my youth. On that trip, Nancy and I also had dinner with my very good high school friend, Dick White, his wife, and some of their friends in South Bend. It was all a welcome tonic for my moodiness and restlessness during the summer of 2007.

After Bobby's death, Nancy filled an important hole in my social life. Not only did she make the trip to Rosemary Beach, but she also saw to it that family events and celebrations occurred on schedule, that my financial puzzles were solved, and that she was my partner at Kirkwood Theatre Guild performances. Nancy's successful business career began just after college with a part-time job at the YMCA, and she broke new ground as she rose through the ranks to become a pioneering female executive managing the Kirkwood and Webster Groves branches of the Y. Over the course of two years, she opened an after-school, "latch-key" program that cared for as many as 250 children a day at her Y. Nancy advocated for the development of "Leaders Clubs" for teens among the St. Louis Ys, and subsequently she was appointed the Zone Coordinator for teen programming in all the Ys in four midwestern states. The Leaders Clubs were so successful because they captured the teens' thirst for adventure when they travelled to meet with other "leaders" in various midwestern cities. When management at the Y changed, Nancy moved to become Director of Parks and Recreation for the city of Fenton, a prosperous suburb just west of Sunset Hills. Not only did Nancy accompany me on that trip to Rosemary Beach, but she has also supported me in many ways after Bobby's death while also blossoming in her own career.

In the fall of 2007, Tom Chaney, with the help of other alums of the Computer Systems Lab, restored a LINC to working order. It was one of four machines rescued from the dumpster by CSL technician Scott Robinson and then stored in his garage during the intervening decades. Parts from the four were barely sufficient to make just one LINC that actually worked, but Tom and his helpers succeeded so well that it took first place at the Vintage Computer Festival, held at the Mountain View, California,

Washington University Photographic Services Collection, Julian Edison Department of Special Collections, Washington University Libraries

Maury Pepper at the restored LINC console, which took first place at the 2007 Vintage Computer Festival

Computer Museum in November 2007. There is a video featuring the comments of many of the principals who participated in that restoration.[13]

After we all returned from the Festival, I began to examine, with increased enthusiasm, the problem called a metastability failure that occurs when a computer clock arrives out of synchronism with

13 https://www.digibarn.com/history/07-11-04-VCF10-LINC/video-coverage.html

the data. A computer storage element (a flip-flop) must not suffer such a problem because its stored value is then indeterminate, and a *glitch* may result. A glitch is neither a one nor a zero, but an intermediate value that the computer cannot interpret properly. It is like a sour note played by the silicon dance band. Once played, there is no way to take it back.

The history of the glitch dates to 1965 when Severo Ornstein and Mish Stucki, both staff members of Wes Clark's Computer Systems Lab, were designing clockless systems for Wes Clark's project to develop macromodular computer systems. They asked Tom Chaney, another CSL staff member and 4W2 alumnus, what happens when the clock arrives out of synchronism with the data. Tom, the consummate engineer, set out to determine the answer experimentally. He was able to photograph the output voltage of a computer circuit undergoing this extremely rare action—thus catching a *glitch* while doing its mischief.

A few others had speculated about the glitch before, but there was controversy about its very existence. Later in 1972, Tom and Charlie Molnar wrote a paper describing the significant system failures that can result from this fundamentally inescapable problem. They submitted the paper to a prominent computer engineering journal, but it was promptly rejected, with two of three reviewers saying the manuscript should not be published. One said it was an uninteresting, well-known phenomenon, while the other claimed that it was impossible, and the data presented must be incorrect. Eventually, reason prevailed, and the paper was published. Tom became "the father of the glitch," known around the world for his experimental demonstration of the phenomenon. In fact, his vanity license plate read *glitch* until his recent death.

Before his death in 1996, Charlie had written some software to calculate the probability of a glitch occurring in a given circuit. Since I felt this software and other useful tools should be made available to computer engineers, I got together with Tom and his son Scott Chaney to do so. In the late summer of 2007, I joined them in the offices of their firm, STS, located in Bridgeton, Missouri, just west of the St. Louis airport. A WU graduate student I had hired, Mike Grote, also became part of the team. I named the new firm "Blendics," a contraction of Blended Integrated Circuit Systems, and it was based on the idea of coupling synchronous cores of millions of transistors with asynchronous links between them. This technique was called GALS, which stood for Globally Asynchronous, Locally Synchronous. The tools we were developing were: MetaACE, which allowed the integrated-circuit designer to predict the probability of a glitch and redesign if that probability was not infinitesimally small; and PILS, which made it possible for the designer to connect arbitrarily many locally synchronous cores. PILS stood for "Port-Independent, Live and Safe," a Petri Net theorem that Mike and I proved, which described the constraints that made it possible to connect billions of locally synchronous cores, each of which might contain as many as a million transistors.

We filed patents and wrote a proposal to the National Science Foundation (NSF). It was funded and, as a result, we were able to hire Dave Zar, then at WU, and several others. Subsequently, in March 2008, the NSF asked us to attend a workshop in Crystal City, which was aimed at helping new grantees attract venture capital support. Scott Chaney and I went and circulated among the representatives of several venture capitalists. When I started to give my pitch to one of them, Erik Olsen, he held up his hand, saying, "Let me get my boss." In a few minutes he introduced me to John Pyrovolakis, managing partner of the National Innovation Fund (NIF) an Omaha-based venture capital firm. I restarted my pitch, and it seemed to go well. Actually, it had gone very well indeed, and we are still working with John and NIF more than 13 years later.

One aspect of my life that had not gone so well was my health. On the first warm morning of late February in 2009, I had chosen to go for a walk in the neighborhood. A patch of black ice looked to me like dirty concrete, and I slipped and fell. I knew immediately that it was bad because my eyes and my feeling about where my foot should be pointing were not in agreement. When I tried to move, the pain was severe. My next-door neighbors happened by, and we agreed to call 911 and alert my daughter.

I was taken by ambulance to the ER at a nearby hospital, where Nancy met me. It was soon determined that I had broken my right hip. The next morning, a surgeon pinned the hip back together, and those pins have served me well ever since. The physical therapist who assisted in my recovery taught me some leg exercises that I still practice each morning.

That was not my only medical adventure. Four years later, in

2013, the pacemaker that had been installed in 2002 suddenly failed, pushing me into heart failure. Doctors implanted a new biventricular pacemaker that included an automatic defibrillator, and it cured my cardiac problems nicely. In fact, my cardiac output returned almost to normal, and it has stayed that way.

Finally, my PSA score that measures my prostate cancer shot up in 2014 and I was introduced to hormone therapy. Since my radiation therapy in early 2005 was supposed to last seven years, this recurrence was pretty much on schedule. Various hormone and medical treatments curtailed the spread of the cancer.

These medical adventures, happily treated, are a testament to the excellent healthcare here in St. Louis. Maybe my doctors can arrange to keep me poking at my laptop until I finish a few more chapters of this book! Now, back to the Blendics story. Since we were looking for customers in Silicon Valley, Dave Zar, George Engel, and I made many trips there. We also presented papers at the annual "ASYNC" conference, The International Symposium on Asynchronous Circuits and Systems, which has been held annually since 1994. But we didn't find any customers.

These trips to the "Valley" did give me many opportunities to visit my half-sister, Candy, in Marina, a small town just north of Monterey and about 45 minutes south of San Jose. Candy lived there with her second husband Mike Owen. For years, she did the menu book for the Marina, Monterey, and Carmel area: a large-format book found in local hotels and motels, which showed the menus of the nearby restaurants. It was one of the many businesses that were displaced later by the ever-growing availability of the Internet.

Despite our many trips to the Valley, Blendics did not work out well, but it did spin off two companies and remains alive as a holding company with a 10% interest in each of the spinoffs. Neither of them is cashflow positive as I write, but both have great potential, and I will discuss them in the next chapter. Meanwhile, I will try to explain why Blendics did not fulfill our dreams of a highly successful startup.

In a nutshell, it is the all-too-familiar tale of venture capital. Fewer than one in ten venture-funded companies succeed. The reason why Blendics failed is not because we were poorly funded; in fact, we received substantial funding from the NSF in November 2007 and again in August 2011 from John Pyrovolakis and his NIF.

Instead, the problem was the clock dependence universally hidden within the EDA tools. Why that was so requires a bit of technical explanation. Those readers with an allergy to such explanations may want to skip the next few paragraphs.

EDA tools operate like a highway engineer, who lays out all the city streets and the highways between the cities. In the Blendics scheme, the synchronous cores are designed like city streets. The IC engineer lays them all out while observing the rules of the various synchronous cores (in our analogy, the local municipalities). The links that connect the cores are a different story, as are the highways that connect cities. In the Blendics scheme, different cores may have different clocks, and a data pathway between cores is clockless, just as an intercity highway will have no traffic lights. However, the Blendics scheme assumes all lanes of the data highway between cores are laid out neatly side by side.

The EDA tools failed to support this simple restriction. Instead, they allowed individual lanes between two cores to wander independently of each other from source to destination. This peculiar fact is a result of the need for a single clock covering all cities and highways in our analogy. Also, this need is so embedded in the EDA tools that we could not apply the PILS theorem. The tool developers did not wish to make a fundamental change to their highly complex products to please a tiny startup in the Midwest. Thus, we had to abandon the basic notion on which Blendics was founded.

To my dismay, almost 14 years after Blendics was founded, a huge chip has been fabricated without the aid of GALS or any other asynchronous technology. Cerebras Systems, a Silicon Valley startup, recently announced an 8.5-inch square chip containing 2.6 trillion transistors partitioned into 850,000 cores. It features a 7-nanometer fabrication process, one that requires the most advanced semiconductor production technology. The purpose of this chip is to power neural networks used in advanced artificial intelligence (AI) algorithms. Our 2004 Clockless Computing speakers would have been amazed.

Maybe clockless computing will yet find its way onto the information technology scene, but it will have to revolutionize the ever-growing, electronic design automation (EDA) industry to do so. With a square chip, fully as big as this page is wide, already developed—one using clocked techniques throughout—it is hard to see any path that clockless computing might follow. The huge Cerebras Systems chip takes advantage of the identicality of each of its cores to deliver a clock signal with uniform timing to almost a million cores. It solves the yield problem by merely avoiding the use of any misbehaving core. The need to produce chips with more heterogenous cores is another problem.

Perhaps a technology called 2.5D is a more likely candidate for the future of very large integrated circuits with heterogenous cores. Again, I will use an analogy to explain. First, picture a silicon pepperoni pizza. The dough corresponds to the silicon that serves to provide connectivity between the pepperoni slices. In turn, the pepperoni slices correspond to small silicon chips (or chiplets) that sit on top of that dough and connect to it through tiny metal bumps. The dough provides no logic functionality, only simple connectivity. Use of a high-performance SerDes (Serializer/Deserializer) can ameliorate any inter-chiplet timing problems.

Companies pioneering this 2.5D technology have shown that it keeps the huge EDA ship on its clocked course, and it also solves the yield problem of large 2D chips and the cost and complexity problems of true 3D chip technology. Look for the growth of these

Five LINC pioneers—Mary Allen Wilkes, Howard Lewis, Jerry Cox, Wesley Clark, and Severo Ornstein—at the 2013 BCL/CSL Reunion

companies as they pioneer the adaptation of existing clocked design tools to this promising 2.5D semiconductor technology—and it's all done without the need for clockless computing.

However, consider the human brain. It is a prime example of clockless computing and performs its tasks with energy efficiency that is far superior to today's clocked computers. Perhaps neuromorphic computing will show the pathway to clockless computing at last by ending the EDA industry's regime of clock-based computing.

Leaving my speculations about clockless computing and getting back to my recollections of events, I would like to say a bit about the BCL-CSL Reunion that was held on my 88th birthday weekend, 24 and 25 May 2013. I'm not sure how it landed on that weekend, but its purpose was to celebrate the 50th anniversary of the founding of the two labs, BCL and CSL, in 1964. Nizar Mullani had the spark that triggered the event, though the arithmetic was off by a year. I asked Nancy to take over the logistics and she did an amazing job. About 140 alums of the two labs attended. On Friday night, we had a reception and dinner and on Saturday morning a "Legacy of the Labs" panel:

Moderator: William Danforth, MD
(Chancellor Emeritus of Washington University)

Panel members:
- William Raub, PhD (Past Director of Biotechnology at Division of Research Resources, NIH)
- Bruce Walz, MD (Chairman, Radiation Oncology, Saint Louis University)
- Marcus Raichle, MD (Washington University neurologist and early PET researcher)
- Ivan Sutherland, PhD (Pioneer in graphics and asynchronous computing)
- Santanu Das, DSc (Founder and past CEO of TranSwitch)
- Garland Marshall, PhD (Founder and Past CEO of Tripos)

Plus:
- Tribute to Charles Molnar, ScD
- Donna Molnar reading remarks by their son Stephen Molnar, PhD (Distinguished Engineer, Nvidia)

The reunion concluded with tours and talk. I think all the returning alums enjoyed seeing each other. Sadly, the timing was good in that many have now, almost a decade later, passed away or are unable to travel. A video of the reunion is available.[14] This video includes the above panel and does a great job of summarizing the effect of BCL on Washington University and the effect of LINC on the world of computing.

---

14   (BCL-CSL 50th Reunion Part 1 = https://youtu.be/IvygbT1pe9U and BCL-CSL 50th Reunion Part 2 = https://youtu.be/4pn24cP6Nyw)

Chapter 20
Q-Net Security | 2015-

We applied some of our Blendics technology to our spinoff, The Atreyu Group,[15] a Wall Street firm that offers real-time risk surveillance. This technology allows managers to be sure their traders are avoiding mistakes that could cost their companies millions, and it does so without delaying the trade opportunity for so long that any advantage will be lost. The Atreyu Group is currently flirting with a cashflow positive balance sheet, a good thing. Blendics will own a 10% stake in Atreyu and enjoy a large profit if it is acquired by an interested larger firm.

The second spinoff from Blendics first showed signs of life in late 2014. In one of my frequent phone calls with my longtime friend, Wes Clark, we began talking about the hazard posed by hackers to the nation's critical infrastructure. Wes saw this national hazard as a fundamental Internet design flaw. I was also motivated by the book, *Lights Out: A Cyberattack, A Nation Unprepared, Surviving the Aftermath* by Ted Koppel, published in early 2015.

During our discussions, we considered several possible solutions, eventually arriving at a rough plan. I filled in some details and in June 2015 gave Blendics $50,000 of my own money to explore the topic further. Wes, George Engel, Jeremy O'Driscoll, and Dave Zar all pitched in for the drafting of a patent. By the fall of 2015, we had filed our patent, and felt we had the solution to an important national problem. Furthermore, John Pyrovolakis recognized its importance and offered to purchase the rights to our cybersecurity developments for the same amount, plus interest, that I had invested.

---

15   https://www.atreyugroup.com

Wes suggested that we call it "Q-Net Security": Q for the Quartermaster, the fabled purveyor of secret technical gadgetry in the James Bond books and movies. We set up a Q-Net Security (QNS) website and pivoted Blendics activities to QNS, retaining another 10% stake in the new company for Blendics.

In the startup world, a "pivot" is a popular term used when the original idea fails to blossom, and the assembled team can be repurposed to a new and more promising opportunity. It was clear to Wes and me that the ability of scoundrels to remotely attack software systems was unbounded. As long as a computer system had the characteristics that Alan Turing described in his famous 1936 paper, "On Computable Numbers," it would be hackable. You will remember that Turing only presented the mathematical description of that machine, while Wes had built the TOWTMTEWP to make the Turing Machine a reality. All general-purpose computers built both before and after the TOWTMTEWP are equivalent to a Turing Machine in that they can compute anything that is computable when given enough memory and time.

This means that remote attackers can find a way to execute malicious code, providing they can access the memory that stores a computer's instructions. Because modern computers accept input from the Internet and store it in their instruction memory, they can never be proved to be safe from this kind of attack. The content of their memories is ever changing—and without the burdensome control of that memory content, there will always be a way for attackers to insert malware. Reports of the never-ending stream of successful attacks gives pragmatic proof to this statement.

So, how did we propose to provide provable cybersecurity protection? The answer is hardware that eliminates the need for software. We called it a Q-Net Input/Output unit or QIO and incorporated all the necessary cybersecurity functions in its hardware: random-number generation, encryption, decryption, and the delivery of keys from the source of a message to its destination. It could be packaged in a small box about the size of a fat remote TV control unit. This has led to the familiar name, Q-Box, which is used interchangeably with QIO. Installation consisted merely of placing the QIO in line between the Internet and the computer that needs protecting.

A packet of keys is sent from the source QIO to the destination

QIO. Each such packet was called a JitKey packet, or a "Just-in-time Key" packet and is cryptographically wrapped to avoid revealing any of these keys. Such JitKey packets are sent frequently enough to provide different keys for each of 40 successive packets. Thus, even a lucky guess of a key would reveal only a single packet's worth of sensitive information.

We needed to build a prototype and decided to do that in software so that we could work out bugs in our design before committing to hardware. Dave Zar did that, but there were enough unanswered questions that I dug into developing a design document, which I completed in the summer of 2016.

Another significant event occurred in the summer of 2016: Q-Net Security hired Andrew Quirin, a graduate student from SIUE, who was recommended by Professor George Engel. Clearly, Andrew was a star, and he took on the job of implementing in software the system described in my design document. The hardware version, whose construction was led by Scott Chaney, would follow. The software system had revealed many issues that would be incorporated in that hardware version. We also built a software version of a Q-Net Policy Manager, a headquarters unit designed to manage as many as 10,000 QIOs. With a handful of software-based QIOs and a QPM, we could demonstrate the system to potential customers. However, the completion of the hardware implementation of both the QIO and QPM was still far in the future.

In the summer of 2015, Wes, Maxine, Nancy, and I travelled together to the Heinz Nixdorf Museum in Paderborn, Germany. The occasion was the museum's recognition of Mary Allen Wilkes as one of the woman pioneers in computing. Others include Ada Lovelace and Grace Hopper who had, of course, passed away. Mary Allen gave a short speech in German. What a tour de force! We gave one of the four remaining LINC computers that Scott Robinson had rescued from the dumpster to the Heinz Nixdorf Museum, where it has been displayed as the first personal computer. We were all delighted with the entire celebration. Sadly, though, in March of 2016 Wes Clark passed away suddenly. Many of his friends gathered in Brooklyn for a celebration of his life. All spoke of his leadership and his amazing ability to see the future of computing and networking. (This tribute is available on YouTube.)

Some of his belongings found their way to the QNS offices in

St. Louis, particularly an incomplete *nuppet* stage and the TOWT-MTEWP, which needed repair. Wes had made up the word *nuppet* to describe a puppet-like character operated by moving a magnet just below the stage; he derived the name from a contraction of "not a puppet." The stage was elaborate but incomplete with footlights, places to fly scenery, and much detailed but incomplete stagecraft. Wes left no plans, and we were at a loss as to how to proceed. Eventually, we shipped it back to Maxine.

On the other hand, the TOWTMTEWP had been a feature of Professor Doug Clark, Wes's eldest son, in his lectures to Computer Science freshmen at Princeton University. Since Doug's retirement, it had fallen into disrepair. Tom Chaney and I were asked by Maxine to see whether we could bring it back to life. We did just that with the help of a summer student, Justin Moses, and a WU research associate, John DeHart, who had been a student in CS working with the original software Turing machine that ran on the WU Computer Centers IBM 360. With the help of my son, Randy, we were able to develop interest in the TOWTMTEWP at The Henry Ford Museum in Detroit. It now resides there and was featured in a video moderated by Mo Rocca and broadcast as part of the museum's series, "Innovation Nation."

Also in 2017, my good friend from my youth, Lisa (Skillern) Smith and her daughter Lisa VanAmburg wrote a limerick for me on the news that Scott Chaney and Ron Indeck were headed to Santiago, Chile, to demonstrate our software prototype.

> There is a fine fellow named Cox,
> Who prefers to think outside the box,
> An inventor so clever
> That the hackers can never
> Break into computers he locks.

I was delighted. However, the anticipated sale to Chile fell through because of an inconvenient revolution there, one that brought interest in QNS and Chilean commercial activity generally to a halt. That was the first of many unexpected events that have delayed the successful deployment of the QIO.

Nevertheless, our company, QNS, has grown. By September 2017, Ron Indeck had become our fulltime CEO, leaving behind his successful previous company, VelociData, Inc. I retained the position of President and Founder, while my daughter Nancy became QNS Finance Director. The firm grew significantly in size, and as its potential increased, John Pyrovolakis increased the commitment of NIF financial support to QNS: first to $5M and then later $10M.

I will now move to a discussion as to why the QNS solution to the cybersecurity problem is different from anything else currently on the market. As usual, I will use an analogy to help those without the necessary technical background. Think of your computer as your castle, one with a long line of visitors, each carrying packets of information from other castles, near and far. Some of these visitors intend you harm, so your operations minister, the lord chamberlain, checks them all at his desk just inside the drawbridge. However, some of the attackers instead climb the castle walls, hunting for vulnerabilities.

Your Computer is a Castle; Attackers are Everywhere

ChrisRauArt

Inevitably, some window or door has been left ajar, and one of the attackers slips in and then masquerades as one of your stewards. Other castle servants, who receive instructions from this imposter, may view him as a legitimate steward—with the result that the attacker effectively takes control of one or more functions of the castle.

The above sketch illustrates this situation in a whimsical way, but it suggests events that can happen in a general-purpose computer. In fact, imagine that the castle (a general-purpose computer) controls a portion of the kingdom's critical infrastructure or the transfer of money to and from neighboring castles. Wherever cybersecurity is a high priority and activities are managed by a general-purpose computer, as this analogy shows, there is opportunity for cybercriminals.

Notice that there is a moat around the castle, but it is of little value if attackers are allowed across the drawbridge to be screened by the chamberlain. The drawbridge is analogous to your network interface controller (NIC); once across the moat, the attackers can find a poorly protected nook or cranny and corrupt, destroy, or encrypt the castle's records. They can also exit via the rear gate carrying valuable records and march alongside all the benign visitors and emissaries that you have sent to do your bidding elsewhere in the kingdom.

Instead of allowing the visitors and their packets past the moat, it is better to check them as they approach it. As the sketch above suggests, a Q-Knight is stationed there who has been selected because of his obsessive-compulsive demeanor. He insists on a thorough check of all incoming travelers. The Q-Knight's duties are completely different from those of the chamberlain, who performs myriad functions and acts as the castle's operating system. The Q-Knight does one thing only: authenticate and authorize visitors.

Thus, in our whimsical analogy, the OCD-tainted Q-Knight, stationed at the entrance to the drawbridge, carries out these authentication and authorization checks. No attacker can outwit the Q-Knight, and all visitors who fail the checks or arrive without credentials from another trusted castle are cast aside. The moat keeps the rejected attackers from reaching the castle wall.

☙☞

Your Computer is a Castle; Protect it with Q-Net Security

ChrisRauArt

In the real world, it is best to employ special-purpose hardware whose only job is to authenticate all incoming traffic, making sure each packet is authorized and flawless. Only then will the payload be decrypted and transferred into your computer. Q-Net Security carries out this agenda outside your computer using special-purpose hardware that is designed for that function alone. This QIO, a TV remote-sized device, performs a fixed sequence of steps swiftly, without any possibility of compromise.

Both the U.S. Army and Air Force have initiated contracts with QNS. Berkshire Hathaway Energy Renewables have purchased a few units for trial and now expect to order many more. Our investor, John Pyrovolakis, and the NIF fund have committed an additional $3.5M funding beyond the original $10M to carry QNS through 2022. By then we should be in good shape for a profitable merger or acquisition. This extension of funding helps QNS overcome the delays in deliveries of semiconductor chips that almost all technology companies have experienced during 2021-2022. The future for QNS looks bright.

Chapter 21

Music, the Auditory System and My Belief | 2021-

Music has played an important role in my life since childhood. In grade school, I took cornet lessons and attempted to play in a neighborhood dance band. I could find the right notes but not at the right time. Other, more solitary pursuits occupied me in my spare time: cartooning, egg coloring, playing with a puppet theater, and listening to music on the radio. I missed the group activity of the neighborhood dance band but resigned myself to being a consumer of music and not a maker.

Touring big bands came to South Bend, and by the time I was a senior in high school, the Palais Royale ballroom had hosted many of them. I was in awe of the Lionel Hampton and Stan Kenton bands when they came to town, and I stood spellbound in the admiring crowd. On my return to South Bend from MIT after I had received my draft notice, my friends and I made a trip to Chicago to hear the Les Brown band featuring singer Doris Day. Seeing all of these big bands live was memorable and exciting. Elrose and my father arranged other unforgettable events for me: George and Ira Gershwin's *Porgy and Bess* played in Chicago, and Gilbert and Sullivan's *H.M.S. Pinafore* came to the Granada Theater in South Bend. Later, all these rich musical experiences led me to visit many popular jazz venues in Boston.

In the late '40s, the musicians who played at the Savoy on Mass Ave just south of Boston Symphony Hall were traditional jazz artists: Pops Foster, Sidney Bechet, Bunk Johnson, and George Wein. Traditional jazz, sometimes called Dixieland jazz, featured solos from one of the frontline players: trumpet, clarinet, and trombone. The rhythm section players typically used the piano, bass, and drums to drive the beat. Some frontline players took turns with their solos, while the other frontline players wove an intricate counterpoint.

The music made by a traditional jazz band reminds me of an accomplished group of six acrobats always catching the trapeze as it swings between them, precisely in time with the beat. While the lead acrobat does amazing tricks on his trapeze, the rhythm section keeps all the trapezes swinging together, and the other frontline players take their cue from the lead acrobat. They weave in and out in an extemporaneous manner, always surprising but never seeming contrived. For me, each recording of a topnotch traditional jazz band is an ever-exciting treasure.

Three such groups touched my life. Trumpeter Max Kaminsky, as you already know, played at the Ken Club in Boston on the occasion of my first date with Bobby. The second group was the Jim Cullum Jazz Band. Cornetist Cullum played for many years on the Riverwalk in San Antonio and kept playing almost until his death at 77 in 2019. Bobby or Nancy and I visited San Antonio to enjoy their music many times until our last visit in 2015.

Starting in the early 1970s, the Saint Louis Annual Ragtime and Traditional Jazz Festival took place over three days in June aboard the *Goldenrod*, a restored showboat moored on the St. Louis riverfront. The Goldenrod was the largest showboat on the Mississippi, and it may have inspired Edna Ferber's novel and the famous musical, both named *Show Boat*. The Jim Cullum Jazz Band was a regular feature at the Goldenrod Festival. Bobby and I attended frequently over the quarter century of its lifetime. What a joy!

Not only did I get to see and hear the Jim Cullum Band there, but I also saw my third favorite band, *Tiger Rag Forever*, featuring my close friend, Rich Dammkoehler, on trombone. Rich was one of the three faculty members who joined me in founding the WU CS department. On cornet was Bill Wilkinson, who played some fantastic solos that can be heard now on the *Tiger Rag Forever* albums. Even though they were a local group, their recordings have held up remarkably well for me over the half century since I first heard them. One of my favorites is "Doctor Jazz" with vocal by Rich and cornet solo by Bill (from the *I Hear Tigers* album).

I am also very fond of the tunes in the *Great American Songbook*, which included the hundreds of songs written between 1920 and 1960 for Broadway theaters and Hollywood movies. Famous composers, such as the duos Rodgers and Hart, as well as George and Ira Gershwin, created many enduring hits. Prolific lyricist Johnny Mercer wrote the words to dozens of memorable songs, Cole Porter and Irving Berlin wrote both words and music, and female singers such as Ella Fitzgerald, Peggy Lee, Anita O'day, and Billie Holiday gave their unique interpretations to tunes from the *Great American Songbook*. I loved them all, but I am particularly fond of Ella, a consummate and wonderful musician.

Clearly, I prefer the songs and singers I grew up with. I listen to classical music with pleasure, but I do not have the same vocabulary for classical music that I do for pop. I suppose that makes me a musical simpleton, but there is no accounting for taste: *de gustibus non est disputandum*!

How is it that the human brain can appreciate something as complex as a traditional jazz recording or a Bach cantata? I learned about human audition during my years as a graduate student at the MIT Acoustics Lab and while at CID from my colleagues Davis, Eldredge, and Hirsh. Later, I learned more just by observing the experiments that Russ Pfeiffer and Tom Goblick carried out when they took over Charlie's cat lab. The auditory system is an amazing neurophysiological system whose major components can only be sketched here.

These major components include the external ear, the middle ear, the inner ear or cochlea, and the auditory cortex. Let me briefly discuss the function of these components one by one:

- The external ear is what we can see on each side of our heads. The biggest part, the pinna, funnels sound into the ear canal, where it then travels on to the ear drum.
- The middle ear receives sound from the ear drum and provides optimized energy transfer between the air in the ear canal and the fluid in the cochlea. Through evolution, this energy transfer has developed to precisely equal what is needed to match the differing characteristics of air and fluid.
- The cochlea contains a membrane, lined with nerve cells, called the basilar membrane. Sound sets up a traveling wave on this membrane, with high-frequency sounds peaking at the end of the basilar membrane near the middle ear and low-

frequency sounds peaking at the distant end. That makes it somewhat like a piano keyboard with the high notes near the middle ear and low notes near the far end.

- About 30,000 nerve cells, called hair cells, line the basilar membrane. It is as if the keyboard had 30,000 keys, with each group of neighboring keys responding to a different frequency.
- Neural impulses from these hair cells travel to a part of the brain called the auditory cortex, located below the surface of the scalp just behind the external ear.
- Patterns of neural stimulation dance around on the auditory cortex allowing the listener to recognize speech, music, and all sorts of familiar sounds.

In the animal kingdom, the human auditory system is by far the most complex of all such systems, but some animals can hear higher pitches (bats), while others can pick up lower pitches (elephants). Nevertheless, the human auditory system is an obvious triumph of natural selection. The scientist in me wants to believe that Darwin and evolution explain the marvels of this system, but it is such a wonder that my scientific conviction wavers. The auditory system has a bigger dynamic range than the best high-fidelity system. Sounds so faint that they are barely above the thermal noise background can still be heard by young ears. The energy transfer from the sound waves in the ear canal to the fluctuations of the basilar membrane is provably optimal. How could natural selection achieve such amazing results?

My training is in physics and not in philosophy. However, I believe my uncertainty about natural selection, good luck, and the existence of miracles makes me an agnostic. The laws of physics that govern the universe were thought to be immutable by Spinoza and later by Laplace and many others. Their thinking assumed a deterministic world in which each event is predetermined by its antecedents. There is no place for free will in such a deterministic world. I don't like that world, and if I need to live with some agnostic uncertainty, so be it.

As a freshman at MIT, I was required to take an English course taught by Professor William Green, generally known among the freshmen as "Wild Bill Green." He was a daringly stimulating lecturer; he also asked us all to write a paper about free will and our thoughts about its existence or impossibility. I choose to defend its existence, perhaps because I wished it so, but also because I was already aware of the inevitable presence of small amounts of random noise in all electronic systems.

Only four years later, mathematician Claude Shannon revolutionized the world by explaining how all signals could be transmitted noise-free by using digital coding. The random noise is still present, but Shannon showed under what conditions its disturbing effect could be completely overcome.

Nevertheless, the brain does not use Shannon coding. Random noise is present even if its value is small. Therefore, I believe that two brains having exactly the same sensory input over a lifetime can reach different conclusions. This is clearly in contrast to the deterministic thinking of Spinoza and Laplace and leads me to continue to believe in free will.

Another philosophical question that I puzzle about is the role of luck in one's life. Luck is defined as a force that causes good things to happen to us by chance and not as a result of our own efforts. Many say that we make our own luck or that luck favors those who are prepared. However, I believe I have, on the whole, had extraordinarily good luck throughout my life.

I will illustrate my good fortune by drawing a comparison with the life of my close high school friend, Dick White. For geometry, Dick and I had Miss Kitson, who awakened our love of mathematics and sent us both to the state math contest. Dick took 12th place there, and I took 13th. Dick was valedictorian, and I made the honor roll. So academically we were close, and, if anything, Dick was my better.

Our religious education was similar: he was brought up as a Catholic and I was a regular attendee at the St. James Episcopal Church in South Bend. Neither of us attended church regularly in later life.

Because of pulmonary problems, Dick was not drafted, and instead he enrolled in engineering at Iowa State. Because of the accelerated academic calendar during the war, he was able to earn his BS early and go on to graduate school in electrical engineering before the end of the war. He married, but then tragedy struck. Dick was diagnosed with TB and sent to a sanatorium; his father paid the medical bills and supported Dick's budding family.

After treatment Dick recovered, but he felt obliged to return to South Bend and help out in the family business. Eventually, he established his own business and did well. Bobby and I visited the Whites on our trips through South Bend. Dick and his wife visited us in St. Louis, too. Dick passed away within a year and a half of Bobby.

I find it hard to discount the effect of good luck on my life. Did the hand of the divine touch me? I don't know. Is agnosticism a poor substitute for careful thought? Perhaps, but I have done my best to find an alternative and remain reverently agnostic.

Chapter 22
My Family | 1951-

It is time to catch up on my family. If we all were able to get together, there would be 22 of us, but sadly Bobby did not live to see the whole tribe. Thus, there are 21 now, and this chapter seems like an appropriate place to take stock.

My three wonderful children posing in our living room in 1969.

The chart below lists first names and birth dates only. All those on the right are surnamed Cox. On the left, Nancy has the last name Battersby, Kim has Spenard, and Erin has Rau. Daughters-in-law and sons-in-law throughout the chart are shown in italics.

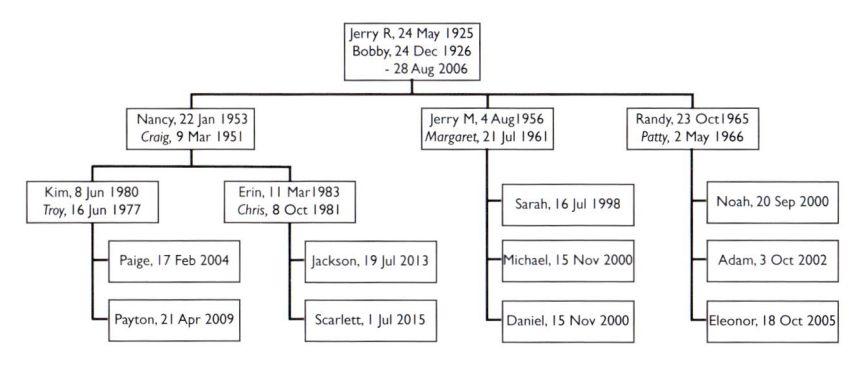

Jerry R, 24 May 1925
Bobby, 24 Dec 1926
- 28 Aug 2006

Nancy, 22 Jan 1953		Jerry M, 4 Aug1956	Randy, 23 Oct1965
Craig, 9 Mar 1951		*Margaret, 21 Jul 1961*	*Patty, 2 May 1966*

Kim, 8 Jun 1980	Erin, 11 Mar1983
Troy, 16 Jun 1977	*Chris, 8 Oct 1981*

Paige, 17 Feb 2004	Jackson, 19 Jul 2013	Sarah, 16 Jul 1998	Noah, 20 Sep 2000

Payton, 21 Apr 2009	Scarlett, 1 Jul 2015	Michael, 15 Nov 2000	Adam, 3 Oct 2002

| | | Daniel, 15 Nov 2000 | Eleonor, 18 Oct 2005 |

In-law names are in italics

After the busy career described earlier, Nancy retired from her position as Director of Parks and Recreation for the city of Fenton. However, she couldn't sit still for long, so she took up grant writing, and she particularly enjoyed writing grants for Memory Care Home

Almost everyone in the family celebrating my 90th birthday on a Mississippi steamer just north of St. Louis

Solutions (MCHS), a St. Louis-based Alzheimer's Disease non-profit that supports home-based caregivers. The grants that Nancy wrote doubled MCHS's external support. But she was also working part-time at Blendics and at Q-Net Security (QNS). As that work increased, she had to give up grant writing, along with her position as an officer in the St. Louis Chapter of the Grant Professionals Association. Nancy's title then changed, and she became the Finance Director for both Blendics and QNS. Craig was employed at restaurants and at a nearby printing company for most of his working life, but he has now retired and supports Nancy with shopping, yard work, cooking, and helping to mind their grandchildren whenever they visit.

Nancy and Craig's daughters, Kim and Erin, have married and produced four great-grandkids: two girls, Paige and Scarlett, and two boys, Payton and Jackson. They are a joy for me to watch develop. All four great grandkids are healthy, with their individual personalities already clear. For example, Payton inherited the technology gene and runs all the audio-visual equipment at his mother's church; Paige is active in sports and cheerleading. Her team has won titles in national competitions. Kim is an ordained Wesleyan church pastor and supervises the youth ministry at her church. Troy Spenard runs a very successful autobody shop in Warrenton, Missouri, just 50 miles northwest of Sunset Hills, where the Spenards have made their home.

Nancy and Craig's younger daughter, Erin, lives with her husband Chris Rau in a suburb of Kansas City. Erin is an executive with Trane Technologies Inc., a manufacturer of commercial HVAC systems, while Chris is a high school art teacher and graphic artist whose website is *chrisrauart*. Erin and Chris have two great youngsters, Jackson and Scarlett.

My son, Jerry, has the middle name, Mills, which we chose to recognize my grandmother. We also wanted to make sure he would not be Jerome R. Cox, III, since being "the third" would surely embarrass him in grade school. Jerry has a great love for wood and amazes everyone with what he can do with it. He designs fine furniture for a local company, NewSpace, and some of his art can be found at coxstl.com. Jerry fell in love with and married Margaret, an untamed whirlwind who has yet to slow down. She is currently in charge of activities for those who enjoy independent living at Meramec Bluffs Senior Living Community.

Jerry and Margaret's oldest child is Sarah, now taking a gap year or two after college before entering law school. She is saving the money she earns as a legal assistant. Her long-term goal is a seat on the Supreme Court. Sarah has twin brothers: Michael, a theater major at Missouri Baptist University, who clearly has theatrical talent, since it is hard to take your eyes off him when he is on stage; and Daniel, who did very well in high school, followed his passion by enlisting in the Army and is now deployed to the U.S. Embassy in Baghdad, Iraq.

Son Randy's full name is Randall Allen Cox: Randall, a family name from Elrose's side of the family, and Allen to honor the

Reverend Allen Swartz, the minister who married Bobby and me and maintained a life-long friendship with Bobby's parents. Randy and his wife Patty have three children, two boys and a girl. After many years spent in a suburb of Detroit working for the auto industry, Randy has switched to information technology, where he serves as one of the vice presidents of Siemens and leads a group whose goal is to establish its Internet-of-Things (IoT) business sector. Recently, he completed a climb to the 19,341-foot summit of Mount Kilimanjaro in Tanzania. This was an item on his bucket list, and the family is all happy that he is safely down.

Patty is a woman of many accomplishments: a business major, an attorney, a professor of marketing, a runner, a soccer devotee, and a mother of three. The oldest of the children is Noah, now a junior at the University of Michigan majoring in business. His brother, Adam, is following in his footsteps, just beginning his freshman year at the U of M. Their sister, Eleonor, is the athlete of the three, taking after her mother in that regard. The unusual thing about these three Detroit grandkids is Squirrel Town.[16] There are about twenty YouTube videos, and even a book, describing the construction and teardown of Squirrel Town, located in Randy and Patty's backyard and built of castoff materials over eight years by Noah, Adam, and neighbor kids. Squirrel Town had more than a dozen buildings that were about half the size of real buildings. Some of the buildings had multiple rooms and multiple stories. They included a city hall, a jail, several stores, and a bank. Squirrel Town also had a mayor, political campaigns, elections, allegations of election fraud and everything the kids could think of to make it operate like a real town. It covered an acre or two of Randy and Patty's backyard, and there could be five to ten kids playing their various roles inside the 20 or so buildings.

Ultimately, it had to be torn down because many of the buildings were falling apart and had become a danger to the next generation of local youngsters who might play inside. So, prior to Noah and Adam heading away to college, all remnants of Squirrel Town were removed and the yard was returned to its original green condition. You have to see the videos of both the construction and teardown of Squirrel Town to appreciate the industry of those kids.

16   https://www.youtube.com/playlist?list=UUagmAWZGHjOFQ2OZWvOAtxQ
      Squirrel Town by Noah Cox also available at Amazon.com

So, I have 15 kids, grandkids, and great-grandkids in my family, as well as five in-laws. Wow! When I was growing up, there was just my mother, father, and me, until my mother passed away. I had no idea how wonderful a family of loving kids could be. Perhaps my mother is my better angel and is looking down on me and the Cox tribe with her serene smile, making sure that the breaks go our way.

My family report would be incomplete without mention of my half-brother and half-sisters. My half-brother Randy passed away in 2012 following complications from a fall on his stairs. Nancy and I attended the funeral in Girard, Pennsylvania. My half-sister Candy also passed away in 2018 after an extended battle with lung cancer. Nancy and I visited her in Marina, California, just a month before she died, and she remained cheerful until the end. Half-sister Anita is still in good health and visits from time to time, along with her husband Jim Hunt.

As the 15 family members listed in my tree grow and mature, they surprise me over and over again with new talents and adventures. Each of them has been allowed to pursue his or her own passions, and I applaud that freedom of choice. My only regret is that I will not be able to see all the youngsters find their way into adulthood.

Chapter 23
Epilogue | 2022-

As I was finishing the final chapters of this memoir, I learned once again about the fragility of life. On 26 August, while getting ready to go to the hospital to have my pacemaker generator replaced, my hip gave way, and I fell and broke my hip on the garage floor. After a few weeks in the hospital and in rehab, I am now living with Nancy and Craig in their lovely home in Wildwood, a western suburb of St. Louis. My three kids (Nancy, Jerry, and Randy) have been wonderful to me during this difficult time. I am now getting used to depending on a wheelchair.

This is a time to reflect on my life and the new challenge of healing my body and being able to walk again. My heroes are all gone now: Hallowell Davis, Wesley Clark, and William Danforth. They were all exceptional men, and I was privileged to learn from each of them. They each changed the world in their own way.

Davis developed the field of evoked response audiometry, which has played a part in the detection and early education of deaf children. As a result, children born deaf today can expect to listen, talk, and read along with their hearing grade-school peers.

Clark, a pioneering computer designer, created the first computer that could be managed by a single individual and in the process revolutionized the application of computers to medical research. Clark's LINC computer triggered a movement away from large, centralized processors to today's computing that is increasingly at the network edge.

Danforth turned a university that catered to a regional student body into a nationally recognized research university. Today,

Washington University students are attracted from around the world. Danforth also stimulated technology growth in the metropolitan St. Louis area and created the world-renowned Donald Danforth Plant Science Center.

Each one of these three demonstrated that you can make great contributions to society without strife. I was privileged to be able to call them all my friends. Not only these three heroes but so many friends whom I have encountered on my journey through life have given me joy. They all have demonstrated the value of my motto: "Work Hard, Be Kind."

My vanity license plates proclaim my motto while making it visible to aggressive tailgaters.

I too have worked hard, but almost always at something I enjoyed. Was that luck or am I easily amused? Hal Davis taught me his appetite for adventure. Wes Clark taught me to look beyond the horizon. Bill Danforth showed that much can be accomplished with a gentle touch. Were my encounters with these three amazing men just good luck? Whatever brought us together—predestination, karma, or luck— I am forever grateful.

Finally, I must mention with a tear my late wife, Bobby. She blessed my life from the "first talk" to the last and, what's more, gave me my three wonderful children. Of all the gifts I've received in a lucky lifetime, that has been the greatest gift of all.

ACKNOWLEDGMENTS

First, I must acknowledge my daughter, Nancy Cox Battersby. Several years ago, Nancy created *"Our Family History,"* a 161-page book documenting our family history stretching back on my wife's side to Robert 6th Lord of Annandale, Earl of Carrick de Bruce, born in 1243 in Scotland. Not only has Nancy traced our roots, but she has also kept me happy and supported me in so many ways since the passing of my wife, Bobby, in 2006. She has also helped me research many questions that have arisen during the preparation of these pages and provided suggested improvements along the way. The book would not have been possible without her help. I have two sons. The older is Jerome Mills Cox and the younger is Randall Allen Cox. They both have read portions of the book, offered suggestions, and helped me recover many family memories.

Candace O'Connor has done an amazing job of editing these pages and turning my rough manuscript into something I hope is readable. She has asked frequent questions along the way that a reader might ask. I have tried to answer them as best I can remember. Her skilled editing was never a burden but was always done with a warm touch.

The rest of the publishing team includes Karen Dodson, Publisher; Marcy Mamroth, Art Director; and Caroline Chicoine, Attorney. Working with them all was a pleasure.

Finally, thanks to others who have read particular chapters and offered suggestions and corrections: Jill Arnone, Bill Gerth, Lois Goldring, Gil Jost, Maxine Rockoff, Don Snyder, Van Stoecker, and Mary Allen Wilkes. The cover features a painting by my half-brother's wife, Theresa Cox-Kendig, that she did recently from a photograph of me taken in 1970. The two castle sketches were done by my grandson-in-law, Chris Rau.

Page 42

A nonstandard, humorous unit of length created as part of an MIT fraternity prank named after one of Jerry's fraternity brothers Oliver R. Smoot

Page 45

Phil's old Radios, one of the world's first websites for antique radios and televisions featuring an RCA 630TS radio that Jerry constructed from a kit in 1947

Page 55

A Massachusetts Institute of Technology (MIT) musical comedy written largely by a Dutch friend of Jerry's, Art Van Stolk, called "O Say Can You Si" about the adventures of two MIT students in South America

Page 61

A multi-flash picture of Jerry's wife, Bobby Cox, skipping rope, an image that has been published far and wide and now resides in the Smithsonian Museum

Page 115

The Secret History of Women in Coding, featuring Jerry's colleague Mary Allen Wilkes (New York Times, February 19, 2019)

Page 128

EXPLORER – The World's First Total-Body PET Scanner

Page 134

Features information about the physical version of Alan Turing's theoretical university computer created by Wesley Clark and Bob Arnzen in "The Only Working Turing Machine There Ever Was Probably (TOWTMTEWP)"

(The Henry Ford's Innovation Nation)

Page 149

Computers in Cardiology (now called Computing in Cardiology [CinC]), an organization founded by Jerry and Paul Hugenholtz to recognize the growing role of computers in electrocardiography

Page 190

History of the Laboratory Instrument Computer (LINC) (National Institutes of Health Office of NIH History & Stetten Museum)

Page 227

Atreyu Trading; a Wall Street firm that offers real-time risk surveillance, established in part with Blendics technology

Page 219

LINC@45 Video Coverage on DigiBarn TV (DigiBarn Computer Museum)

Page 243

Squirrel Town: 21 videos produced by Jerry's grandson Noah and others that highlight the construction and teardown of more than a dozen buildings that were half the size of real buildings; *Squirrel Town* is also available in paperback on Amazon.com

Page 226

Biomedical Computer Laboratory-Computer Systems Lab 50th anniversary, Part 1

Page 226

Biomedical Computer Laboratory-Computer Systems Lab 50th anniversary, Part 2

Note: Folios with italicized "*f*" indicate figures in the text.

A

Abstract Database System (ADS), 155–156

Acoustics (Beranek), 79

Acoustics Lab. *See* MIT Acoustics Lab

Adams, John, 35–37, 35*f*, 36*f*, 37, 46

Advanced Research Projects Agency (ARPA), 109

adventure in Moscow, 136–143
  panel discussion on biomedical computing, 136, 138
  panelists, 136

Adventures of Ozzie and Harriet, The, 163

Allen, Fred, 16

Allies, 29, 29*f*, 30, 32

Ambos, Merry. *See* Richon, Merry Ambos

Ambos, Nicole, 154

American National Standards Institute (ANSI), 43

American Radio Relay League (ARRL) Handbook, 16

Amplitude-Zone Time-Epoch Coding (AZTEC), 117–118

Amsler, Marty, 37–38

Amsterdam, Morey, 46

analog-to-digital converter (ADC), 89, 95

Apodaca, Tony, 166

Applied Research Laboratory (ARL), 167, 180, 184, 187–188

Armstrong, Arthur, 37–39

army, 25–33
  combat, 30–32
  discharge at Fort Sheridan, 32
  Infantry Division (88ᵗʰ), 29
  discharge post, 32
  replacement depot, 28
  reporting to re-assignment officer, 31–32
  training, 25–27
  troopship for the U.S., 32
  uniform, 25*f*–26, 32

Army Specialized Training Program (ASTP), 26–27

Arnzen, Bob, 134, 134*f*

Arsenic and Old Lace, 147

Arthur, Martin, 118

Asynchronous Transfer Mode (ATM), 188, 204

As You Like It (Shakespeare), 20

ATM Lattice Cell, 188

Atreyu Group, 227

Audio Analgesia (AA), 83–84

Auditory and Non-auditory Effects of High-Intensity Noise (ANEHIN), 79–82

auditory system, 63, 116, 234–239

B

Ball, Bill, 154

Barry, Dave, 116, 136–137, 139–140

Batista, Fulgencia, 80

Battersby, Craig, 161, 161*f*, 200, 207–208, 241–242, 241*f*, 245

Battersby, Erin. *See* Rau, Erin Battersby

Battersby, Kim. *See* Spenard, Kim Battersby

Battersby, Nancy Cox, 12, 67, 73, 75–77, 92, 105, 112, 130–131, 143–144, 161, 185, 206–208, 231, 235, 241*f*, 242, 245

Battle of the Bulge, 38

Baum, Frank
  Wonderful Wizard of Oz, The, 11

Beatles, 113, 122

Bechet, Sidney, 234

Becky Thatcher, 148

Behrer, Remsen, 119

belief, 108, 205, 234–239

Bell, Gordon, 151–152

Bell Labs, 165, 181, 188, 206

Benny, Jack, 16

Benson, Bob, 158–159

Bentley, Roy, 119–120, 122, 125, 132

Beranek, Leo, 49–50, 49*f*, 63-65, 93
  Acoustics, 79
  completion of Master of Science under supervision of, 64
  exam committee, 66

Berle, Milton, 45

Berlin, Irving, 236

Bernal, Ron, 203–207, 204*f*

Berry, Dick, 100

Best, Dick, 35, 37

Big Band music, 52

Biomedical Computer Laboratory (BCL), 95–96, 100, 102–119, 103*f*, 110*f*, 120–127, 130–132, 140, 144, 146–147, 153–154, 158, 168, 177, 181–184, 211, 224*f*, 225–226, 262
  annual progress report, 131–132
  classes in computer programming, 110

closure of, 184
  graduate students, 102
  international notice, 132
  research assistants, 110
  research collaboration with School
    of Engineering, 182
  retirement of director Lew Thomas, 184
Blaine, Jim, 146, 181–183
  meeting on progress at ERL, 184
  NIH Shared Instrument Grant (SIG)
    Program, 182–183
Blendics, 216–228, 241
Blood Sweet and Stanley Poole, 92
Bogart, Humphrey, 28
Bokek, Ein, 168, 170, 170*f*, 171
Boston Marathon in Hopkinton,
    Massachusetts, 72
brain mapping, 190–192, 194. *See also*
    genome mapping
Brazier, Molly A.B., 95–96, 100
Brewster, Teddy, 147
Bridge Too Far, A, 148–149
broadband, 182–183. *See also* network/
    networking
Brown, Arlen, 19
Browning, Gen. Frederick, 149
Browning Automatic Rifle (BAR), 29, 29*f*
Bryan Hall, 154, 157, 212
Buczek, Patty. *See* Cox, Patty Buczek
Bugnitz, Tom, 159

C

Campbell, Wilbur, 24
Carroll, Lewis, 8
Castro, Fidel, 80
Center Development Office (CDO),
    97–100, 103–104, 106, 108–109
Central Institute for the Deaf (CID),
    22, 69, 73, 75–86, 88, 90–94, 96–97,
    100–101, 110, 119, 127, 129, 141, 163,
    183, 196–197, 236
  annual salary at, 78
  collaborators, 110
  Electroacoustic Lab, 73, 83, 94
  Family Center, 90
  Hal Davis's offer of job, 75
  meeting with research staff, 76
  research at, 91, 93
  tests conducted by, 84
Chadwick, Dottie, 54, 62, 66–67
Chaney, Scott, 220–221, 229, 230

Chaney, Tom, 219–220, 230
Chang, Bill, 129, 173, 178
Chang, Tony, 173–176, 178
Chesler, David, 123
childhood. *See* early childhood
Chorus Line, A, 147
Churchill, Winston, 161
Cisco, 203–207
Cisco Carrier Routing System, 205
Clark, Bob, 196–197
Clark, Doug, 230
Clark, Wes/Wesley, 102, 116–117, 130,
    135, 141, 191–192, 210–212, 216, 224*f*,
    227–230, 245–246
  ARPA grant, 109
  Average Response Computer (ARC), 96
  Caribbean cruise, 186*f*
  Computer Design course, 110, 165–166
  Computer Systems Lab, 220
  discussion on macromodules, 109*f*
  faculty appointments, 105
  grant from NIH, 103
  Heinz Nixdorf Museum in Paderborn,
    Germany, 229
  invited to convince the Merrill Lynch
    managers, 177
  LINC computer, 97, 99, 190
  LINC Evaluation Program, 98
  at Lincoln Lab, 95, 95*f*, 104, 108
  LISP programs, 134
  Marriage with Mary Allen Wilkes, 115
  MTC, 107
  TOWTMTEWP, 134*f*
  visit to China, 173, 177–178
Clockless Computing symposium, 216–217
Collins, Francis, 195–196
Colthurst, Sir Charles, 150
Columbus Athletic Club, 172
Columbus Bar Association, 172
committees, 66, 103, 121, 129, 151–154,
    164–165, 182, 189–198, 201
  brain mapping, 190–192
  genome mapping, 190
Communications Biophysics Lab (CBL),
    69–70, 95–97
Compton, Karl T., 44
computed tomography (CT), 122–126,
    128–129, 211–212
Computerized Medical Systems (CMS), 115
Computer Science department, 151–167,
    156*f*, 176
  research program, 153

women in, 160, 167*f*

Computers in Cardiology (CiC), 144–152, 178, 178*f*, 186
  meeting held in Florence, Italy, 149

Computer Systems Lab (CSL), 106, 109, 111, 116, 130, 133–134, 173, 210, 219–220, 224*f*, 225

Coneybeer, Rob, 203

Cook Nuclear Power Plant, 217–218

Corely, Dick, 182

Corning Glass Works, 181

Coronary Care Unit (CCU), 117–118, 214

COTS (Commercial off the shelf), 164

Cousteau, Jacques, 60

Cowan, Max, 192

Cox, Adam, 207, 241*f*, 243

Cox, Allison. *See* Niebauer, Allison Cox

Cox, Anita. *See* Hunt, Anita Cox

Cox, Barbara Jane Lueders (Bobby), 51–63, 67–68, 71–74, 76–77, 92–93, 105, 126–127, 130–133, 143, 145
  45th wedding anniversary, 200
  back pain, 207, 209–210, 213
  Caribbean cruise, 186*f*
  CID LINC, 100
  death of her mother, 90–91
  discharge of, 212
  dissertation document, 71
  dream house, 100
  electrocardiogram, 211
  enlarged aortic aneurysm, 212–213
  ex-boyfriend (Keith Hunton), 96
  expecting second child, 82
  family reunion, 77
  family Thanksgiving dinner, 178*f*
  family tree, 241*f*
  funding of the Computer Science and Engineering Department, 207
  at funeral, 172
  graduated from Katharine Gibbs, 53
  health deterioration, 217
  in her wedding finery, 59*f*
  hired a belly dancer, 162
  labor pains, 66
  meeting at Rotterdam, 132
  multi-day trip to Missouri, 77
  multi-flash picture: skipping rope, 61, 61*f*
  O's estate, 163
  passing, 214–215
  photographic portrait, 90*f*
  pregnant, 63, 131
  relocation at 8–9 Garden Circle, 65
  relocation to St. Louis, 75
  role in home decoration, 79

search award, 202*f*
stepfather, 56, 91, 144, 162
trip to Europe, 112
Twelve Angry Women, 92
weekend trips to Boston, Massachusetts, 56–57
wish to have her body cremated, 214

Cox, Allison, *See* Niebauer, Allison Cox

Cox, Daniel, 207, 241*f*, 242

Cox, Eleonor, 207, 241*f*, 243

Cox, Elrose "Candy." *See* Owen, Elrose "Candy" Cox

Cox, Elrose Randall, 13–17, 14*f*, 21, 21*f*, 23, 32, 48, 57, 77, 172, 197–198, 234, 242

Cox, Ferris Randall Rockhold, 16, 21, 21*f*, 172, 184–185, 197, 244

Cox, Helena Jane Mills, 1–2, 4, 8, 9*f*, 10*f*

Cox, Jerome, Sr., 9, 18, 18*f*

Cox, Jerome A., 1

Cox, Jerome R., III, 242

Cox, Jerry M., 83, 83*f*, 92, 105, 112–113, 130–131, 144–145, 161–162, 166, 185, 198, 206–207, 208*f*, 214–215, 241*f*, 242, 245, 247,

Cox, Lillian Rockhold, 1

Cox, Margaret Wolfe, 166, 198, 207, 215, 241*f*, 242

Cox, Michael, 113, 207, 241*f*

Cox, Nancy Jane. *See* Battersby, Nancy Cox

Cox, Noah, 207, 241*f*, 243

Cox, Patty Buczek, 207, 208*f*, 215, 241*f*, 243

Cox, Randall Allen (Randy), 12–13, 36*f*, 131, 144–145, 147–150, 147*f*, 161–162, 185–187, 201, 206–207, 208*f*, 209, 214–215, 230, 241*f*, 242–243, 245, 247

Cox, Sarah, 207, 241*f*, 242

Cox-Kendig, Theresa Surovick, 185, 247

Crocker, Zenas (Zee), 51, 53

Cudworth, Allen, 76–77

Cudworth, Cynthia, 77

Cultural Revolution, 173–174

Cunningham, Jack, 114, 132, 136–139

Cybernetics (Wiener), 69

D

Dam, Andy van, 152

Dammkoehler, Rich, 154
  Tiger Rag Forever, 235

Danforth, John, 209

Danforth, William, 130, 159, 202*f*, 209,

225, 245–246

Das, Santanu, 225

Davis, Florence, 73

Davis, Hallowell, 69, 73, 76–77, 82, 84, 86, 89, 91, 94, 100, 128, 157, 197, 236, 245–246
  assignments given by, 79, 83
  development of the cochlear implant, 90
  electroencephalogram (brainwaves), 87
  job offer from, 75
  Navy flight, 81

Davis, Jim, 173–174

Day, Doris, 234

Dead Sea, 168–170, 170f

Dearnley, Irv, 34–35, 37

Debakey, Michael, 119, 136–137, 142

Defense Mapping Agency (DMA), 91, 163–164

DeHart, John, 230

Delta Upsilon (DU) fraternity, 34–39, 42, 94

Dempsey, Dean Edward, 96, 100–101

Dessau, Brigita, 112–113

Dessau, Erling, 112–113

De Tomaso Pantera, 151

Dewart, Allen, 18

Dickinson, Becton, 115

digital. See going digital

Digital Equipment Corporation (DEC), 88, 94, 110–112, 141–142, 152, 158, 182–183

Digital Imaging and COmmunication in Medicine (DICOM), 184

Distant Early Warning (DEW), 70, 77

Distant Early Wiener Warning (DEWW), 70

Dittia, Zubin, 202, 204, 207

"Doc" Edgerton. See Edgerton, Harold

doctoral dissertation, 64–74
  hectograph technique, 71
  reciprocity calibration process, 70

Donald Danforth Plant Science Center, 209, 246

Dorsey, Tommy, 52

Drama Club at Riley High School, 20

2.5D technology, 224–225

Duckworth, Charlie, 73

Dunscombe family, 150

E

early childhood, 1–13
  about father and his job, 2–8, 9f, 11–12, 14–16, 21
  about maternal grandparents, 1–2
  about pet dog Zipper, 7, 7f
  adventures during, 4, 10, 35
  amusements with neighbor, 8
  birth information, 3
  death of grandfather and grandmother, 1, 6, 10
  death of mother, 1–2, 11
  death of uncle Harold Mills in the Battle of Belleau Wood, 2, 6
  family, 1, 6
  friends, 1
  illness of mother, 4
  kindergarten, 5, 5f
  at Rosemary Beach, 8, 9f, 11f, 12f, 13, 17, 21–22, 76, 217–219
  schooling, 5, 7, 10–11

Eatherton, Will, 202, 204, 207

Ebsworth, Barney, 186

Edgerton, Harold (Doc), 47–48, 47f, 57–60, 61f, 63

Edwards, Roy, 120

Eldredge, Don, 22, 76, 91, 93–94, 236

Eleanor Rigby, 114

electrical engineering (EE), 39, 51–53, 57, 64, 79, 100, 102, 106, 109, 121–122, 129–130, 151, 158, 173, 193, 217, 238

Electroacoustics Lab, 73, 83

electronic design automation (EDA), 217, 223–225

Electronic Radiology Laboratory (ERL), 146, 180–189

Eliot Society's Search Award, 202f

Engebretson, Maynard, 88–90, 97–100, 102, 112, 119

Engel, George, 217, 222, 227, 229

Essen, David Van, 192–194

Ethernet, 181, 211

Everything You Always Wanted to Know About Sex* (*But Were Afraid to Ask) (Reuben), 17

evoked response audiometry (ERA), 89–91, 98, 128, 197, 245

F

Faddis, Mitch, 211

family, 1, 4, 11–12, 16–17, 27, 32, 46, 67, 73, 75–77, 83, 90–91, 93, 95, 100, 112, 130–132, 144, 150, 162–163, 172, 201, 205, 214–215, 218, 240–244

Fast Packet chipset, 188–189, 202–203,

206–207
Feder, Robin, 196–197
Feldman, Nancy, 22
Ferber, Edna
  Show Boat, 235
Feshbach, Herman
  Methods of Theoretical Physics, 64
Fingerhut, Andy, 202, 204, 207
First on the Agenda, 201
Fisher, John, 24, 39
Fitzgerald, Ella, 236
Fleming, Dick, 209
Foldy, Leslie L., 71
Forrester, Jay, 106
Fort Benjamin Harrison, 25
Foster, Pops, 234
Fourier, Joseph, 123
Four–Week-Wonder, 110–112, 110*f*, 166, 220
Fozzard, Harry, 116

G

Gardner, Murray, 66
Gardner, Wallace, 84
Garrett, Jack, 78–79
Garrett, Mabel, 79
General Electric (GE), 124, 181
genome mapping, 190, 194–196
Gershwin, George, 236
  Porgy and Bess, 234
Gershwin, Ira, 236
  Porgy and Bess, 234
Gerth, Bill, 111, 114–115, 247
Gibbs, Katharine/Katy, 37, 53, 57
Gilbert, W. S.
  H.M.S. Pinafore, 234
Gillette, Will, 155, 194
Glaeser, Don, 100, 102, 119
Globally Asynchronous, Locally
  Synchronous (GALS), 221, 223
Goblick, Tom, 236
going digital, 87–101
  modules, 88
  tone pip, 87–89
Golden Fleecing, The, 92
Goldring, Dave, 96
Goldring, Sid, 96, 98–99
Goldstein, Max, 82
Gray, Alex, 166

Graziadei, Jim, 42
Great American Songbook, 235–236
Greatbatch, Mennen, 118
Great Hall of the People in Tiananmen
  Square, 175–176*f*
Green, William, 237
Green Chartreuse, 20
Grote, Mike, 220
Growth Networks, Inc (GNI), 199–209
Guckel, Henry, 109
Gustav Line, 29

H

Haggett, Ann Page, 54, 62, 65–66, 144
Haggett, Dick, 62, 65–66, 144
Hall, Bryan, 154, 157, 212
Halstead, Ward, 22
Hanson, Bee, 131
Harbison, Myrna, 154
Harvard, John, 34
helicopter parenting, 8
Hello Dolly, 113
Hermits, 18–19, 24
Higgins, Carol, 127
high school, 2, 14–24, 30, 76, 90, 160–161,
  172, 201, 208–209, 218, 234, 238, 242
  9th grade at James Madison, 15–16
  Central High School, 16–18, 20
  James Whitcomb Riley High School,
    17–18, 19*f*, 20, 22, 23,
high-speed networking. *See* network/
  networking
Hi-Hat Club, 62
Hirsh, Don, 182
Hirsh, Ira, 76, 78, 83, 89, 92–94, 167,182,
  196, 236
  Measurement of Hearing, The, 76
  Psychoacoustic Lab, 91
Hirsh, Shirley, 89, 93
Histogram, AVerage, and Ogive Calculator
  (HAVOC), 88–91, 94, 96–97, 114, 117
H.M.S. Pinafore (Gilbert and Sullivan), 234
Hoffman, Ed, 126–127
Holiday, Billie, 236
Holiday Magazine, 57, 59–60
Hounsfield, Godfrey, 12, 122–123
Huang, Henry, 124
Hugenholtz, Paul, 132, 136–137, 139,
  146–149

Human Brain Project, 193

Human Connectome Project, 194

Hunt, Anita Cox, 77, 105, 172, 198, 244

Hunt, Jim, 244

Hunt, Leigh, 8

Hunton, Joy Reed, 54, 61–62, 96

Hunton, Keith, 53–54, 62, 96

I

IEEE Communications Magazine, 165

Indeck, Ron, 230

Industrial Hygiene and Toxicology (Patty), 197

Institute of Electronic and Electrical Engineers (IEEE), 118, 146

International Organization for Standardization (ISO), 43

Internet-of-Things (IoT), 243

Israel Defense Forces (IDF), 169

J

Jain, Raj, 207

Jim Cullum Jazz Band, 235

Jobs, Steve, 166, 211

Johnson, Bunk, 234

Johnson, Sherwood, 40

Joint Photographic Experts Group (JPEG), 184

Jost, Gil, 181, 247
  meeting on progress at ERL, 184

Journal of Nuclear Medicine, 127

K

Kahn, Bob, 192

Kajiya, James, 192

Kaminsky, Max, 53, 235

Katherine, Aunt, 10, 55, 59

Kemp, Hal
  "Where or When," 17

Kempner, Ken, 147

Ken Club, 52–53, 235

Keyes, Mary Ellen, 22, 30–31*f*, 32

Kimura, Dan, 155, 208

Kirby, Durward, 15

Kirkwood Theatre Guild (KTG), 92, 199, 218

Kitson, Mary Alice, 19, 238

Knepp, Carol, 22

Koplar, Harold, 84–86

Koppel, Ted
  Lights Out: A Cyberattack, A Nation Unprepared, Surviving the Aftermath, 227

Krippner, Ken, 115

Krygiel, Annette, 164, 166–167*f*

Kuhl, David, 120

Kuhnle, Brent, 24, 39

Kumar, Arun, 183, 187–188

L

Lambda Chi Alpha (LXA) fraternity, 24, 34

Lambda Chi brothers, 39–40, 42–45, 51–52

Lang, Bill, 93

LaQuess, Corky, 53

Larson, Ken, 121

"latch-key" program, 219

Lauterbur, Paul, 129

Law of Feedback Control, 146

Lee, Peggy, 236

Lenoski, Dan, 203–204, 204*f*, 207

Lester, Jerry, 46

Let's Make a Deal (TV program), 200

Lewis, Howard, 224*f*

Liberty Mutual Insurance Company
  job at, 63, 67–68, 72–73, 75–78, 85, 187
  Loss Prevention Department, 64
  loss-prevention engineers, 72
  policyholders, 72
  Workmen's Compensation policy, 68

Licklider, J.C.R., 65, 76, 84, 108–109

Life magazine, 44–45

Lighthall, Harry, 40–41
  Lights Out: A Cyberattack, A Nation Unprepared, Surviving the Aftermath (Koppel), 227

Li'l Abner, 18

LINC, 95, 95*f*, 96–100, 103–106, 108–110, 112, 114–117, 120, 122, 130, 141, 154, 190, 192, 219, 219*f*, 224*f*, 226, 229, 245, 263*f*

LINC Assembly Program (LAP6), 115

Lindbergh, Charles
  WE, 11

Little, John D. C., 45, 121
  Voo Doo, 43–45, 43*f*, 121

Livingston, Bob, 190–192, 194

Loss Prevention Department (Liberty Mutual Insurance), 64

luck, defined, 238

Lueders, Bobby, *See* Cox, Barbara Jane Lueders (Bobby)

Lueders, Eleanor, 55, 90–91

Lueders, Oscar, 55–56, 144–145, 162–163

Lusted, Lee, 96

Lynch, Merrill, 177

M

Macromodular Computer Design, 216

Macromodules/macromodular, 109, 109*f*, 116, 133–136, 216, 220

Mansfield, Peter, 129

Markham, Joanne, 121

Marshall, Garland, 116, 154, 225

Martha Mary Chapel, 57, 57*f*, 58, 58*f*, 60

Martin, Joseph, 192–193

Mason, Jeannie, 51, 54

Mason, Sam, 51–52, 54–55, 57, 66–67, 145–146

Massachusetts Institute of Technology (MIT), 21, 24–25, 31–32, 34–53, 55–56, 60–61, 65–67, 70, 72, 76, 79, 93, 95, 97, 102–103, 106–109, 115, 121–122, 129–130, 145–146, 151, 177, 234, 236–237
  303 Walker Memorial Hall, 45
  engineering education, 48
  experience in acoustics, 79
  Fariberz Maseeth Hall (MIT Grad House), 34
  instructors, 51
  president of the MIT chapter of Lambda Chi, 45
  Radiation Laboratory, 35
  veteran's disability, 35

McCormick, Bruce, 191

McDonnell–Douglas, 114

McGavin, Darren, 92

McGoon, Earthquake, 18

McKelvey, James/Jimmy Morgan, Jr., 131, 162, 166

McKelvey, James/Jim, 129, 131, 151, 158

Meckel, Margot, 17

medical information system (MIS), 156

Meek, Wanda, 102

Memory Test Computer (MTC), 106–107

Mercer, Johnny, 236

Merrill Lynch, 177

MetaACE, 221

Metal Oxide Semiconductor

Implementation Service (MOSIS), 188, 217

Methods of Theoretical Physics (Morse and Feshbach), 64

MGB GT, 133, 136, 142–143, 179

Milan, Joe, 114

Mili, Gjon, 60

Mills, Ada, 2, 6

Mills, Harold Colthurst, 2, 6, 150

Mills, Helena Jane, *See* Cox, Helena Jane Mills

Mills, Mary Dunscombe, 1–2

Mills, Rev. Seth A., 1–2

Milne, A.A., 8

Minsky, Marvin, 117

MIT Acoustics Lab, 48–51, 59–60, 63, 65, 69–70, 72, 76–77, 93, 97, 236.
  See also Massachusetts Institute of Technology (MIT)

MIT Lincoln Laboratory, 70, 77, 95, 95*f*, 97–98, 104, 106, 108

Molnar, Charlie, 97–99, 102, 104, 108, 116–117, 129, 134–135, 190, 194, 225, 236
  doctoral dissertation, 105, 109, 115
  LINC, 95, 95*f*
  Sensory Biophysics Laboratory at the School of Medicine, 151
  system failures, 220
  visit to Fort Detrick, 191

Molnar, Donna, 116, 191, 225

Molnar, Stephen, 225

Monte Cassino Abbey, 28–29, 29*f*

Montgomery, Gen. Bernard, 148–149

Moon, Marc, 212–213

Moore, Steve, 184

Morse, Philip, 64, 121, 126
  Methods of Theoretical Physics, 64

Moscow. *See* adventure in Moscow

Moses, Justin, 230

Mrs. Miniver, 20

Mullani, Nizar, 127–128, 225

music, 52, 84–86, 113–114, 133, 139–140, 169, 216–217, 234–239

Myers, Chris, 182

Myers, Elizabeth, 8, 17, 20, 30

Myers, Larry, 8, 12*f*

Myers, Lee, 113

Myers, Mary, 8

Myers, Michael, 113, 188

Myers, Paul, 8
Myers, Phil, 8
Myers, Ralph, 8
Myers family, 8, 11
Myers kids, 11, 17

N

Nash, Ogden, 8
National Academy of Sciences (NAS), 192–194
National Advisory Committee on Aeronautics (NACA), 49–50
National Bureau of Standards, 69
National Geospatial–Intelligence Agency (NGA), 91, 164
National Institutes of Health (NIH), 94–95, 97, 102–106, 111, 114, 125, 136, 147, 153, 164, 168, 172, 190, 193–196, 225, 262
   Biomedical Computer Laboratory (BCL), 100–101
   Computer Study Section, 95–96, 112
   Division of Computer Research and Technology (DCRT), 146
   Division of Research Resources, 101, 154
   funding/grant, 97, 104, 184
   LINC Evaluation Program, 98
   National Heart, Lung, and Blood Institute, 180
   Shared Instrument Grant (SIG) Program, 182–183
National Science Foundation (NSF), 94, 181, 212, 221–222
National Sports Car Championship in 1952 and 1955, 40
Neff, Dewey, 22
Nelson, David, 163
Nelson, Harriet, 163
Nelson, Ozzie, 163
Nelson, Ricky, 163
network interface controller (NIC), 232
network/networking, 108, 165, 167, 180–189, 204–205, 212, 229, 232, 245
New England Center for Computer Technology and Research in the Biomedical Sciences, 103
New Enterprise Associates (NEA), 203–207
New York Times, 115
Niebauer, Allison Cox, 185
Nielsen, Don, 89, 97, 196
Niemoeller, Art, 76, 80–81, 85, 93, 127

Niemoeller, Janne, 127
Nolle, Floyd, 102, 116–119, 214

O

O'Day, Anita, 62, 236
O'Driscoll, Jeremy, 227
Office of the Network Coordinator (ONC), 182
Oliver, Charles, 116, 118–119
Olsen, Erik, 221
Olsen, Ken, 94
Olson, Maynard, 190, 194–195
The Only Working Turing Machine There Ever Was, Probably (TOWTMTEWP), 134, 134*f*, 228, 230
optical communication, 181. *See also* network/networking
Ornstein, Severo, 98, 109, 110*f*, 116, 173, 220, 224*f*
O Say Can You Si (van Stolk), 55
Oslo, Maynard, 190, 194–195
osteomyelitis, 31
Ostrow, Harold, 147
Otoacoustic Emissions (OAE), 89–90
Owen, Elrose "Candy" Cox, 21, 21*f*, 48, 59*f*, 113, 172, 185, 188, 197–198, 222, 244
Owen, Michael/Mike, 188, 222

P

Page, Ann. *See* Haggett, Ann Page
Pake, George, 101, 103, 120, 124–125, 129, 210–211
Papian, Bill, 97–98, 103–105, 107, 109
   Advanced Development Group at the Lincoln Lab, 108
   director of the Computer Components Lab (CCL), 109
   Project Whirlwind, 106
parenting. *See* helicopter parenting
Parulkar, Guru, 188–189, 202–204, 204*f*, 205–206
Patty, F. A.
   Industrial Hygiene and Toxicology, 197
Pepper, Maury, 219*f*
Pfeiffer, Russell R., 129–130, 151, 158, 236
Phelps, Mike/Michael, 124–129
   role in PET development, 127–129
   vision for positron imaging, 128
Picker X-Ray Corporation, 123–124

Pigeon Drop scam, 105

Plummer, Bessie, 11, 11f, 15–17, 23

Poisson, Siméon Denis, 121

Pollack, Sy, 154, 159

Porgy and Bess (Gershwin and Gershwin), 234

Porter, Cole, 236

Positron Emission Tomography (PET), 120–135, 193, 225, 263

Post-Dispatch, 86

Potchen, Jim, 120

Powers, Bill, 96, 111

Pratt, Arnold W. (Scotty), 146–147, 168–170

premature ventricular contractions (PVCs), 119

Prewitt, Judith (Judi), 168–171

Primakoff, Henry, 71

Proceedings of the IEEE, 118

Procyk, George, 37

Program in Audiology and Communication Sciences (PACS), 197

Project Zeus, 180–189

Pyrovolakis, John, 221–222, 227, 231, 233

Q

Q-Knight, 232

Q-Net Input/Output (QIO), 228–230, 233

Q-Net Security (QNS), 227–233, 241

Quirin, Andrew, 229

R

Radiation Physics Laboratory, 121, 126–127

Radiological Society of North America (RSNA), 122, 184

Radiology, 127

Raichle, Marcus, 192–193, 225

Randall, Elrose. See Cox, Elrose Randall

Random Point Processes (Snyder), 158

Rapmund, Garrison, 190–192, 194

Rau, Chris, 209, 240, 242, 247

Rau, Erin Battersby, 161, 161f, 207–209, 240, 241f, 242

Rau, Jackson, 241f, 242

Rau, Scarlett, 241f, 242

Raub, William (Bill), 101, 111, 136–137, 139, 225

RCA 630TS television, 45, 45f

Reed, Joy. See Hunton, Joy Reed

Research Lab of Electronics (RLE), 49, 146

Reuben, David
  Everything You Always Wanted to Know About Sex* (*But Were Afraid to Ask), 17

Rhee, Gwangsoo, 194

Richardson, Bill, 62

Richon, Merry Ambos, 154, 201

Rick's Café, 28

Riley Drama Club, 20

Riley High School, *See*, James Whitcomb Riley High School

Ripley, Ken, 147–148

Robinson, Scott, 219, 229

Rocca, Mo, 230

Rockhold Lillian. *See* Cox, Lillian Rockhold

Rockoff, David, 177

Rockoff, Maxine, 121, 168, 177–178, 186f, 210–212, 229–230, 247, 262

Roestel, Arne, 115

Rogers, Francis, 56

Roosevelt, Teddy, 147

Rosenblith, Walter, 69, 76, 95–97, 102, 108

Rott School, 145

Ruderman, Mort, 110, 112

S

Sandel, Tom, 98, 105, 130, 173

Satterfield, Jim, 89, 97

Savoy Café, 52, 62

Sensory Biophysics Laboratory at the School of Medicine, 151

Shakespeare, William
  As You Like It, 20

Shannon, Claude, 238

Show Boat (Ferber), 235

Shriners Hospital, 102

Shultz, George, 40

Shuman, Bill, 41, 53

Silverman, Dick, 81–83, 93–94

Silverman, Sally, 94

Simon, Bill, 98

Simpson, Bud, 98–99

Single Photon Emission Computed Tomography (SPECT), 120

Skillern, Lisa. *See* Smith, Lisa Skillern

Skillern, Penn G., 7–8, 11, 12f, 21f, 48, 114

Skillern, Penn G. Jr., 7, 17, 114

Skillern, Scott, 7, 76

Skillern family, 7, 9f, 11, 13, 17–18, 21,

48–49

Smith, Diane C.P., 192

Smith, Lisa Skillern, 7, 11, 12*f*, 17, 21*f*, 48, 76, 114, 230

Smoot, Oliver, 42, 42*f*, 43

Snyder, Don, 121–123, 126, 128, 130, 247
  Random Point Processes, 158

Society of Photo-Optical Instrumentation Engineers (SPIE), 183

Spenard, Kim Battersby, 12, 161, 161*f*, 207–208, 241*f*, 242

Spenard, Paige, 208, 241*f*, 242

Spenard, Payton, 208, 241*f*, 242

Spenard, Troy, 36*f*, 208, 241*f*, 242

Sperlinga, Jay, 52

Stage Door, 20

Starmer, Ellen, 180

Starmer, Frank, 180–181

Starr, Arnold, 190

St. Louis Internet Access Collaborative (SLIAC), 212–213

Stolk, Art Van
  O Say Can You Si, 55

Stone, Fred, 101

Stucki, Mish/Mishell, 98, 109, 116, 220

Sullivan, Arthur
  H.M.S. Pinafore, 234

Sullivan, Ed, 45

Sulston, John, 195–196

Surovick, Theresa. *See* Cox-Kendig, Theresa Surovick

Sutherland, Ivan, 108–109, 116, 164, 177, 192, 216–217, 225

Swartz, Allen, 163, 243

Swartz, Lee, 57

SynOptics, 188–189

T

Taylor, Richard, 53

Teas, Don, 89, 97

Tech, The, 43

Ter-Pogossian, Michel, 121, 124–126, 154, 192
  death from heart attack, 129
  invention of PET, 128
  Radiation Physics Lab, 127
  role in PET development, 128–129

Thomas, Jane, 173

Thomas, Lew, 153–154, 173

decision to retire as director of BCL, 184

Tiger Rag Forever (Dammkoehler), 235

Tom Sawyer, 148

Townes, Charles, 103

TOWTMTEWP, 134, 134*f*, 159, 228, 230

Trial Advocacy Program, 177

trips, 56, 78, 167–179, 186–187, 202, 207, 222, 239

Turing, Alan, 97, 134, 134*f*, 159, 228, 230

Turner, Helen, 165

Turner, Jon, 165, 167, 180–181, 187–189, 194, 202–207, 204*f*

Twelve Angry Women (Cox), 92

U

U.S. Congress, 27, 35

U.S.S. Forrestal, 81

V

VanAmburg, Lisa, 230

Veiled Prophet Ball, 84, 86

Voo Doo (Little), 43–44, 43*f*, 45, 121

VTEL, 184

W

Walz, Bruce, 225

Warner, Homer, 96

Washington University, 65, 76, 79–80, 82, 89, 94–96 100, 103, 109, 111, 114–116, 122, 126, 128–129, 134–136, 156, 161, 165, 173–174, 185, 195, 200, 206–208, 210, 216, 225–226, 246, 262–263
  150th anniversary, 216
  biomedical computer lab (BCL), 95–96, 100, 102–119, 103*f*, 110*f*, 120–127, 130–132, 140, 144, 146–147, 153–154, 158, 168, 177, 181–184, 211, 224*f*, 225–226, 262
  class obligations, 80
  Computer Labs, 109
  Faculty Club, 200, 215
  IBM 650 computer, 94
  School of Medicine, 96, 101, 146, 151, 182, 193
  work on PET, 128

Waterston, Bob, 195–196

Watson, James, 194–196

Waxman, Bruce, 95, 111–112, 114, 164, 177

WE (Lindbergh), 11

Wein, George, 234

"Where or When" (Kemp), 17
White, Dick, 19, 19f, 24, 218, 238–239
Wiederhold, Gio, 153, 155
Wiener, Norbert, 69, 70
  Cybernetics, 69
Wilkes, Mary Allen, 98, 105, 109, 115, 134–
  135, 177, 224f, 229, 247–248, 263, 263f
Wilkinson, Bill, 235
Williams, Charles R. (Chuck), 63, 68, 72,
  74–75
Williams, Kirk, 206–207
wire-wrap guns, 111, 141
Wolfe, Margaret. *See* Cox, Margaret Wolfe
Wolfe, Paul, 166
Wolff, Steve, 181
Wonderful Wizard of Oz, The (Baum), 11
Wrighton, Mark, 202f
wuarchive, 182

Y

Yak, George, 12, 15–17, 20–22, 76

Z

Zar, Dave, 217, 221–222, 227, 229
Zeelenberg, Cees, 147
Zuckerberg, Mark, 182
Zyda, Mike, 166

TRIBUTES

Jim McKelvey, Entrepreneur | Co-Founder of Block (formerly Square)

I can't think of a kinder or harder-working man than Jerry Cox. He has been an inspiration to me for my entire life.

Joseph November, Author | *Biomedical Computing*

Work Hard, Be Kind is not just the memoir of a computer scientist's remarkable career. It's a humor-packed and lavishly illustrated romp through the formative years of medical computing. And it's a necessary read to any young person hoping to make the world better by bringing technology to bear on the challenges of medicine. Jerry Cox carefully explains the engineering, science, and medicine involved in each major development he chronicles, and reveals to us the personal side of what it was like to see those developments through. Refreshingly, Jerry shows that it was not easy. He is candid about the setbacks one often experiences as a pioneer, and about the strength it takes to persevere as well as the importance of having a supportive family and good friends. One leaves this book with a strong sense of why indeed "work hard, be kind" are good words to live by.

Severo M. Ornstein, Author | *Computing in the Middle Ages*

Jerry's memoir provides the reader with some understanding of the ways in which technology has invaded medical research and practice over the last half century. In addition, it reveals one who has followed his own dictum: "work hard, be kind." It provides ample evidence of a life well lived that should serve as a model for others. Throughout he exhibits modesty and generosity as he works determinedly throughout his long life on a stunning array of vital medical/scientific enterprises. Without delving too deeply into technical detail, the reader is made to understand the impact of his many projects, whose history is often leavened with heart-warming anecdotes. Always at the story's core is his devotion to his wife, Bobby, and to his burgeoning family. His life-story is likely to elicit not only admiration but even a hint of envy in those hoping to follow his stellar example.

William Raub, NIH official who funded biomedical computing research

Under Jerry Cox's leadership, the Washington University Computer Laboratories did more than any other entity to introduce computer technology into medicine and biology. Jerry ensured that the laboratories became an extraordinarily productive training ground for engineers, physicians, and scientists interested in biomedical computation. In the words of an overwhelmed site visitor, "the bench is deep."

Jerry Cox is an eclectic innovator, superb leader, and a marvelous human being. I have never known his equal.

Maxine L. Rockoff, early developer of computer-aided instruction

To Jerry: It has been a stimulating joy to read *Work Hard, Be Kind.* Thank you for giving me this privilege. As I read the book and think of my own life and the ways it has intersected with yours, I see two distinct segments. The first was from 1968 to 1971 when you were my boss at BCL. The second was from 1981 to the present after I moved to New York solo and restarted my life with Wes.

One highlight of Segment 2 was our trip to Paderborn in 2015, just a few months before Wes died. What joy to have you and Wes and Mary Allen sharing the LINC days!

Thinking back to my years at BCL, I am struck by the camaraderie and collegiality that you engendered throughout the community of people who worked there. Whether it was conceiving and typing up a new grant application or gathering data for a grant that was already in place, you recognized and acknowledged every contribution. Instead of competition, there was cooperation. It was unique. I'm so glad you have undertaken this monumental task of writing your autobiography! It tells the story of an admirable man whose trajectory through life has benefitted every human being whose life it touched. It will also be available for those who follow who are wise enough to recognize the guidance it provides.

Mary Allen Wilkes, pioneering systems programmer

He was only going to stay two years but found himself pioneering the fledgling field of biomedical engineering for the next several decades, fostering countless breakthrough developments that made Washington University an international leader in electronic radiology, biomedical computing, and computer networking. In the 1960s he built the first instrument capable of detecting deafness in newborns and put small computers in biomedical research labs for the first time. His teams developed the first computer-based system to monitor cardiac arrhythmias, and invented data compression techniques and PET scan technology still used today. And now in the 2020s he has developed novel anti-hacking technology for the internet. With characteristic, and certainly undue, modesty, Jerry Cox, inventor, entrepreneur, lover of jazz, and creator of always pronounceable acronyms, interweaves his many professional contributions with delightful personal recollections of family and colleagues. It has been a pleasure to read his stories which he tells with warmth and grace while explaining the technologies with welcome clarity, invoking billion-piece dance bands to illuminate the problem with clocked computer chips and medieval castles to demonstrate today's threat from malware.

A smiling Mary Allen Wilkes pictured with LINC at home in July 1965.